OVER OUR DEAD BODIES brings together the voices of deeply concerned women – historians, novelists, journalists, poets, women in the peace movement and the peace camps, women in politics and arms factories. Offering informed argument, personal accounts, poetry and polemic, as well as a comprehensive chronology of the nuclear age and a glossary of terms, this book insists that questions of peace and war are questions of morality and politics, and that we are all capable of judging the issues. There is no simple formula for avoiding nuclear war, but the authors argue, from a wide variety of positions, that the question is too important to be left to the 'experts'. Nationalist leaders have not prevented wars in the past and we can't trust them to do so now. The message of this book is one of hope – so long as we understand, argue and *act*.

Dorothy Thompson was born in 1923 and grew up in London and France. She studied history at Girton College Cambridge, interrupting her studies with war service as an engineering draughtswoman, and graduating in 1945. In 1948 she married and while her three children were young, worked part-time in adult education and on various sociological surveys. Since 1968 she has worked in the Department of History at Birmingham University, apart from spells as a visiting professor at Rutgers, Pittsburgh and Brown Universities in the USA. The author of several books and articles, particularly on her specialist subject, Chartism, Dorothy Thompson is a member of the national executive of the Society for the Study of Labour History and of the editorial board of *Social History*. She has been active in the peace movement for many years, and is a member of END. She now lives in Worcester with her husband, the historian E.P. Thompson.

OVER OUR DEAD BODIES

Women Against the Bomb

Edited by Dorothy Thompson

Virago

Published by VIRAGO PRESS Limited 1983,
41, William IV Street, London WC2N 4DB

Printed in Finland by Werner Söderström Oy,
a member of Finnprint.

British Library Cataloguing in Publication Data
Over our dead bodies.
  1. Deterrence (Strategy)   2. Atomic warfare
  I. Thompson, Dorothy
355′.0217   U162.6
  ISBN 0-86068-348-6

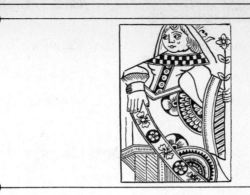

CONTENTS

ACKNOWLEDGEMENTS

Every contributor owes a debt to the many expert and talented writers whose works we have consulted in the course of writing our chapters. Where possible, individual debts have been acknowledged, but if any have been overlooked, we ask indulgence from our colleagues in the peace movement. In a written text it is not usually possible to indicate the debt owed to television and news programmes, but anyone concerned with peace knows how great a debt we owe to a small number of dedicated workers in the mass media, in radio and television services here and in the United States, who have managed to break through the apathy, timidity and commercial-mindedness of the programme controllers to demonstrate the urgency of the kind of problems we are discussing here.

Every piece in this book has been written especially for it, with the exception of the first two poems by Janet Dubé which are part of a longer sequence, *Meditations for Our Children*, published earlier this year by Janet, and obtainable from her. Help with individual chapters has been mentioned in the notes. We have all been helped by comments from each other, but perhaps especial mention should be made of the very great amount of work done by Suzanne Wood and Evelyn King in typing, copying and generally putting the manuscripts in order, often from very scruffy drafts.

The charts on pp. 19, 20, 21 and 25 are reproduced by kind permission of the Medical Campaign Against Nuclear Weapons, and are taken from their pamphlet *The Medical Consequences of*

Nuclear Weapons: the table on p. 23 is reproduced by kind permission of the Radical Statistics Group, and published in *The Nuclear Numbers Game*. The maps on pp. 98 and 99 and the chart on p. 97 is reproduced from *Ambio*, Vol XI, no. 2–3, 1982, published by the Royal Swedish Academy of Sciences. The map on p. 90 is reproduced by kind permission of Mary Douglas Publications.

INTRODUCTION

The writers of this book are united by a common concern with the threat of destruction which faces our civilisation. The book has been produced quickly, with a sense of urgency, and it is clear that we write at a time when the world around us is changing rapidly. Between the writing and our appearance in print it may be that popular revulsion will have lessened the dangers, that action will have been taken to reduce world tensions, to destabilise the military blocs and to open up possibilities of world peace and world co-operation. It could also, alas, be that tensions will have increased, more conflicts will have developed, more hideous weapons of destruction manufactured. Whichever happens, our arguments remain valid and will, we hope, have won wider recognition by the time they appear.

Some chapters in the collection are personal statements, some concern themselves with the examination of particular problems or aspects of the central problem. Chapters have deliberately been kept short, and each is self-contained. The nuclear threat is a subject on which it is difficult to concentrate for long without becoming depressed or defeatist. Nevertheless, we think that in the end our message is one of hope and of guarded optimism. Perhaps for the first time in history, the majority of people the world over are concerned to prevent the outbreak of a major war. If we consider that some nations and some leaders are going the wrong way about it, it would still be arrogant and stupid to suggest that people who are not actively engaged in the peace movement do not care about their own and their children's futures. We hope that the information and the arguments that we present here will convince them that the present philosophy of preserving peace by preparing for war is outdated and suicidal, and that peace can only be gained by acting and thinking in peaceful ways, and in seeking means other than war of resolving conflicts of interest between nations and individuals.

Contributors to the book speak from a number of different standpoints. Differences of age, experience, religious and philosophical viewpoints exist among us, as they do among the peace movements of the world. But we are agreed on the central question of the dangers we face, and of the need for protest and for action. For some of us the title of the book represents the stance we want to take. For others there is perhaps something over-dramatic in it, although we certainly don't differ about the seriousness of the questions being discussed. We have tried to avoid jargon — particularly the weapons' jargon by which so many 'experts' try to obscure the basic moral and political questions. However, some technical terms have to be used, and we have added a glossary which we hope covers most of these.

Each chapter has been written independently, and is the responsibility of its author. But all of us have had the benefit of comments and criticism from the other contributors and from other women in the group who have not written chapters. Although the editor accepts responsibility of selection for the volume as a whole, again, most of the decisions have been cooperative ones, and we are agreed on the value of each piece, even those with whose standpoint we are not totally in sympathy.

Whatever our viewpoint, we are united on one thing: the questions we are considering are far too important to be left to self-selected 'experts'. Women, even more than the average 'non-expert' citizen, tend to mistrust their own judgements. We often feel that we are unfitted by our education and training to form an opinion on questions of defence strategy and weaponry. Many of us have a block when it comes to reading about such things, and give in with too much humility to 'experts' who have the arrogance to take charge of matters affecting our lives and our children's lives. So we are asserting here that everyone must listen to the arguments, must make up her or his own mind. The opinions and feelings of women, as workers, as thinkers, and as carers and nurturers of the young and the old must be heard. We are central to any political and moral decisions that have to be made. Whatever the viewpoint of any of the writers and organisers of this book, we are united in saying that women must speak out, and that their voices must be heard. We don't claim that we have all the answers. We don't claim that the solution to any of the problems discussed will be easy. We certainly don't think that we are the only people in the world who are passionately concerned to find a way to achieve peace. But we do insist that the most important matter of our time must be decided by every citizen. Arms manufacturers, nationalist leaders and self-glorifying politicians have never prevented wars in the past: we have no reason to think that they will prevent the final catastrophe.

Nearly two thousand years ago, the Roman conquerors of Britain were accused, in words that are prophetic for our times, of making a desert and calling it peace. The radioactive desert that would be Europe after a nuclear war could never be reclaimed.

Dorothy Thompson, Upper Wick, 1982

Editorial team: Alison Assiter, Jeanette Buirski, Angela Carter, Jill Craigie, Gay Clifford, Sheryl Crown, Janet Dubé, Jenny Edwards, Lisa Foley, Inge Goodwin, Sue Hirst, Philomena Hingston, Evelyn King, Jill Liddington, Connie Mansueto, Lesley Merryfinch, Bel Mooney, Marjorie Mowlam, Ann Pettitt, Lynne Jones, Joan Ruddock, Beryl Ruehl, Diana Shelley, Edith Simon, Myrtle Solomon, Kate Soper, Fran Stevens, Marian Sugden, Hilary Wainwright, Maxine Wombwell, Suzanne Wood, Dorothy Thompson (editor).

BEYOND THE WASTELAND

In the park in Budapest children were playing on swings, chasing each other, queuing for the slide, hurtling down the chute with screams of pleasure. Behind them, silhouetted against the sky loomed the vast Liberation Monument, erected by the Russians to commemorate their victory over the occupying German forces – before the liberators became the oppressors, before 1956, before the Cold War.

The monument is a symbol of Hungary's fate; and yet women in a group of Hungarian tourists carefully tidied the flowers someone had left at its foot. And still more children came in a crocodile to view the monument. The little girls clung adoringly to their women teachers' hands at the foot and the rear of the little procession; the boys pushed and argued in the middle – like children anywhere. Something about those children – about their appearance – puzzled me. Then I realised. It was simply that they could have been dressed by Tesco and Marks and Spencer; they looked more like an English school party than a group of French, German or American children would have done. Little Lazlos and Karoly and Irena giggled and whispered. Then my companion said, with brutal irony, 'They're communists, those children. Let's nuke them.'

It is only by seeing it thus, concretely, that the true horror of possible nuclear war is driven home. That is why the propaganda machine does all it can to prevent us from reaching that clarity of vision. If people are persuaded to think of their enemies as

6 Over Our Dead Bodies

different, dehumanised, it makes the possible annihilation of that enemy much easier to accept; and it is a short step from seeing it as acceptable to thinking that it might even be desirable. The hatred of Zionist for Palestinian is as nothing compared with the hatred of a red-necked middle American for 'commies' he has never seen – unless they are those peaceniks who demonstrate. And the hatred of that redneck is itself as nothing compared with the abstract political hatred for The Other embodied by two piles of bricks and mortar: the White House and the Kremlin.

How has this come about? In 1873 Nietzsche wrote: 'The great tidal wave of barbarism is at our gates'. Yet it did not come – unless you can count many wars, the Somme, Dresden, Belsen, My Lai, and the late twentieth-century disease of political terrorism. But not the ultimate barbarism: that still lies ahead. For the first time in – how many centuries? – we are in a state where men actually believe that the end of the world is possible. Not the end of *a* world, of a particular civilisation, but of *the* world. Apocalypse now – indeed.

Just after Hiroshima, Bertrand Russell told the House of Lords: 'As I go about the streets and see St Paul's, the British Museum, the Houses of Parliament and the other monuments of our civilisation, in my mind's eye I see a nightmare vision of those buildings as heaps of rubble with corpses all around them. That is a thing we have got to face, not only in our own countries and cities, but throughout the civilised world.' Thirty-eight years later we can share that nightmare vision: the Louvre, the Budapest Museum of Fine Arts, the Parthenon – all gone. No children left to sing 'London Bridge is falling down'.

'Ah, but . . .' the doubter will argue, settling back on the bar stool and folding arms knowingly, 'the fact that it hasn't happened shows how much we need the bomb. We're still here because it's a deterrent.' This and other theories will be countered elsewhere in this book. I want to argue that, just as exposure to horror can brutalise the witness, and experience of suffering can numb the sufferer, the fact of living our lives under the shadow of a mushroom cloud brutalises and numbs us. There does not need to be a holocaust for the 'baroque arsenal' to start corrupting the sensibilities of those who, deliberately or by default, put their faith, not in God or Man, but in that monstrous bastard child of science and barbarism, of reason and ignorance – the nuclear bomb.

As an experiment, I read something to a young woman of my

acquaintance, a twenty-year-old who works with children and wants nothing else than to have a family of her own one day. It was an extract from the transcript of Jonathan Dimbleby's ITV documentary 'The Bomb', in which two Japanese women remembered the day when the Americans dropped their affectionately named offspring 'Little Boy' on Hiroshima.

Mrs Yamasaki: I heard my sister's voice crying, 'Help me, help me'. I could just see her fingertips, this much, and I said, 'I'll help you.' I started to clear the rubble. And then I heard a voice saying, 'Mother, it's getting hot.' It was my eldest child who was eight. She was trapped too. My sister said, 'It's getting hotter. You're the only one of us who is safe, you must go, get away.' But I said, 'My sister, if I can't get you out, I can't reach my child. Please let me see your face.' But I couldn't free her, only part of her arm, up to here. It was dreadful. I couldn't bear to leave them but the flames forced me back. I escaped out on to the road. I'd left my child to die.

Mrs Tomoyasu: (after searching for twenty-four hours for *her* daughter) I heard her voice, calling 'Mother, Mother'. I went towards the sound. She was completely burned. The skin had come off her head altogether, leaving a knot of twisted hair at the top. My daughter said, 'Mother, you're late, please take me back quickly.' She said it was hurting a lot. But there were no doctors. There was nothing I could do. So I covered up her naked body and held her in my arms for nine hours. At about eleven o'clock that night she cried out again, 'Mother,' and put her hand around my neck. It was already ice-cold. I said, 'Please say Mother again.' But that was the last time.

I have read those extracts again and again and still I cannot type for tears. Yet my young acquaintance's response was not emotional. She said that it was terrible, but she did not like to read things like that because there was no point. It is a very human response to the pain of others: to turn away, unable to cope with the enormity of grief on a large scale. I suspect that perhaps women are more prone to this numbness than men — immersed in the day-to-day, pausing only to look at their children playing with a sudden presentiment of doom as the Radio One news chirps merrily of international tension, then continuing their tasks in the numb certainty that 'it will never happen'. I would walk from house to house and tell Mrs Smith and Mrs Jones that unless they learn to be angered for the sake of Mrs Yamasaki and Mrs Tomoyasu, and to weep for those who still weep, then there is more and more likelihood that it *will* happen, and to their own daughters, their own sons.

People hug their alibis like teddy bears — the stuffed, unreal things that give them comfort in the night: 'We can't do anything about it . . . There's no point in protesting . . . If we got rid of ours, the Russians would send one over, wouldn't they? . . . there are so many now you can't get rid of them . . . nobody wants to use them so they won't ever be used . . . it's a deterrent, innit? . . . look, the nuclear status quo has held up for thirty-eight years . . . what's the use of worrying about it? . . . eat, drink and be merry, for tomorrow we may be radioactive.'

It is as if a large part of the population feels helpless, and another large part attempts to rationalise its helplessness − or its indifference. In accepting that they have no choice over their own destiny people deprive themselves of one of the most basic elements of human dignity − to choose, understanding the consequences of that choice.

Yet in order to make choices you have to be informed, and there are well-oiled wheels which turn and turn, ensuring by their machinations that information is hard to come by. Where is the serious debate about nuclear war in the media? Where is the sustained questioning of the nuclear strategy of the Western world? Nowhere. Instead, in the popular press especially, there is a sustained smear campaign against those who do ask questions. Last year, in a month which saw the Pope's visit to England, and another, less auspicious visit by Ronald Reagan, what was noticeable was that both men spoke of peace − in fact Reagan told the Pope that his trip to Europe was 'a pilgrimage of peace'. Nobody in Fleet Street jeered − presumably because they knew he was not telling the truth. There was something grimly hilarious about Reagan, suddenly metamorphosed from hawk into dove, saying to the German Parliament: 'To those who march for peace, my heart is with you. I would be at the head of your parade if I believed marching alone would bring about a more secure world.' But there was nothing funny about the way a certain section of the press responded to the huge Campaign for Nuclear Disarmament rally taking place at the same time. The *Mail on Sunday*'s headline asked, 'Whose Hands on the CND Banner?' and the *Sunday Express* gave its own predictable answer, in a headline that denounced, 'This sick charade that is masterminded in Moscow'. You would have thought that the thousands of sincere, decent, ordinary marchers would have had grounds to sue Winston S. Churchill, who, in a paranoid article that masqueraded as analysis, called them 'the tools of Moscow'.

The innocent might well be justified in assuming that such articles mean that these employees of the newspapers concerned are deeply and sincerely anti-CND. In fact, of course, they are not anti anything, except closing time. No, the sub-editors who write the headlines are carrying out the wishes of their editors who are obeying the proprietors whose concern is to placate the government and the military establishment, in the hope perhaps of receiving a peerage – a just reward for services to journalism, and to truth.

If you were to search the media for anything to allay fears about a nuclear holocaust, what you would discover would only make those fears worse. For the serious newspapers report the subtle shifts in strategy, usually without comment, in the same language that the establishment uses: a grammar of evasion. Its effect is to brainwash people into accepting the possibility of a nuclear war. Once, if you remember, we were assured that that nuclear status quo was necessary as a deterrent – the very existence of nuclear weapons was a cast-iron guarantee that they would never be used. But now the language is of 'tactical nuclear war', 'pre-emptive strikes', 'limited nuclear war' and 'counterforce', phrases which imply that someone, (preferably us) can strike first somewhere else and survive. 'Theatre war' is another good phrase: it means that Russia and America watch in the wings whilst a nightmarish Elizabethan revenge tragedy is played out on Europe's stage and the superpowers survive in a world that is only partially devastated – to show each other that they must not steal each other's lines.

Such language makes the idea of nuclear confrontation a reality. Slowly and insidiously, what was unthinkable becomes thinkable and all the glib phrases politicians have at their command, (very, very many) are absorbed into our common language, so that the thinkable becomes acceptable. It filters through into the most unlikely places. One day, for instance, you open the pages of the *Guardian* to discover a fashion writer starting an article on home dressmaking with the cheery thought that after the big bang we will all have to learn fundamental skills like sewing again. Articles on fallout shelters appear in colour supplements. Another day you go into a restaurant for a simple hamburger, (in my case into a place called Sweeney Todd's, in Bath) to find this on the menu:

The Nuclear Holocaust Kit
A Sicilian Pizza scorched with Jalapeno peppers, contaminated with hot chilis, mutated with pimentos, defoliated with peperoni, and neutralised with a pint of bitter.
ST Corp Health Warning
NUCLEAR HOLOCAUSTS CAN SERIOUSLY DAMAGE YOUR HEALTH.

The young manager spread his hands wide in a shrug when certain of his customers objected that the item was in poor taste – good though the food might be. 'Why do you take it so seriously?' he asked in irritation. 'We can't do anything about it, so what's wrong with making a joke? The trouble with people like *you* is you've got no sense of humour.'

Where, you might well ask, is the joke? It is extraordinary that the same man might hesitate to put a pizza called 'Bar Mitzvah Boy – garnished with salt beef and crisped in a gas oven' on his menu, or to feature a dish called 'Terminal Cancer – the last word in crab sandwiches', or even a 'Passchendaele Pie – chunks of meat flavoured with poppy seeds, buried in a French pastry case'. Yet the suffering of the people of Hiroshima and Nagasaki is a subject fit for joking, the long-term damage done to their unborn children is turned into a light-hearted food description, and those who object to the possible extinction of humankind being trivialised in this way are chided for being too serious. That is what I mean by the bomb brutalising, even when it is not used.

Almost the worst by-product of this process is the sad damage that is done to meaning. Those who ask for analysis are patronised as 'naive'; those who want us to step back from the brink are called 'extreme'; those who, like me, are passionately and conservatively patriotic are denounced as 'tools of Moscow'; those who care about the future of their children are labelled sneeringly as 'lefties, peaceniks and fellow-travellers'; those who meet and talk and develop concrete plans for halting the arms race are labelled 'unrealistic'. When I was seventeen I went to the dentist wearing a CND badge, and found to my terror that the drill-waving man had nothing but angry contempt for 'ban-the-bombers'. It is always the same; nowadays there are county councils who forbid CND to meet on school premises because it is supposed to be a 'contentious' organisation.

Yet what *is* the bone of contention? That nuclear war is undesirable? That is what CND believes; one can only assume that those who prohibit those meetings believe, in some perverted way, that nuclear war is desirable — otherwise there would be nothing contentious about the issue. It is another moral perversion, that the respectable view is that of the nuclear status quo; the view that nuclear weapons (and so by definition, now, nuclear war) are necessary.

Though a nuclear war in our hemisphere would eliminate the civilisations of Europe, China, Japan Russia and the USA — though that is *known* — still the powers on both sides posture arrogantly, stating clearly that destruction is the price worth paying for their respective ideologies. It goes without saying that any mother in Russia would prefer to see her children chewing gum, wearing Levis and training as cheerleaders than that they should be dead; whilst her equivalent in America might groan at the thought of a future of communist shortages and dreariness but would infinitely prefer that to no future at all.

Government, Western or Eastern, takes no account of such innocent preferences for life, for continuity even despite possible oppression. It ignores the view, which is surely shared by very many 'ordinary' people, that it would be preferable to be invaded by Russia, and to mount a full-scale resistance movement against the occupying force with the hope of one day vanquishing them, than to attempt mutual annihilation. At least there would be hope. At least there would be a future.

Yet, with monstrous arrogance and ignorance the propagandists shriek 'all or nothing', like the young man who in a frenzy of jealousy, kills the girl he loves rather than see her with another man. Here, for example, is Francis Pym, then Secretary of State for Defence, who was asked in the film, *The Bomb* whether he would, in the old cliché, 'rather be dead than red':

Dead . . . than red? (pause) At the end of the day our peace and our freedom and our democracy have had to be preserved over the centuries at the cost of many dead. Fifty million lives were lost in the last war by conventional means in defence of peace and freedom. People over the centuries, our forefathers, have been prepared to go to fantastic lengths in order to preserve their freedom. And the view has been that it is better to, if you like to express it in these rather emotive terms, to be dead than red. But the purpose of course is to preserve our parliamentary democracy, and that I am sure people through the ages will always wish to do.

First, notice the quite fantastic assumption, in the context, that there will always be 'people through the ages'. Then observe that amidst all the orotund phrases, like 'peace, freedom and democracy', Pym never once confronts the question in real terms. Death is never a reality to those who trade in the empty rhetoric of ideology, just as the enemy is never human. Finally, note that Francis Pym, a member of Her Majesty's government, is actually saying that he would be prepared to 'go to fantastic lengths' (like dropping a thousand 'Little Boys' on Moscow, and Budapest, and Bucharest, we must assume) 'to preserve our parliamentary democracy', knowing, as he must, that retaliation would be instantaneous, and the Houses of Parliament would be a heap of rubble haunted by the bland and fatuous pratings of Thatcher, Pym and Nott.

You do not have to be religious to see the spiritual sickness in this – the kind of vaulting arrogance personified by Faust and Satan in literature and synonymous with a wholesale rejection of the Sermon on the Mount, of the humility of Christ. You do not have to be a bible scholar to see chilling parallels between the language of apocalypse and the description of contemporary annihilation:

And the second angel sounded, and as it were a great mountain burning with fire was cast into the sea; and the third part of the sea became blood; and the third part of the creatures which were in the sea, and had life, died; and the third part of the ships were destroyed . . .

(Revelation viii)

Scarcely had the bomb fallen than a dazzling light spread over the sea and a thick column of smoke rose, reaching the proportions of a high mountain and spreading out at the top like a mushroom. The sea changed colour. It is estimated that the explosion killed submarine creatures by the thousand. Several large vessels were sunk and a number damaged.

(newspaper account, 1946)

It is not a frivolous analogy; it is the revelation handed down to us by the men who first developed atomic weapons.

More and more I find myself feeling that some sort of religious sense would be better than this universal blankness. Would it not help mobilise public anger against the wicked waste of resources entailed in stockpiling the nuclear arsenal, and public rejection of the mass slaughter that is its logical consequence, if people *did* believe in something more than 'preserving our parliamentary democracy', or, less abstract, the next pay rise, the chance of a summer holiday in the sun, or the advisability of a video recorder? In the nineteenth century, you could take a group of people and be sure that seven-eighths of them believed in God, and the other one-eighth were passionately committed to the wonder of science and reasoning, which could fill the moral void which God had left. Now both those beliefs have gone: Christianity redundant in a materialistic world, and rationalism dumbfounded at the Frankenstein monster unleashed upon the world by scientific knowledge. What we are confronted by is the greatest sin, and the greatest absurdity: that humankind, lacking faith, should still have the vanity to destroy, not just itself, but the planet, and all life upon it – possibly by accident, or through madness, or pride, or fanaticism, or simply (irony of ironies) to 'preserve' . . . something or other.

To be optimistic, it seems to me that the growth of the peace movement across the world, and its great energy, *is* evidence of an alternative faith. It is an assertion of feeling against arid political pragmatism, of sense against madness, of life against death. It accepts the difficult truth of Yeats' dictum 'In dreams begin responsibilities', knowing that the dream of leaving the waste land behind is the responsibility of every human being. The way forward must be to step back; for to continue forward will be to take ourselves back, and back . . . into extinction, beyond death itself.

And we have a right to our own private deaths. Though death is as taboo a subject as God, each of us lives with the knowledge that we must die one day, but the with simultaneous comfort that our children, or if we have none, those of our friends, relatives and neighbours will outlive us. The man in Birmingham faces his solitary death in exactly the same way as the man in Budapest, knowing that long after he is silent the shouts of children will echo in the parks of his city, as they always have. It may be unconscious, but I believe that the sense of continuity and oneness matters to people; it gives a point to existence and fleshes out the secret hope of immortality. The nuclear threat denies us even that.

Ultimately, the essential thing about us as human beings is not what political system we live under, or what we achieve in worldly terms, but the ties of affection that bind us to those we love, *and* the respect and sympathy we have for those whom we know to have the same ties, the same needs – wherever they might live. The liking, and loving, the bearing of children, ageing and mourning – and hoping – are common experiences that stabilise the hectic world. So the horror of Hiroshima, which forced Mrs Yamasaki to abandon her child, called civilisation into question. The philosophy which *we* are forced to live by – that there could well be justification for wiping out millions upon millions of our fellow humans — has no place in civilisation. And when a young woman mutters, as I have heard, that there seems no point in bringing children into such a doomed world, that thought, removed though it may be from the actual experience of the Japanese mother, or the reality of international affairs, strikes a small blow at all that is most valuable about human life: the joyful will to love that transforms all the ordinariness of the everyday into something infinitely precious and permanent.

That is the power of the nuclear bomb — to pollute our atmosphere, our language, our minds and our souls. It is a power that must be met with power, which is why, finally, I must add a word on peace, or rather pacifism. I am not a pacifist. I would fight to save the people I love; I also admit that there are principles in defence of which I would condone the use of conventional force. But, as every thinking soldier must know, nuclear war would make him redundant; no place for individual heroism or endurance or military skill when the final conflagration makes a holocaust of this earth. So I think we must move beyond pacifism, in as much as it implies passivity, and counter the threat with the kind of heroism, endurance and skill which wins military medals. The women at Greenham Common have shown how it can be done. If it is necessary to chain ourselves to railings, to write letters, to take to the streets, to counter propaganda at local level by exhaustive argument, to show civil disobedience if necessary, then it must be done. I have to ask myself this question: if I am ready to fight for my loved ones and for my deepest principle, a respect for life, then how am I to deal with the gravest threat to both? By giving in and crying?

No. If we are to meet the challenge and step into that frightening area of responsibility beyond the waste land, anger is necessary, and action. I do not feel peaceful any more. I am prepared to declare war on those who juggle with the future of my children, and of your children — and the future of those children I watched playing happily in the park in Budapest.

Anne Pettitt

HOW I LEARNT TO START WORRYING AND HATE THE BOMB
The Effects of a Nuclear Bombardment

There are certain myths concerning nuclear war to one or all of which the vast majority of us suscribe: they enable us to live a life of relative unconcern in the face of probable annihilation. Dissect those myths to reveal the horrific reality within, and our everyday lives are shown to be precariously balanced between sweet oblivion and intense anxiety. Have we all learnt to stop worrying and love the bomb? I was amazed to read that the poster of the mushroom cloud is number nine in the top ten poster selling list — the image of death poised somewhere in the public consciousness between Jasper Carrott and Sting.

The rewriting of these myths necessarily involves a shift of consciousness and it is mainly for this reason that I look to the women's movement for a committed stance, for there, as a cornerstone, is the desire to determine one's own life, to choose life before death and to create a society in which human relationships can be based on mutual respect rather than on oppression and fear. The threat of nuclear war is the ultimate oppression, the terrifying expression of the struggle for power of male-dominated institutions. Women still play the predominantly caring role towards children: I know that I somehow feel most responsible for my children's well-being, for their diet, health and so on — I take *care* of them. It was experiencing that particular feeling of anxiety at the thought of them dying slowly and agonisingly while I looked on helpless that exploded the first myth for me — that it will at least be quick.

The Big Bang! One blinding flash and then you're gone, back to sweet oblivion again. How many times have I heard people say, 'Well, it will be quick.' Here is a quotation from a survivor of Hiroshima, a child at school when a one-kiloton atomic bomb was dropped on the city on a summer's day in August, 1945:

We ran to the swimming pool, dragging a classmate whose leg had been injured and eyes blinded. What I saw there. There was already one dead in the water. He must have fallen in, blinded by the burns all over his body. Another was trying to put out someone else's burning clothes with the blood that was pouring from his own wound. Yet another jumped into the water with his clothes on fire and drowned there unable to move his burned body. Another was beyond recognition, with his face swollen to two or three times normal size. Two of my friends clung to my arms. The surface of their bodies had been burned all over, and their skin had peeled off and was hanging loose from their elbows like the sleeve of a kimono. Their bodies slippery and red, they clung to my weak body. Their eyes were gone, and they could see nothing.

The bomb over Hiroshima was relatively small, one kiloton means that it had the explosive power of 1,000 tons of TNT. As the destructive power of the weaponry has increased, so have our units of measurement: modern nuclear weapons are now measured in megatons, or the equivalent of one million tons of TNT. An optimistic estimate by Whitehall of the scale of first attack we might expect is 200 megatons, and it would more likely be twice that figure. But are we now getting academic? Is 200 megatons acceptable where 400 is not? Lord Belstead, when Minister in charge of Civil Defence, was quoted as saying that while 'only fifteen million' British people would survive a full-scale nuclear attack, the figure could be doubled if people were to follow instructions. Put another way, twenty-four millions would die. To be drawn into the numbers game is to lose sight of reality. Can anyone really comprehend what it means to have twenty-four million people die on a small, overcrowded island in an extremely short period of time? Without any of the sophisticated sanitary, medical and communications systems functioning?

But the scientific language we use to describe the holocaust weaves an illusory world of its own in which we can think the unthinkable, manipulating numbers and words which have little meaning. Of course there are many factors which will determine the precise scale of destruction of the nuclear strike — the nature and tonnage of the weapons; whether they are exploded in the air

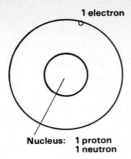

1 electron

Nucleus: 1 proton
1 neutron

(an airburst spreads heat and blast effects over a wide area) or on the ground (which increases local radioactive fallout and destruction of buildings); the nature of the target, densely packed cities and nuclear power stations being most vulnerable; such factors as weather conditions, winds to spread the radioactive fallout or clouds to filter off some of the radiation in an airburst.

There is no mystery in all this, but the scientific descriptions allude to a world inaccessible to the layperson in which decisions concerning our very existence are best left to the 'experts'. In effect, we are robbed of our responsibility.

The ancient Greeks thought that everything in this world was ultimately composed of minute, indivisible particles they called atoms. This theory more or less held true until scientists in our century discovered that the atom was not a single entity but was composed of even smaller particles arranged in a miniature of the solar system. This is a diagram of the simplest known atom, of hydrogen.

The nucleus of the atom gives it its mass and weight by virtue of the proton and neutron particles it contains. Electron particles revolve around the nucleus in fixed orbits. This system has its own internal energy and degree of stability. When we talk about uranium and plutonium atoms we are talking of much larger and less stable systems with numbers of protons and neutrons in the hundreds, viz. uranium 235. If one bombards the nucleus of an atom with other particles, say neutrons thrown out from other less stable atoms, then one can split apart this atomic structure. This is the principle of fission atomic weapons. A tremendous amount of energy is released as heat, light, sound and 'radiation', the general name for the highly penetrating alpha, beta, gamma and X-rays which cause biological damage. The fusion bomb, such as the hydrogen bomb, uses the intense heat produced in the fission process to fuse atoms together with further release of energy. This is how the sun generates its intense heat, but most of the harmful radiation from the sun is filtered off as it travels through our atmosphere. The hydrogen bomb blasts it into our midst.

Let us consider a one-megaton bomb over Central London; this is where I live and where fourteen per cent of the population of this island live. At the point of detonation of the bomb, or ground zero, the blast effects of the explosion would be immense. Within a radius of two and a half miles everything would be flattened, a few jagged remnants of reinforced buildings might remain on the perimeter. Up to five miles away all domestic housing, shops and light industrial premises would be destroyed. Eight miles away the walls of steel frame buildings would be blown away (this type of construction is used a great deal in modern council and private sector multi-storey dwellings). Even at thirteen miles away from ground zero windows would be blown in and people injured by flying broken glass.

I live on the outer edge of Islington, about six miles from the city centre. What, then would be my scenario? (You can construct your own: choose the most likely target near to your home and locate your distance from ground zero on a local map. Charts on pages 19, 20 and 21 will tell you the predicted effects.) What the nuclear barons have in store for me is not too nice. The human body is relatively resistant to the effect of blast. I would probably escape the ruptures and haemorrhages of the lungs, gut and ear drums experienced by those nearer to ground zero; instead I would almost certainly die of multiple injuries, fractures and ruptured internal organs, caused by my house collapsing on top of me. There would be high winds blowing rubble and debris before them as if these lumps of stone had no weight at all. There would be thousands trapped and dead or dying around me and no rescue teams and no hope of any in the foreseeable future. No painkillers. Nothing except the pain and the fear.

The fireball, at the centre of the explosion, would be hotter than the sun and one and a half miles in diameter. Those at the centre of the inferno (the 'lucky ones') would be vaporised, those who had had the foresight to provide themselves with a shelter would be incinerated, roasted alive. The intense bright glow of the fireball could be seen up to fifty miles away, brighter than the sun at noon. People who looked at this glowing sun would have the lining of their eyes burnt away and would be blinded. The intense heat, like the blast effects, diminish with distance. Where I live, this heat, if I were to have no protection from it, would still be great enough to burn the entire skin of my body to shreds. We have all heard of first, second and third degree burns: can the imagination stretch so far as to comprehend such extensive burning, extrapolate from the scald or the burning match to a burn which leaves our very insides exposed? There are specialised burn units set up in hospitals to deal with third degree burns. In one American case a young man whose motorcycle petrol tank had exploded

The extent of over-pressure effects after a 1 megaton (Mt) airburst (1200 ft; 366 m) over central London.

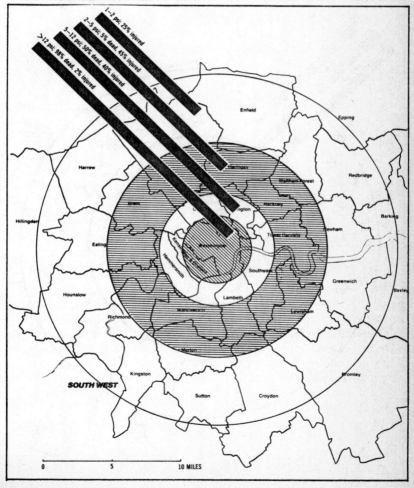

underwent six major operations in which eighty-five per cent of
his body was covered in skin grafts. He was given, in all, about 500
units of blood, antibiotics, placed in an absolutely sterile environment, administered with pain killers. There are facilities in the UK
for treating about 500 such cases and, in the event of a nuclear
attack, this minimal provision would be reduced by the simple fact

Areas receiving sufficient radiant heat after a 1 Mt airburst at 1500 ft
(457.5 m) over central London to cause skin burns and flash dazzle.

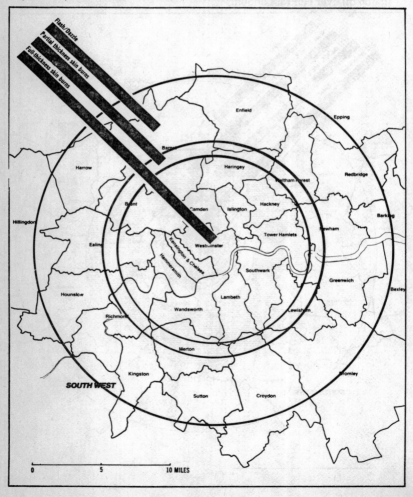

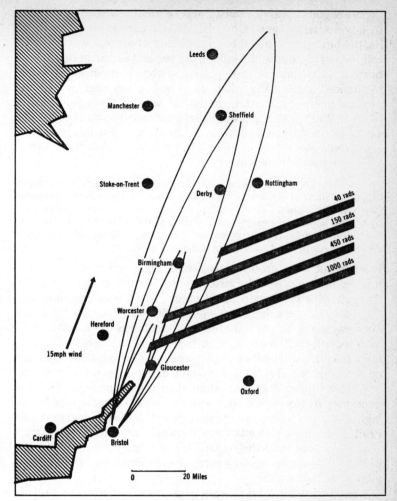

Approximate dimensions of 2 week accumulated radiation dose contour after a 1 Mt 50 = fission yield groundburst on Bristol in a 15 mph wind.

that in a nuclear war very many doctors, nurses and hospitals would be wiped out too.

It was estimated in Operation Square Leg (the NATO exercise which dealt with a hypothetical yet 'realistic' nuclear strike against Britain) that only 24,000 hospital beds out of the 60,000 normally available would remain. One must remember at this point that these are conservative, realistic and 'rational' statistics worked out by government experts who may well have an interest in presenting the best rather than the worst picture of nuclear war. On their estimate of two and a half million injured and a quarter of a million burnt it is obviously futile to place any hope in medical provision. (A stance, incidentally, that is becoming stronger within the medical profession itself, inspiring the Medical Campaign against Nuclear Weapons.) Supplies of vital medical equipment and drugs would be destroyed and transport of what is left incapacitated. You would simply die in agony. In Hiroshima, only three out of forty-five hospitals remained:

Dr Sasaki had not looked outside all day; the scene inside was so compelling that it had not occurred to him to ask what had happened beyond the doors and windows. Ceilings and partitions had fallen in; plaster, dust, blood and vomit were everywhere. Patients were dying by the hundreds but there was nobody to carry away the corpses . . . thousands of patients and hundreds of dead were in the yard and driveway.

Further out from ground zero, about eight miles away, second degree burning would cause severe blistering, open wounds through which infection could enter. The sterile dressings and antibiotic powders that even a domestic scald necessitates would not be available to any but a few, so these burns would not heal. In both second and third degree burns there is the risk of loss of body fluid, but who will be there to replace these with transfusions and intravenous drips? Flash burns would occur in people exposed up to thirteen miles away. In addition to the burns from the heat generated by the explosion, fire storms would rage, fanned by the high winds. No medical or fire service could hope to deal with this. Printed on page 23 is a chart which reveals some vivid information – at four miles from the explosion the living room curtains and perhaps the settee would ignite; at 4.7 miles away the stripped pine would smoulder.

A reaction to all this is to want to get away – out of the city, out of the country. The myth that there is a safe place to go is persuasive. (It was ironic to read of the woman who took her family to the Falkland Islands to try and escape what she saw as inevitable nuclear war in Britain.) With the proliferation of nuclear weapons beyond the superpowers and the rapid expansion in the demand for nuclear plant in both East and West, one can say that if the world is not exactly blown to bits, if the heat and blast don't get you then the radiation will. Never before has war threatened such

Some effects of heat from explosion of a 1 megaton weapon

Distance from ground zero, in miles		Thermal radiation	Effects of thermal radiation
Surface explosion	Explosion at 8,000 ft	cal/cm^2	
4.0	4.5	20	Dark furnishing fabrics catch fire
4.5	5.0	18	Dark-coloured cotton catches fire
4.7	5.6	15	Unpainted wood chars
5.0	6.1	13	All unprotected skin would have third degree burns
5.4	6.9	10	About half the unprotected people would have third degree burns
5.8	7.5	8	Newspaper catches fire
6.5	8.6	6	About half the unprotected people would have second degree burns
8.0	11.5	3	About half the unprotected people would have first degree burns

a destructive effect on future generations of life on this planet. The most insidious vehicle of death in nuclear war is immediate and long-term radiation. We cannot see, hear or feel this radiation — the X-rays, alpha, beta and gamma rays — we can only see the symptoms.

Radioactivity occurs naturally as background radiation — radiation from the sun and from such elements as uranium which exist in the earth's crust as unstable isotopes, that is, unstable forms of the atomic structure which emit 'radioactivity' as they decompose. When a hydrogen bomb explodes, particles of radioactive materials are thrown out into the atmosphere which cling to dust and other airborne debris and fall to earth as the dust settles. This is known as fallout. In the immediate vicinity of the blast, radiation levels are very high and are fatal within hours. Further out from the centre, the fine particles deposit a fine cloud of radioactive dust over a wide area. The wind blows the dust over many miles, through windows, onto crops, into reservoirs and rivers, over everything we touch. The ionising radiation emitted from these particles and from the explosion itself are all biologically damaging. The basic building blocks of living things are the cells: millions of bone cells, blood, nerve, skin, gut cells unite to form that complicated system, the body. As old cells die, or children grow, the division of 'parent' cells produces new cells. At this stage the cell is most vulnerable to the effects of radiation. When the foetus is developing within the womb the fertilised egg cell has to begin the long process of repeated cell division to produce the end-product, the baby. Cells and babies are part of the material world, so bombard their atoms with neutrons, X-rays, gamma, beta rays and the delicate atomic structure, and hence function, of the cell will be destroyed. We don't *know* this is happening, not until the symptoms of radiation sickness appear, or the number of deaths from cancer increases or genetic deformities appear in greater numbers in future generations.

When the body is exposed to radiation, the response depends upon the dose. What then is a lethal dose of radiation and is there a 'safe' dose? It is very hard to say. The young, the old and the sick are more susceptible: it is a fact that a certain dose will kill some people and not others. What we can say is that at a dose of 450 Rads, fifty per cent of young, fit adults could be expected to die. Or to put it another way, you'd have a fifty-fifty chance of living. This is known as the LD 50. To put this figure in perspective, the International Commission on Radiological Protection uses five Rads a year as a maximum limit of exposure for radiation workers. (This figure, by the way, is regularly revised downwards.) This is approximately fifty times the level of background radiation.

An official description of radiation sickness is as follows: the first symptoms are headache, nausea, dizziness and frequent vomiting, then acute diarrhoea and fatigue. This lasts for several days and is followed by apparent recovery, but two to three weeks later the symptoms return along with internal bleeding. Breathing becomes difficult, hair falls out, sores appear under the skin; there is fever, total fatigue and finally death. These symptoms appear at doses of 150 Rads: the chart on p. 25 shows the development of these symptoms with increase in dose. The neutron bomb, a new development, is designed to produce the maximum dose of radiation with lesser effects of heat and blast. It is aimed at killing people (and the environment) with the least damage to property.

To give some idea of the widespread effects of fallout — if just a one-megaton bomb was dropped on Bristol, in the south west, with a 15 mph wind, the effects of radiation being cumulative, people as far away as Birmingham could receive the LD in two weeks. Remember that the conservative estimate for a nuclear attack was

Types of radiation sickness

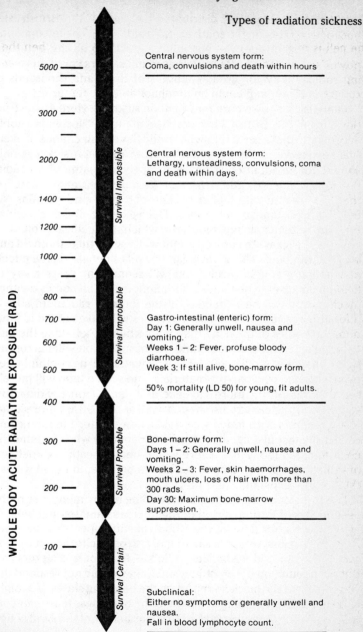

WHOLE BODY ACUTE RADIATION EXPOSURE (RAD)

Survival Impossible

5000 — Central nervous system form:
Coma, convulsions and death within hours

3000 —

2000 — Central nervous system form:
Lethargy, unsteadiness, convulsions, coma and death within days.

1400 —

1200 —

1000 —

Survival Improbable

800 —

700 — Gastro-intestinal (enteric) form:
Day 1: Generally unwell, nausea and vomiting.
600 — Weeks 1 – 2: Fever, profuse bloody diarrhoea.
500 — Week 3: If still alive, bone-marrow form.

50% mortality (LD 50) for young, fit adults.

400 —

Survival Probable

300 — Bone-marrow form:
Days 1 – 2: Generally unwell, nausea and vomiting.
Weeks 2 – 3: Fever, skin haemorrhages, mouth ulcers, loss of hair with more than 300 rads.
200 — Day 30: Maximum bone-marrow suppression.

Survival Certain

100 —

Subclinical:
Either no symptoms or generally unwell and nausea.
Fall in blood lymphocyte count.

two *hundred* megatons, distributed throughout the British Isles but concentrated on the south east. No area would be left uncontaminated. Or consider the possibility of a bomb hitting a nuclear power station. The nuclear fuels used in reactors carry on releasing radioactivity for greater lengths of time, and thousands of square miles of land could be uninhabitable for centuries.

There is no known cure for radiation sickness. Here are instructions from the British civil defence manual: 'Hospitals should accept only those casualties who would have a fair chance of eventual recovery ... People suffering from radiation sickness only should not be admitted. There is no specific treatment for radiation injury.' Bacteria and viruses are far more resistant to radiation than we are and with higher background levels, new strains will develop, resistant to antibiotics. The epidemic diseases such as typhoid, bubonic plague, diptheria, which the medical profession has tried for years to control, might well regain their foothold and become rampant. The sophisticated level of debate on the effects of whooping cough vaccination will seem light years away as death from disease becomes a commonplace. The body's defence mechanisms will be damaged by the ionising radiation, so will offer little resistance. The public services will have ceased to function, the bodies of the dead may not be buried, let alone the bins emptied and streets swept. Standards of sanitation will mirror our worst images of mediaeval slums. The water will be contaminated by sewage and radioactive materials, and scarce food will merely serve as reason for more violence and death. Some radioactive products of nuclear explosion such as strontium 90 are more lethal when taken in with food and drink, as they enter the food chain causing cancer in a significant number of people who consume the contaminated foodstuffs. There would be no escaping the effects of radiation – it would be in the air we breathe, the food we eat, the house we live in.

The British people appear to have some happy memories of the Second World War: a period of togetherness and mutual help, of 'down the shelter' and 'In the Mood', of stiff upper lip when your backs are against the wall. Japan had a strong cultural value of 'no surrender' too – the Kamikaze pilots – to point to a stereotype. But the population of Hiroshima and Nagasaki did not respond this way. An official American report on the bombing states, 'As might be expected, the primary reaction to the bomb was fear – uncontrolled terror, strengthened by the sheer horror of the destruction and suffering witnessed by the survivors.' The people were profoundly shocked and rendered helpless. Acute depression and fear does not make for a busy population, obeying the instructions in their civil defence manuals and generally keeping in line. In short, in such circumstances, all social organisation breaks down. Communication between the survivors is minimal: most telecommunication and electronic systems cease to function and people are afraid to leave their homes for fear of contamination. People become isolated, living with the dead and the dying. It has been shown that isolation is a markedly effective way of inducing disturbed behaviour. It is the stuff of nightmares with which no human being could be expected to cope. I was moved to find that some friends of mine have already decided to commit suicide if they 'survive' a nuclear war as they would have no desire to live in a post-holocaust world. Recent American research on the attitudes of children to a nuclear future shows them to be distressingly nihilistic.

How about the few remaining heroes who climb out of the wreckage and look towards new horizons? In approximately six years there would be a marked increase in the number of deaths from leukaemia, particularly in children. Other forms of cancer have a longer latency period, perhaps up to twenty years. Cancer of the thyroid, lung, bone and breast in particular would be more prevalent.

Research has been done into the incidence of cancer in the population which survived the Japanese bombings, on workers in the nuclear fuel industry, on uranium miners and on children who were X-rayed when in the womb. These last three groups received what was considered a 'safe' dose, that is, a very low dose. But the effects of radiation are cumulative so workers in nuclear industries are especially vulnerable. Also the local population who live near a nuclear plant or near to where waste is stored may receive low doses over a period of time.

So, radiation is not a threat of the future: it is with us now. This was driven home to me while I was researching this chapter. I came across the work of Dr Alice Stewart in which she had examined the records of children who had died of leukaemia and found that a significant number had been X-rayed when in the womb. The chill that I felt when I realised that I had been X-rayed when I was eight and a half months' pregnant was difficult to cope with. I had *known* it was wrong but had put my faith in the experts.

Of course, it was a rational decision but I had not been given a full choice, I had not been told all the facts, and I had not bothered, or at least thought, to question their wisdom. I was willing to let responsibility rest with the experts. Well, I wouldn't do that now. What happens to me and my children is my responsibility — I must be my own expert now.

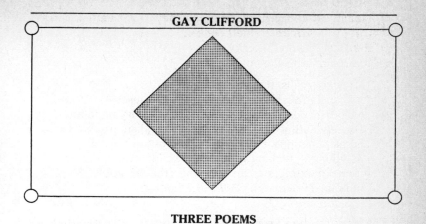

THREE POEMS

The cellars of Sidon *

Tyre is down
Hundreds lie dead in the cellars of Sidon
Cities my cities and your ruins
Rubble and walls, but carbonised bodies:
Stones replaced but never veins.
Jesse broken, his prophetic tree
Scorched dry as vines near Pompeii.
Hundreds dead in the cellars of Sidon.

And other cities where the dead don't rot
For fine nice weaponry we now have got.
Dust in the streets which can be easy swept
Bricks seen again, not those who birthing wept
Shadows on walls and Dresden bombed to hell
Through smoke a question: Did we do this well?
Like porcelain bits the bones say what is gone
Dead in the cellars of Sidon.

Cities your cities, they are ruined dead,
Yet what is that beside a shattered head.
What of obstetrics which made war from labour
And conned the workers to our children's murder?
We say Dark Ages but how dark are these
When swollen piles of calcined bodies freeze.

Limepit waited carts of Plague or the Black Death
Our clean arms salesmen bank on others' breath.
Remember when the city's gone
What's in the cellars of Sidon.

The ochre walls, the gentle terraces
The cafés towers mosques and whore-houses
Apses, arcades and beams, worn clothes drying in air,
Leisurely eating, child's voice, alleys and shops and hair,
The plants in tins, roses and bergamot,
The laughing fucking walking speaking lot.
When we extinguish this and when they're gone
Think on Tyre *and the cellars of Sidon.*

20 July 82

* The poem refers to an event during the invasion of the Lebanon by Israel
in 1982, when many thousands of people were killed. The cellar in Sidon,
filled with dead bodies, was reported in the newspapers in July 1982.

for Victor Jara: vox populi *

I was other   that is why I cared
to find voice   or acts   shared
now am only   gaps   and blackness
Victor Jara   they cut his hand
his fingers one & one & said: play.

And in the stadium of others' dying
his blood drowned his guitar.   But they
thought it only crying,   those who say
that others' death in blood can only count.
No one can die where with green pitch
a playing field courage comes to play
and plucks with ruined stumps   tunes
for us   others   those who need,   say
those with cut bodies   violenced
whose braveness makes them share enmity
for others   illimitable   silenced.

15 July 1981

* Victor Jara, a Chilean poet and folk-singer, was machine-gunned by the
Pinochet regime in 1973 during their brutal overthrow of Allende's socialist government. Since 1973 it is forbidden to mention his name in Chile.

Secret heroine from Joseph Conrad

She went out on the streets, faced facts of war
picked herself through rubble, wondered it seemed far
going to work on broken bricks, the new ruined town.
She'd been at Taylor Woodrow, now worked further down
across the main road, the place where they made arms.
Somehow construction work was no different from munitions.
Her employer about the same, she accepted old conditions.
He did not even need the grace to see any harm
the morning she came in tears, did not take her hand,
but she cried over the new designs, and about the fighting,
drafted mistakes in the model, under inadequate lighting.
We got to test it, and the pit replaced the land.
Our own people fell in, and we minuted alarm.

I'm haunted still and still don't love her less
She drew the detail wrong, but knew the real mess.

When the pit gapes and all the idols fall
When every icon's shaken from its wall
When every birth must simply be aborted
When all our bravery's gone or been distorted
We could remember just who built those walls
And not ignore ourselves who dug the pit.
In our conceptions we construct ourselves
and Gods we make, may be appalled by it.

23 May 81
2 June 81

THE BALANCE OF TERROR
Deterrence and Peace-keeping

Very few people actually *want* nuclear weapons. No one wants them to be used. The argument that most people find most convincing for keeping them is that actually having them means that they will never be used. If each great power knows, it is argued, that the other will respond in kind immediately a nuclear weapon is used, then no one will ever be mad enough to use one.

This is the argument of *deterrence*. By deterring the other side, a powerful nuclear armoury guarantees that there will be no nuclear war. How convincing an argument is this?

From policemen's truncheons to splendid armadas, straightforward deterrents have for centuries been an accepted and acceptable instrument of law, both civil and international. Their effectiveness relies either on the threat of physical force or on negative sanctions — negative sanctions can be the removal of personal freedom by imprisonment or enforced activity, or in the case of nations, instruments such as economic embargoes. Either way, the deterrent has to be seen to be sufficiently unpleasant to make the potential wrongdoer think twice before going ahead with an unlawful action.

Deterrence and threat of punishment have usually been proportionate to the potential crime. A regiment of soldiers isn't stationed outside a nightclub, where a couple of 'heavies' will do. The dangers of escalation clearly enter into the argument even at this level: British policemen still prefer to go unarmed, except on specific assignments, fearing that were they to carry guns there would be more shoot-outs with criminals, and more policemen shot. Deterrence is a familiar element of civilised life, to do with personal and social restraint.

There has always been an element of deterrence too in international relations and national defence. In the nuclear age, however, it has reached proportions so unprecedented that many people claim that deterrence is no longer the name of the game.

How and why has this happened? Is national defence any longer served by current deterrence theory and current arms holdings, or is the scale of nuclear armament itself the greater danger the world faces?

We have seen in other chapters some of the effects of the two atomic bombs dropped on Japan. Though scientists from many countries were involved in the development of nuclear science in general, and of the atom bomb in particular, only the USA ended the Second World War and began the peace with the full capacity to produce such a bomb. This means that for a number of years the USA had the advantage of being the sole possessor of a nuclear 'deterrent'. We can take with a pinch of salt Dr David Owen's statement that the Soviet Union had the advantage in conventional forces at the end of the war. This may have been so on a count of heads, although with twenty million dead, the Soviet Union's shortage of manpower has been widely acknowledged. But modern armies need vast industrial backup if they are to be militarily effective. 'If one lesson was learned in the last war on arms production, which is now almost apparently forgotten,' Douglas Jay said recently, 'it was that defence potential depends on industrial capacity.' The industrial capacity of the USSR was seventy per cent destroyed in the Second World War, due in large part to the scorched earth policy, i.e. the deliberate destruction of anything which could be of value to the enemy, whereas that of the USA was unscathed, and in Noam Chomsky's words, the USA enjoyed 'enormous global dominance' with which to start the peace.

By 1949, the USSR had produced her own nuclear weapon, and by 1954 Britain had followed suit. Even so, a glance at the map, and at the geographical location of the members of the NATO alliance, will show that it would have been possible early on for the USA to launch nuclear weapons on to the soil of the USSR from its allies' territory, but that the reverse was not true, for the USA was and is distanced from her 'enemy', the USSR, by the Atlantic Ocean.

In 1957, the launch of the first Soviet Sputnik demonstrated the fact that she was able to deliver a nuclear weapon not only from aircraft but also by means of an intercontinental-range ballistic missile. Only from that point on, have theories evolved of 'rough parity' or 'balance of power', at least as far as nuclear war is concerned. From that point on, too, the nuclear arms race has spiralled. Ideas of 'minimum deterrence' lasted in the West only as long as the West was ahead, first in solely possessing the weapon, and second in delivery capability. Once the Soviet Union had also developed these, the build-up was rapid, and according to Lord Zuckerman, by 1962 'had already gone well beyond the rational requirements of any mutual deterrent threat'. Now, both sides call for a 'balanced' reduction of arms. When and how to start seem to be major problems, down to what size seems to be another.

Estimates as to what a minimum yet still effective nuclear deterrent could and should be start at a low level, numerically speaking, yet of course even they involve suffering and destruction of appalling dimensions. McGeorge Bundy, former Special Assistant to the President for National Security Affairs in the USA, has said:

In the real world of real political leaders — whether here or in the Soviet Union — a decision that would bring even one hydrogen bomb on one city of one's own country would be recognised in advance as a catastrophic blunder; ten bombs on ten cities would be a disaster beyond history; and a hundred bombs on a hundred cities unthinkable.

Herbert York, director of Defence Research and Engineering, Department of Defence, under Presidents Eisenhower and Kennedy, agrees: 'from one to ten are enough whenever the course of events is being rationally determined.'

Much more recently, Lord Zuckerman has argued that, in the absence of extensive defence deployments, logic decreed that just one missile-armed submarine ought to suffice. This, while sounding low, would mean 160 destroyed cities and perhaps twenty million dead, were it to be an American Poseidon submarine, for they carry 160 independently targetable warheads.

Sadly, today's stockpile of deterrents belongs not to the 'real world of real political leaders' but to a dangerous fantasy unrelated to the real problems facing humanity, nor are they being 'rationally determined' or decreed by the logic guiding Lord Zuckerman. The superpower spiral began as a race for political and economic power, is fuelled by industrial and military interests and today is out of control.

There have been several stages in this development away from simple minimum deterrence, in which the lead has almost always been taken by the USA. At the same time, the military and political doctrines backing these stages have changed, so that in 1954 (that is, even before Soviet ability to retaliate or to attack American soil had developed), John Foster Dulles proclaimed the doctrine of 'massive retaliation'. Once both sides were able to deliver substantial, though not numerically equal, nuclear attacks on each other's home territory, nuclear strategy developed a more complicated series of responses. Simple deterrence was replaced by strategies which took into account the possibility of 'first strike' by the opposing side. This would aim at nuclear military targets with a view to making retaliation impossible; at the same time, both sides tried to make their installations invulnerable so as to provide an equally devastating response, or 'second strike'. This was, if you like, deterrence in two stages: an admission that simple deterrence might fail, but that if it did, the enemy must first consider whether the answering destruction would nevertheless make a first strike worthwhile.

Since the Soviet Union has proved more or less able to match or to answer the technical developments of US nuclear weapons, a balance of power — or of terror — seems to have been accepted by both powers as a form of deterrence. Called 'Mutually Assured Destruction' by the then US Secretary of State for Defence, Robert MacNamara, this policy called on the American side for the nuclear capacity to eliminate half the industrial capacity of the Soviet Union and a quarter of the population. This amounted to destroying the largest 200 cities and towns of the USSR, where one-third of its population live.

To meet the requirements of retaliation as well as attack, both the USA and the USSR have three sections to their nuclear strategy: land-based missiles, long-range aircraft and a missile-carrying submarine force. This is considered sufficient to leave at least one and possibly two of the sections intact should the 'enemy' strike first, to launch a retaliatory attack.

In MAD scenarios, second strike is aimed at cities, to maximise horror, which in turn would prevent the first strike happening in the first place. With the increasing efficiency and accuracy of weapons systems, it is now more possible to 'take out' military and industrial targets and so theoretically lessen the loss of life while striking against the war capacity of the enemy. This strategy, which goes back to the Schlesinger doctrine, is known as PD 59 (after Presidential Directive 59, issued by President Carter in 1979). Any illusion this may create of a more 'humane' nuclear strategy can quickly be dispelled. Many 'military' targets are centres of intelligence and command. The command centres of the West include London, Paris, Bonn, Brussels and Washington. An attack on any one of these would destroy millions of lives as well as centuries of civilisation.

No one knows precisely the number of nuclear warheads that exist in the world today. An authoritative report of the United Nations (Comprehensive Study on Nuclear Weapons 1980, report of the Secretary General to General Assembly of the United Nations) puts the figure at probably 'in the excess of 40,000', ranging in explosive power from 'about 100 tons up to more than twenty million tons equivalent of chemical high explosives'. The report goes on:

The largest weapon ever tested released an energy approximately 4,000 times that of the atomic bomb that levelled Hiroshima, and there is in principle no upper limit to the explosive yield that may be attained. The total strength of present nuclear arsenals may be equivalent to about one million Hiroshima bombs, i.e. some thirteen thousand million tons of TNT. It is often pointed out that this is equivalent to more than three tons for every man, woman and child on earth.

The range of weapons, to quote Zuckerman again, includes 'free-falling bombs, warheads for ballistic missiles, artillery shells, depth charges, nuclear-tipped torpedoes . . . small weapons have also been devised for use in field warfare.' We have come a long way from the notional minimum deterrent of one nuclear-armed submarine or one to ten hydrogen bombs.

Arguments as to whether the USA or the USSR are 'ahead' in this or that range are irrelevant. In discussing the situation after Reagan's 'zero option' and Brezhnev's Bonn visit in November 1981, E. P. Thompson wrote: 'In these times of grotesque overkill, the arguments of balance are trivial at every level except that of "face". If there are enough nuclear weapons in Europe to destroy the continent thirty times over, what does it matter if one side can do it fourteen times and the other sixteen?' One thing is certain: the present stockpiles of nuclear weapons make Europe and indeed the world potentially *less*, *not more* safe and secure than before they existed. There had to be a high level of fear and tension between nations for their governments to embark on the nuclear arms race in the first place; and fear and tension are hardly the atmosphere in which to make cool, calm judgements. Tension and fear favour panic, errors, miscalculation. One slip, and the whole ghastly train of events can be set in motion. There will never be the option of using up all the stocks; humankind will be finished first. Yet what do we see? Incredibly, more nations are joining the 'nuclear club', and the prospect of engaging in limited nuclear war is catered for in NATO plans, and therefore also in those of the Warsaw Treaty Organisation. What are the implications of these two developments, especially for Europe?

Side by side with superpower weapons of mutual destruction, defensive and offensive intercontinental missiles aimed at one another's territory, there have existed since the 1950s both the doctrine and the weapons for quite another scenario. In 1958, Henry Kissinger propounded the theory that the current US military thinking, of all-out attack against the Soviet Union, would lead to virtual suicide by both superpowers. This would be just as true if the war were to be launched in support of America's allies: 'However firm allied unity may be, a nation cannot be counted on to commit suicide in defence of a foreign country.' In his 1971 'State of the World' message, President Nixon took up the theme, saying that the USA should find alternatives 'appropriate to the nature and level of provocation . . . without necessarily having to resort to mass destruction'. Ken Coates has suggested that this theory implies that the 'total destruction of both superpowers might be a second-stage option to be deferred during negotiations which could be undertaken while Europe burns.' So while its populations have been fed a diet of deterrence theory − which, by and large, they have swallowed − more active scenarios have existed for decades. And the irony is that it is Europe, with roughly half of its countries the allies of USA, the other half the allies of USSR, which is the chosen battlefield.

It is difficult to say whether the technical ability to produce much more accurate and finely targeted weapons came before the theory of limited war, or whether the weaponry was devised to fit the theory. It seems to be a sad fact that once man has devised some new technique, warlike or not, he very soon devises an excuse to use it. Weapons and defence systems in the last two decades have been transformed by satellite reporting, radar targeting and tracking and firing by means of automatic computer, pre-set programmed instructions. This dramatic increase in accuracy has made it possible for war games strategists to envisage the concept of 'limited', more localised or tactical war. Certain weapons have been developed with this in mind. The controversial cruise 'Tomahawk' missile, due to be deployed in Western Europe under NATO agreement in 1983 is essentially a development of the wartime pilotless aircraft, the Vl. It carries radar and computer systems, as well as an altitude map in its 'memory store'. Its military advantages are that it is low-flying and sub-sonic. Altogether, the tactical armoury of NATO has been given as 7,000 warheads, ever since MacNamara as US Secretary of State gave a figure. The USSR has its own 'tactical' armoury estimated at some 3,500 to 5,000 warheads.

The military advantage of 'limited' or theatre war has already been indicated: from the superpowers' points of view, it confines the nuclear conflict to a smaller geographical area and need not involve the territory of either the USA or USSR, and deaths and destruction could be correspondingly smaller. In this respect, the USA is at a greater advantage than the USSR, whose Western territory is within Europe, where the 'battlefield' scenario is assumed to take place. At the same time, Soviet military thinking does not subscribe to the view that, once started, a 'limited' nuclear war could be contained, but rather that there would be rapid escalation.

People in Europe, as they have become aware of the existence of plans for potential 'limited' nuclear war on their continent, as an alternative to 'all-out' nuclear war, have become more sharply aware of the wider nuclear debate. One of the consequences of this awareness has been a questioning of Britain's independent nuclear deterrent. Just how independent *is* this deterrent? It is difficult to know, for stationed on British soil or around her coasts are no fewer than four sets of systems, soon to be added to, unless the decision to deploy the Cruise missile system can be reversed. Some of the weapons systems involved are under United States' sole command, and some under NATO's. There are some tactical weapons belonging to Great Britain and a small independent strategic force of four nuclear-propelled submarines fitted at present with Polaris missiles. These are to be replaced eventually by up to sixteen American D5 ballistic missiles (or 'Trident') with fourteen independently guided nuclear warheads. Even disregarding our dependence on the Americans for production and delivery, to what extent can this country claim to be independent, when two other military High Commands are involved?

The second question relating to the independent deterrent theory is against whom and on what occasion would the British — or the French, for that matter — use their deterrent alone, that is, without joint agreement with the Americans? The 'enemy' is presumed to be the Soviet Union, yet it is difficult to imagine a scenario in which the British would be prepared to go ahead without the USA. Furthermore, the scale of retaliation of which the Soviet Union is capable, say with her SS20s, would be of such colossal proportions that that calculation alone should deter any British government from engaging in a nuclear exchange with the USSR.

The only other type of conflict, the USSR apart, in which the British might become involved and the USA not, would be one concerned with some remnant of our colonial past. This seems to be the issue which makes Americans hesitate because of their own origins and history. But the use of nuclear weapons as a British response to a neo-colonial conflict is so unthinkable that we are left to guess again about the uses of an independent 'deterrent'.

One explanation for British and French retention of an independent nuclear 'deterrent' advanced by two such different people as Alva Myrdal and Enoch Powell, is as a compensation for loss of empire. Others, like Patrick Wall, see rivalry between the two powers as an explanation. The British Secretary of State for Defence, John Nott, sees things in even more alarming terms. In a recent House of Commons debate he said: 'I admit that I would feel more than a touch of discomfort if France, with her clear policy of non-commitment to Alliance strategy, were the only West European nuclear power and had a capacity to bring down Soviet retribution on her neighbour across the Channel in circumstances where we had no deterrent response of our own.' So, let's bring it down on ourselves!

It is the relationship between the USA and Britain to which we must return for the reasons usually advanced for the retention of the British independent nuclear deterrent. These reasons are contradictory. For two countries purporting to have such a 'special relationship', there is a curiously high degree of distrust expressed by British politicians of American intentions. This distrust goes back a number of years and is not confined to one party.

Churchill thought that British independence would be helped by

having nuclear weapons of her own; Gaitskell doubted US willingness 'to engage in nuclear retaliation on Britain's behalf' and, by
retaining an independent nuclear deterrent, hoped to maintain
maximum influence with the United States so that decisions would
not be forced on Britain against her will. Other politicians cite
possible future changes in the US Presidency as their cause for
concern. Julian Amery quotes an anecdote: Macmillan, in conversation with President Kennedy is asked, in effect: 'But don't you
trust me to defend you?' and replies: 'I trust you absolutely. I would
not have trusted President Harding out of my sight with my pocket
book.' Anthony Buck seeks to interpret this kind of presidential
change through Kremlin eyes, where Americans might not always
be seen as 'such sure supporters of this country as they are today'.
However much it is disguised as something else – American
pique at our apparent reluctance to spend more on arms, or the
dangers of innate American isolationism – the basic distrust of
American intent stems from widespread doubt as to whether the
Americans would use their nuclear might to 'settle' the crises of
their allies. Such doubts are well-placed; all comes full circle in
Kissinger's frank view that to do so would be virtual suicide for the
USA '. . . in defence of a foreign country'.

A relatively recent extension of the independent deterrent argument has emerged in Britain in debates around 'two centres of
decision-making'. Again, the application of this argument can be
contradictory, seen either as a strengthening bond within NATO, or
as a brake or influence on American decision-making. John Nott
expresses the view that this is something which only Britain can
perform: 'A second centre of decision-making in the form of our
strategic deterrent is a real reinforcement of Alliance strength and
one which, for various reasons, written in history, we alone are in
a position to undertake.' Dr Owen prefers to emphasise the potential for influence:

It is not necessary for us . . . to conceive of this weapons system in terms of
independent action. It is inconceivable that it would ever be used in an
independent sense. Where it does make a contribution to the Alliance is
not just in the number of missiles but in the decision-making framework
within the Alliance. That is an important contribution. It means that any
decision taken by a United States President has to take into account the
fact that there is another nuclear contribution within that Alliance.

The emphasis here is not upon the military value of the independent deterrent so much as its *political function* within NATO. What

is more, David Owen has written on the subject and extended the theory of 'two centres of decision-making' to include circumscription of the putative enemy: Soviet decision-making is 'circumscribed by the French, British and Chinese nuclear bombs, and even by India and Pakistan when they become nuclear weapon states'.

Clearly, there are two dangers in this way of thinking. Firstly, it encourages proliferation. As long ago as 1959, Richard Crossman perceived just such dangers in the independent deterrent argument. 'How can we possibly prevent the Germans, the French and every other nation in the alliance saying, "What the British demand for themselves we demand for ourselves"? The right to distrust the Americans cannot remain a British monopoly.' Soon after this the French did indeed follow suit. Now, there are some fifteen to twenty countries thought to have either nuclear weapons or the capacity to make them. True, these are not confined to Western allies distrustful of us intentions, but include countries with traditions of rivalry or enmity: India and Pakistan; South Africa and black Africa; such states as Nigeria and Libya; Israel and Egypt. Consortia, such as that between Israel, South Africa and Taiwan, pool resources both of material and of technology, and proliferate across more than one continent. Countries refusing to adhere to the Non-Proliferation Treaty include Argentina, Brazil, Egypt, Israel, South Africa and Spain. Virtually all of these countries represent areas of tension and of potential or actual conflict. China produced its nuclear explosion in 1964, India, ten years later – a particular irony, as Nehru was the first to propose a total ban on nuclear tests. The failure is one of international diplomacy. The blame lies largely with those nations who led the way in insisting on their right to an independent nuclear deterrent.

The second danger in the 'two centres of decision-making' concept is less easy to define, but probably more dangerous in its effect. The idea is that a proliferation of centres of decision-making, by limiting the options open to the Soviet Union, is a valuable strategy that somehow contributes to defence by making the 'enemy' more cautious, less certain. This is a foolhardy surmise. Such uncertainty increases the dangers of miscalculation and misconception; of misinterpretation of the others' intentions; generally, it increases tension. Of course, this is perfectly consistent with deterrence theory, which relies on maintaining an atmosphere of tension and uncertainty, as do all games of chance. The argument goes that without that uncertainty, neither side may be deterred. But *with* it, errors and sheer breakdown of the individual or collective nerve become more likely. Only 'utter desperation or fear,' says Lord Zuckerman, could lead to the 'rational' decision to use a nuclear weapon. Yet the extraordinary fact remains that one of the most-repeated catch-phrases used by supporters of the deterrence theory would have us take comfort from this uneasy relationship of antagonistic forces: it is 'the Balance of Power'.

We are led to believe that a more or less equal distribution of power between hostile world forces is a well-tried and historically respectable prescription guaranteed to maintain world peace. David Owen assures us that this is so: 'There is a justified fear of creating an imbalance in forces, for history shows that this is often the trigger for war.' History, as Dr Owen should know, shows us many things, and it is a pity that his use of it is so selective. It is a pity that he limits himself to nuclear examples, for he is in fact claiming something of much greater lineage; the desire to 'retain a balance of force goes deep into the nature of man and nations', he tells us. One regrets that he does not examine the history of the nineteenth century, for instance, when European nations following the Napoleonic wars, tried a number of alliances in their attempts to maintain a balance of power. Perhaps, like the thirty-seven years of 'peace' in Europe, this worked for a time, but the growth of the industrial revolution, national revolutions throwing off old imperial powers, new imperial developments of overseas colonies and capital investment, and new patterns of trade and commerce saw, towards the end of the century, a completely new 'balance of power'. Those old enemies, Great Britain, France and Russia, encircled, through the Triple Entente, a powerful new nation, Germany, which hadn't even existed when the old balance of power had been struck. And those, like David Owen, who add to 'balance of power' the ancient argument, 'Let him who desires peace, prepare for war', should be reminded that the 1914-1918 war was preceded by a massive arms race, particularly in war-ships, and that when that war *did* break out, after more than thirty years of European 'peace', it was the greatest in the history of the world to that date.

This is not the place for a discussion of the complex reasons for the outbreak of the Second World War, but among them could be given lack of will, lack of leadership and an obsession with the 'international conspiracy of communism'. This, a propaganda theme of the German Nazis, prevented many people in Western Europe from identifying the real enemy until it was almost too late. So, yes, let us consider the balance of power, but let us remember too, that the world is in a state of flux, never static. This is true of economics, trade patterns, national interests and therefore of alliances. Most of all, and precisely *because of* today's attempts at a nuclear balance of power, we have the most destabilising factor of all: the nuclear arms race.

Far from being a stabilising mechanism, the balance of power — now known as the Balance of Terror — is straining national and international economies to a quite unrealistic extent. If it is the intention of either or both superpowers to arm to the point where, in trying to compete, the 'other side' is economically crippled, then it is a dubious aim, for such economic instability is itself one major cause of war. The American and Soviet economies are showing signs of strain, as are those of other members of both power blocs. There is a large element of tension in the very psychology of deterrence. This has economic causes too. Both sides have to build up in their populations a 'war' mentality of fear, so that astronomical defence budgets will be accepted. Yet both have to feel aggressive, for exactly the same reasons. Rough parity does not last for long because both sides need to calculate what might be the next stage of escalation, the next 'worst-case scenario', and then reach it.

The present US defence budget is the largest ever: 2.4 trillion dollars have been spent by the US on arms since the Second World War. The US budget for 1980-1985 is estimated to be costing one trillion dollars. The research and development costs for the MX missile for 1981 were an estimated 1.5 billion dollars, even before production started. Plans for the MX have already been modified partly as the result of intense opposition from the locality of the proposed sites. The limit of land-based forces may already have been reached, and the money will go to the development and production of more sea-launched missiles. Does this process give the world security? Or rather is it not a major destabilising factor, inviting disaster of unprecedented proportions?

When Aneurin Bevan, as Shadow Foreign Secretary, pleaded at the 1957 Labour Party Conference not to be sent 'naked into the

Conference Chamber' he did more than betray himself and those unilateral disarmers of the 1950s with whom he had identified himself. He illustrated vividly the political purpose of the independent nuclear deterrent. When the arguments over this or that system of defence are over, there remains one classic cliché: 'We must negotiate from a position of strength.' No one denies that, even after decisive wars, there must be negotiations, but the aim is to do so from as strong a bargaining position as possible. This accepted approach has dogged disarmament and arms control issues throughout recent decades. We are all — well, almost all — multilateralists now; we all agree that the present position is dangerous, but we insist that we make no concessions, no reductions, until everyone else does the same — especially 'them'.

Here lies the snag in this 'dual-track' argument, this negotiating disarmament from a position of strength. It leads to stalemate. No one is prepared to make a move, to change the status quo in any way. What is more, if having nuclear weapons gives an advantage in international diplomatic negotiations, this is another argument for proliferation. And once more, prestige and patriotism become enmeshed in the debate. Mr Nott may have dismissed the argument in the House of Commons (3.3.1981): 'I have little time for arguments based on prestige, seats at top tables and the like'; but more recently, in the same place (16.3.1982) Mrs Thatcher has put it firmly in the centre of defence policy: 'The Government . . . believe in keeping a nuclear deterrent as a safeguard of our strength. We also believe that it is far better to negotiate for disarmament from a position of strength. I agree . . . that we need to negotiate a position on disarmament.'

Leaving aside the rather ludicrous suggestion that, if you want to have a national say in world disarmament your country must develop its own nuclear weapons (for that is the logical extension of this argument), let us look at some things which have actually happened. First, though more countries have joined the 'nuclear club', none has done so in order to strengthen the disarmament lobby, but rather to strengthen its own position in some area of traditional conflict. Secondly, though Britain, France and China have for years now had nuclear weapons, they have been *excluded*, along with the rest, from the talks that really mattered: SALT l and ll, which were arms-limitation talks between the two superpowers, and which in some respects set the limits *higher* than those that existed at the time. Yet the rest of the world would suffer too, should nuclear war break out between USA and USSR.

What is clear is that the dual-track argument of deterrence and detente is unequally applied in practice: far more effort and expenditure are put into 'deterrence' than into detente. There are terrible dangers in this. Peter Jenkins has hinted at something of the kind (*Guardian*, 24 May 1982) in discussing the Falklands war: 'Throughout this whole affair means have dictated ends. Sending a task force on such a scale effectively determined that the Falklands would have to be retaken by force.' There is a strong school of opinion which insists that the two nuclear bombs need not have been used on Japan, that Japan had already put out peace feelers. But the bombs existed; did they therefore have to be used? Perhaps we should change the old proverb to 'Inventions are the fathers of necessity'. The pretext for more and worse weapons can be found. What chance has detente, while it is locked into the same argument as that of deterrence? There has to be a pause in the process of escalation long enough to reach a genuine disarmament agreement and for the reverse process, de-escalation, to begin.

The nuclear dimension has been a hindrance to talks, not a help. In a recent article, Nicholas Sims pinpointed some of the snags. There are now both categories of warfare to be disputed, as well as categories of countries to do the disputing. There are tensions between those governments which emphasise the 'absolute priority' of tackling first the question of nuclear weapons, but others who insist on a parallel restraint on conventional armaments. (To these can be added a school of thought which insists that modern chemical and biological warfare needs priority treatment too.) Secondly, there is the problem of the actual setting up of disarmament negotiations, and the structure of disarmament diplomacy. Four alternatives present themselves as the basis for the forum of negotiations. They are: bilateral talks, that is between the USA and the USSR only; nuclear weapons states only (a basis which, again, is an enormous encouragement to proliferation); multilateral talks, bringing in all thirty-five members of the Committee on Disarmament; or total involvement bringing in all members of the United Nations.

What is clear is that there is widespread dissatisfaction with the method of disarmament and control as vested in SALT l and ll, namely that the two superpowers together decide the rules and then monitor their enforcement. It is they who are to be disarmed, they who are to be monitored. Furthermore, it is often the poorer, weaker countries who have a grievance and who are suffering some sort of repression, or aggression, at the hands of stronger neighbours. It is their world too; they are demanding a voice in the debate. Lastly, and quite simply, there is a massive distrust of the superpowers, and doubts as to whether deterrence and disarmament are, at present, less about keeping the peace and more about keeping the status quo.

In answer to the growing demand in Europe for an end to nuclear escalation, and in particular to plans for Europe as the probable battleground in any 'limited' war, the pro-deterrent lobby is heard claiming that we have had in twentieth-century terms an unprecedentedly long period of peace in Europe, thanks to the existence of the nuclear deterrent. While it is true that there has been no further outbreak on European soil of an all-out war, this argument, and some of the curious claims surrounding it, are worth looking at more closely.

First, some European countries have been involved in a number of wars since 1945, but outside Europe. These have taken place in African and South-East Asian countries where formerly a European nation was the colonial ruler. There is Vietnam, (where the French were finally defeated at Dien Bien Phu in 1954); Algeria, and Suez (where the British and French had rights in connection with the canal). Involvement in others has taken the form of arms sales, and of public support for one side or the other (notably during the Vietnam war).

Secondly, in some of those wars, weapons systems have been introduced which have blurred the division between conventional and nuclear weapons and their delivery systems. Some very sophisticated systems have been 'tested in combat experience, both in Vietnam and the Middle East wars', and in the Falklands campaign. Many of the precision-guided systems can be fitted into non-nuclear-weapons systems.

Thirdly, while there has been no full-scale war in Europe, there have been numerous conflicts which have involved loss of life, conflicts during which the principle of freedom has been invoked. 'I can think of several occasions . . . when tanks might well have rolled in Europe had there not been a balance of terror within Europe. One has only to think of the East Berlin riots, the Berlin blockade, the Czech crisis, and even the recent Polish crisis . . .' said Dr John Gilbert in a deterrence debate. But there have been other occasions, since 1945, when tanks *have* rolled in Europe — in Hungary for example, and Czechoslovakia . . . The tanks were Russian; some were East German. The West made noises, but let them get on with it. We are entitled to ask: has the long peace been due entirely to deterrence, or to that other force which was agreed at Yalta: an ideological and geographical division of Europe between the post-war superpowers; two agreed spheres of influence? Such a division is, of course, cynical. It is doubly cynical to pretend that it doesn't exist.

However much nuclear weaponry the great powers need to ensure their mutual stability, it seems clear enough that Britain gains nothing from her limited but expensive nuclear armoury.

As I write, the 1982 Special Session on Disarmament at the United Nations in New York has ended in gloom, with little or no progress made. The time has come for one nation to give a decisive lead. There would be only one government to persuade, and this could be done through the normal democratic channels. Were Britain to do this, she would be the first nation voluntarily to give up its nuclear war capacity. But she would not be alone in making the decision that her defence was improved without it. Canadian and Swedish scientists were among the international team which contributed to developing the first atom bomb, but both Canada and Sweden made the deliberate decision to exclude such weapons from their own defence systems. It is valid to ask what the alternatives are to the nuclear path; these are examined in another chapter. The unilateralist path is an attempt to end the frustration of inadequate or failed international debate, stale stances and clichéd arguments.

Nuclear weapons exist; it is unreasonable to hope for their total abolition, at least while the present divisions in the world exist. They will be retained by the two superpowers though both of them know that this could be on a scale a fraction the size of present arsenals. Meanwhile, in Europe, a number of regional plans have been advanced over the decades for nuclear-free zones: since 1956, there have been the Polish Rapacki Plan, the Finnish Kekkonen Plan, Romanian suggestions in 1957, 1968 and 1972 for a nuclear-free Balkans area, revived in 1981 by Ceaucescu. Other suggestions have come from the Soviet Union, for a Nordic and a Mediterranean nuclear-free zone. As long ago as 1961, the Unden Plan, formulated by the Swedish Foreign Minister, advocated general development along the lines of nuclear-free zones. These suggestions have either been blocked or sidestepped until now. Could Europe develop the political will, this seems to be the most promising and acceptable way forward as an alternative to the present 'deterrence-detente' statemate. What is first needed is an initiative of courage and commonsense.

So long as deterrents deter, all is well. Once a nuclear conflict begins, their possession is suicidal.

This is a grim picture, but there *is* hope. It begins with accepting reality. In Europe, Russia and the USA, we have seen that there are people aware of the real nature of nuclear weapons. Hidden behind the ideological smokescreens of both superpowers one glimpses millions of people who want to live. And so do we.

THE ILLUSION OF PROTECTION
Civil Defence

'Human beings have the right to exist.' Without this fundamental principle all our social, moral, political, religious and educational structures and beliefs are meaningless and irrelevant. Therefore we have the right to ask the government, the elected representatives of the people, what measures they are taking to uphold this principle within the nuclear context.

Mine is the first generation which has never known a life free of the awareness that our existence can be totally annihilated within hours. We have never had the assurance that this nation could determine its own survival. We have not enjoyed the freedom and peace for which so many lives were sacrificed in the Second World War. Instead, we have lived with a background of nuclear escalation, an insidious Cold War, a propaganda campaign of aggression and mistrust, the consequence of which has instilled in me a sense of nihilism, impotence and despair. It is with this core to my perception of existence that I, and the rest of my generation, and subsequent ones, live our lives. Our only concept of peace has been that you 'deter' war. The true concept of peace, of peoples living in 'harmony' with each other, seems to belong to another, fictional age.

Every weapon devalues human life. Nuclear weapons ultimately devalue human existence. It is not surprising then that the powers that escalate and proliferate nuclear weapons diminish the value of human life in direct proportion. This is clearly evident in their attitude to civil defence.

Devastation is a somewhat mild description of the effects of a possible nuclear attack upon Britain. No word has yet been invented to describe this event adequately. Let us hope we shall never need one.

What could be expected is a formidable array of death and destruction. The NATO exercise 'Square Leg' of autumn 1980 predicated an arsenal of a total of 200 megatons to fall on Britain, or the equivalent of 13,000 bombs of the type dropped on Hiroshima. This megatonnage is considered by many experts to be a cautious estimate. Add to this the introduction of US Cruise missiles, and the level of attack expected is magnified hugely. The Soviet bloc would no longer be aiming at fixed military, industrial and civilian targets, but would probably include a 'blanket cover' bombardment to counter the advantage of Cruise missiles, capacity of being fired from anywhere within a hundred miles of their bases. In 1983 it is proposed to introduce Cruise missiles to two bases, at Greenham Common and Molesworth. A simple exercise demonstrates the vastness of the 'blanket cover' bombardment that this move invites: draw a circle representing a hundred miles radius around both of these sites.

As the days of the MAD ('Mutually Assured Destruction) deterrence theory sink into memory, we now have to live with a new breed of scientifically and technically advanced superweapons; missiles with multiple, computer-guided warheads; increased accuracy, increased capacity, improved launching and siting systems. Gone are the days when MAD was indeed mad. Military, and indeed political thinking, has advanced to the stage where one side could find *winning* a nuclear war conceivable. Current nuclear armoury improvements are largely aimed at the ability to destroy the opposition's missiles in their silos before they can retaliate. To put it plainly, in a time of conflict and tension, the temptation must be to launch your missiles first before the other side can destroy them.

There is a very thin line between conventional weapons and nuclear weapons. Conventional missiles and armoury can now be adapted to house nuclear warheads. In the event of a conventional war in Europe, there must be a considerable temptation to the officers in the field to resort to such armaments.

Successive governments, in their wisdom, have deemed it necessary to provide a triple layer of nuclear defence for this country: we have our alliance with NATO, our own independant nuclear capacity, and the siting of a considerable number of US bases, missile sites, ammunition stores and electronic surveillance posts. Consequently, we vie with West Germany as the country most densely populated with missile targets on this planet.

If, or when, we were to enter a nuclear conflict, we could justifiably anticipate a *massive* attack.

The known effects of a nuclear attack are manifold – initial blast, wind storms, fire storms, blinding from the flash of the explosion, immediate and long-term radiation, epidemics of typhoid, cholera, dysentery, polio, contamination of water, food supplies, livestock and crops, the destruction, crippling and fracturing of fuel supplies, water supplies, sanitation systems, medical centres and supplies, road and rail networks, telephone systems, the immediate death of millions of the population, and the lingering, anguished death of as many more from radiation, injury, disease and starvation.

There are many unknown variables to add to this list of 'hazards' – the possibility of the use of chemical or biological weapons, the increased long-term radioactivity caused by the destruction of nuclear plants, the possibility of a resurgence of plague brought about by the limited effect of radiation upon insects, bacteria and fungi, new forms of disease introduced by bacteriological change, ecological imbalance, the temporary or permanent destruction of radio and other electrical installations and receivers by the electro-magnetic pulse emitted during nuclear explosions, the possibility of triggering off earthquakes and tidal waves by the magnitude of multiple nuclear explosions, the erosion of the ozone layer which surrounds this planet and protects us from the deadly ultra-violet rays of the sun, climatic shifts and changing weather patterns.

As emphasis shifts from deterring a nuclear war towards winning it, with the escalation and improvement of nuclear weapons, with the enormous known and possible effects of nuclear war, we must ask ourselves what steps the government has taken to protect us and uphold our 'right to exist'. Quite simply, apart from outline directives to county and local authorities on supply and distribution of minimal medical and food supplies, the best answer we are offered, other than their claimed, outdated ability to deter war, is to suggest we prepare makeshift shelters and organise self-help groups.

Although there is a fair measure of provision for the survival of the government and associated 'authorities', there is a contemptible lack of provision for the rest of the population. Indeed, the available evidence indicates that the task of governing after a nuclear attack would be severely impeded by the survival of any considerable proportion of the population, when normal standards and structure of society will have broken down into those of 'survival of the fittest'. No surprisingly, then, in the absence of any protection from a nuclear attack, their civil defence policies are aimed at 'control' of survivors.

It is impossible to elaborate on the current attitude of the government towards civil defence without giving a brief historical perspective, for its provision (or lack of provision) is not an overnight decision, but the outcome of post-First World War politics.

In 1914, Britain faced, for the first time in a century, the threat of foreign invasion. However, no comprehensive 'civil defence' plans were formulated until the ruling classes were threatened by civil unrest. Home defence plans, that is defence from an *internal* enemy, were drawn up by Sir Eric Geddes in 1919. A former member of the War Cabinet, he proposed that the UK be divided into districts, each under the control of a Junior Minister designated to coordinate the military, police, 'volunteer' bodies and essential services. This rudimentary structure was first used during the railway strike in 1919 and then in the miners' strike in 1921. The power to use troops in 'states of emergency' under strict parliamentary accountability, was embodied in the 1921 Emergency Powers Act, and proved to be very important during the General Strike of 1926. It enabled the government to swiftly recruit 250,000 Special Constables, to issue instructions to local authorities, to deploy troops and police, and to take almost total control of the media of communication.

The very real threat of a foreign invasion and the vulnerability, for the first time, to large-scale attack from the air, stimulated the government to inaugurate the Air Raid Precaution programme in 1935 and Civil Defence Emergency Plan Y which closely mirrored the home defence plans of the 1920s. The eleven areas of the country were now called 'Regions' and regional commissioners appointed in 1939 remained in office until 1944. The Civil Defence Corps was disbanded at the end of the war in 1945. Civil unrest (strikes by dockers and railwaymen) prompted the government to set up the Home Office Emergencies Committee in 1947, which continued to coordinate home defence plans for strikes and natural disasters until the major reorganisation begun in 1972.

Within this period, several developments took place. The first Cold War era (1945–1968) prompted the passing of the 1948 Civil Defence Act. The Civil Defence Corps was reconstituted and continued until 1968 when civil defence was put on a 'care and maintenance basis and the Civil Defence Corps was disbanded along with the Auxiliary Fire Service and a large section of the Territorial Army.

The early 1950s witnessed the construction of twelve Regional Seats of Government, reinforced to withstand nuclear attack, at *secret* underground locations. These safe hideaways, equipped with the necessary life support systems (food, fuel, ventilation, communication) to protect the occupants during and after a nuclear attack until the danger of radiation had passed, were intended for a select few – government, state agencies and local dignatories – while no protection was envisaged for the people as a whole.

During the late 1960s and early 1970s, in the atmosphere of detente, the government gave more attention again to the threat of the 'internal' enemy and to the political consequences of long-term economic recession in the West. Between July 1970 and August 1972, years which included the first miners' strike of 1972, four 'states of emergency' were declared. Key state agencies were given the authority to reorganise completely the national contingency plans to pre-empt and counter the internal 'enemy' – socialist and trade union organisations. The Emergency Services Division of the Police Department, set up in 1971, took over responsibility from the Civil Defence and Commons Service Department.

By 1974, a process of reorganisation and refinement of planning and attitude saw England and Wales divided into ten regions, several of which were sub-divided to make seventeen sub-regions. This brought the Civil Defence regional boundaries almost exactly into line with the Army's UK Divisional boundaries, and at the same time the police, local government and the Territorial Army were reorganised. This process was justified as a long overdue rationalisation of administrative arrangements, but its effect has been to weld local government, the security forces and the emergency regional network into a single interlocking framework.

Within each region a hierarchy of command exists to be

operated in times of emergency. Power would be in the hands of a triumverate, consisting of the regional commissioner (probably a Junior Minister of the Crown), the regional police commander and the regional military commander. The chain of command fans out to county councils, local authorities and parish councils.

By April 1973 every local authority had appointed an 'Emergency Planning Officer' to head an 'Emergency Planning Team', the training of whom is largely undertaken by the Home Defence College at Easingwold in Yorkshire, established on its present site in 1973.

There has been a mass of circulars issued from the Home Office to local authorities, chief constables and chief fire officers giving instructions on procedure in the event of war or other 'emergencies'. The overall content of the circulars makes it clear that although essential supplies, services and transport would be provided for the state administration it would not be provided for the people as a whole. Indeed, the main concern appears to be 'control' of the population. In one paper entitled 'The Police Service in War' the first item is: 'Special measures to maintain internal security with particular emphasis concerning subversive or potentially subversive persons.' It must be remembered that these circulars are deemed 'unclassified'. They give only a hint as to the measures being contemplated in the highly 'classified' plans which have been drawn up by the military and other state agencies.

In 1979 the British government issued its pamphlet *Protect and Survive*. In the same year it took the decision to order four Trident submarines and agreed to allow the installation of 160 US owned and operated Cruise missiles in Britain. The briefest study of *Protect and Survive* shows it to be no more than a flagrant pretence to reassure the public that a nuclear war would not be as horrendous as generally predicted and that with a minimum provision of self-protection many of us would be safe. Apart from being a lie, there are three other points to be noted: the timing of the publication of *Protect and Survive* indicates that it was aimed to serve as propaganda to counteract the anticipated opposition to Trident submarines and Cruise missiles. (Was the attempt to 'reassure' the public that a nuclear war could be survived really meant to accustom them to the possibility of a war and thereby perhaps to increase its possibility?) But most important, for the first time the government openly showed that it had no plans to protect us against nuclear war; the population is to protect itself.

Far from being 'reassuring', *Protect and Survive* has fuelled public opinion to question openly and to oppose government strategy. The re-emergence of the Campaign for Nuclear Disarmament as a growing and viable force, both nationally and internationally, and the rising number of voices of opposition from numerous peace organisations, medical establishments, scientists of all nations, is adding a ground swell of momentum which is gathering force.

The government's answer to this opposition has been to employ a more insidious form of propaganda, less open to public confrontation. In December 1980, Air Marshall Sir Leslie Mavor, former principal of the Home Office Civil Defence College at Easingwold, was given a new role. Together with a team of un-named 'experts' he has been travelling the country 'briefing' county councillors and local government officers about Home Defence at closed, invitation only, meetings. The prime motive for this campaign is to promote a two-fronted force of reassurance and acceptance. Firstly, he advocates the use of voluntary bodies in home defence; in doing so, he hopes not only to win support for such agencies but also to continue the conditioning process of accepting the prospect of nuclear war. Second, through press handouts or other means, the grossly misleading content of these meetings are reported. Two examples are:

Sussex Express (24 October 80)
ACCORDING TO THE GOVERNMENT IT'S NOT AS BAD AS YOU MAY HAVE THOUGHT SAFE AFTER TWO DAYS
Milton Keynes Gazette (24 October 80)
'. . . if a foreign power used the maximum amount of nuclear weapons at its disposal in a concerted attack on this country, only 10% of Britain would be destroyed and 85% of the population would survive.'

As yet no attempt has been made by Mavor to justify these statements in a public forum, nor has there been any move to correct the impression that these reports must have left in the minds of the local population.

The conclusions to be drawn from this outline of government attitude to civil defence (Home Defence) are these:

There are no adequate plans to defend the population from a nuclear attack.

There are no adequate plans to provide the surviving population of a nuclear attack with essential supplies and services.

Civil defence preparation was originally conceived to combat civil unrest and the current plans are a highly refined and, for the most part, *secret* consequence of this conception.

Civil defence plans have been advanced so far with little or no democratic debate, and as such represent an instance of the power state agencies wield over democratically elected governments.

There are elaborate plans and provision for the protection and survival of members of the government and associated state agencies.

It is with these facts in mind that we must examine what advice the government intends to give in time of war, both publicly and to the state agencies.

There is an amazing disparity between the advice the government offers to the public and that issued to its regional chain of command.

Protect and Survive is so full of loopholes and misleading information that it can be discounted. Its basic message is for us to 'stay put', construct an inner refuge within a room converted to withstand blast, wind, fire and fallout, take provisions for fourteen days, and then wait for the 'all clear' signal and further radio information from the government. It assumes that we live in a suitable dwelling – those of us living in a flat above the third floor, those of us living in bungalows are not catered for. To carry out the protective conversion of our dwelling it is necessary to be fit and strong – the elderly, sick, injured or pregnant among us will be severely handicapped. Even if we have the funds to buy all the materials and food supplies indicated in the booklet, there are not sufficient stocks on the market to be able to supply any but a small proportion of the population. But even supposing we all do follow the government instructions, the protection offered would be viable only to those living on the periphery of an explosion against the immediate effects of an attack. Most would be vaporised by blast or incinerated in their shelters.

In contrast to the message of *Protect and Survive*, government circulars indicate that a more realistic approach to the effects of nuclear war has been envisaged by the state, and plans for the control of the population before such a war and those survivors of it are well advanced.

As far back as 1973 (Circular ES 3/1973), the circular *Home Defence Planning Assumption* envisaged that, 'it can be assumed that the population survival rate would range from 60% in the worst affected areas to 95% in the least affected areas . . . loss of essential services and productive capacity due to installation damage, loss of power supplies and lack of raw materials could be as high as 80%'. It has already been shown that the estimated level of attack today would be much higher.

To avoid the chaos of unofficial mass evacuation from cities and areas close to military establishments we are told in *Protect and Survive* that no area would be safer than any other, and that refugees would not be given food and protection in the area to which they fled. The government has also given itself the power to declare major exit roads 'Essential Service Routes', reserved for the exclusive use of the army, police and other authorised personnel.

Medical resources and personnel would be destroyed in direct proportion to the rest of the population. Circular ES 1/1977, *The Preparation and Organisation of the Health Service for War*, gives instruction for the discharge of all patients who would not fall into the category of 'emergency case', for medical personnel to refrain from searching for survivors requiring treatment in highly radiated areas, and to restrict treatment to those cases who, after limited surgical procedures, could be expected to be alive after seven days. There would be insufficient stocks of painkillers in reserve to ease the suffering of the doomed. Nor would there be sufficient sources of vaccines or inoculations against the antici- pated epidemics. There is no known cure for radiation sickness. Troops would be stationed to guard surviving hospitals and medical centres against attacks by those refused treatment.

Food would be a major factor, if not *the* major factor, in the lives of nuclear survivors. The government advises us to amass supplies of canned and dried foods in the pre-attack period sufficient to last fourteen days. Its civil defence planning is conveniently based on the assumption that this can and will be carried out and contin- gency feeding plans continue from this assumption. It is envisaged that emergency feeding centres would be established using exist- ing food stocks, with the gradual introduction of cereal-based sub- sistence farming. Troops and police would be deployed to guard existing food stocks from 'looting'. The supply, control and dis- tribution of food would be affected by several factors – the scale and location of attack, the numbers surviving, the problems of transportation of supplies when road and railway networks would be crippled, the scale of radioactive contamination of the land, whether an attack occurred before or after harvesting of crops, the length of time before imports, if any, arrived. Starvation would be hard to avoid and the human consequences difficult to control.

The provision of water would pose a very serious problem. Home Office Circular ES 6/1979 states:

It can be said with absolute assurance that any widespread nuclear attack would quickly disrupt the distribution system for domestic and industrial water . . . Outside the areas of total destruction close to the burst of the weapon, particularly vulnerable elements of many systems are water towers, surface reservoirs and pumping stations whether dependent on mains electricity or regular deliveries of fuel . . .

Again, planning relies on the individual pre-attack provision of sufficient supplies of water for fourteen days, after which time plans are based on the distribution of water from communal centres, individual consumption limited to a litre a day.

Adding to the problems of distributing food and water would be the widespread environmental health hazards. Millions of us would be dead or dying, disease would quickly assume epidemic proportions, sewage and refuse would remain unburied and uncollected. Government advice in Circular ES 8/1976 does not mince words: 'Many of the bodies could not be identified, even with scientific assistance, from the remains. It would not be practicable to devote scarce resources to the separate registration and burial to those who could be identified.' Survivors would be organised into working groups to perform mass burials or cremation.

It is within the realm of law and order that government circulars present a grim forecast of the dictatorial powers that the authorities intend to assume to enforce control. There are four distinct areas of concern − the arrest of 'potential subversives' before an attack, the prevention of mass evacuation, action against unauthorised distribution of supplies, and the repression of people opposed to the policies of the regional and sub-regional commissioners. Circular ES 3/1976, *Briefing Material for Wartime Controllers*, contains such instruction as, 'In conditions in which death, destruction and injury were commonplace, such penalties as probation, fines or sentences of imprisonment would no longer be effective . . . in the case of flagrantly anti-social behaviour there might be a need for harsher penalties than would be generally acceptable in peacetime . . .' There are plans for the holding of emergency courts, internment camps and executions.

These indications suggest the level of study and organisation undertaken by the government in the last decade with regard to nuclear war. There are equivalent studies and planning for other areas, including energy supplies, communication, transport, construction work and building materials.

The plans for a post-nuclear-attack society hinge on the assumption that there would be a well-defined pre-attack period of two weeks or more in which the organisational machinery can be set in motion. Current estimates now envisage that it is more likely that nuclear war preparation would be limited to forty-eight hours. No account is taken of the increasing possibility of the onset of a nuclear holocaust by human or technical error.

The conclusions to be drawn from the government attitude to civil defence and its proposed advice are that as a population we are unprepared for surviving a nuclear war.

Two choices remain open to us — we can either take steps effectively to reduce the possibility of a nuclear attack upon Britain, or we can take measures to ensure that the chance of survival of a nuclear attack would be considerably enhanced.

The stationing of nuclear weapons on these shores had led to the targeting upon Britain of a massive number of nuclear weapons. The deterrence theory provides small comfort as a defence. Effectively our nuclear arsenal may not only have no power to deter war but, by its existence, openly increase the chance of our involvement in one.

It is widely believed in scientific and official circles that there can be no effective civil defence against a nuclear attack. Moreover, the minimal protection of extensive in-blast shelters within a country possessing nuclear weapons would indicate to an enemy that that country was preparing for war and could be interpreted less as a defensive measure and more as an aggressive one. Mass evacuation is not an option for Britain because of the density of both population and nuclear targets.

The only rational civil defence policy open to this country is the removal of the nuclear targets from our territory. The benefits of this are twofold. First, the removal of the economic burden of maintaining and improving our nuclear capacity would provide us with the resources to introduce a realistic programme of defence for the whole nation. Secondly, the international repercussions of such an act could be both a first step towards global disarmament

and an active measure, by example, towards the stemming of proliferation of nuclear weapons throughout the world.

We live in a country with a democratic foundation and history.
We have the power and means to influence our destiny. There is
an increasing outcry against the nuclear policies of our government as the awareness of the realities of nuclear war increases.
The attention paid to public opinion by our government, and the
methods used to counteract it, clearly indicate the pressure by
which they can be influenced. We must use this pressure to alter
the manifestos of the political parties to include the nuclear issue,
to bring it into public debate.

Only by educating the population about the probability of a
nuclear war, and its effects, can sufficient pressure be aroused to
influence government policy. Already there are signs that this
pressure is taking effect. Opposition is spreading, with the emergence of 'Nuclear Free Zones' ranging from small parish councils
to the Greater London Council. The latest proof of success is the
abandonment by the government in the summer of 1982 of its
plans to implement the civil defence exercise, 'Hard Rock',
because of the number of councils openly acknowledging that
current civil defence plans are both inadequate and misleading. As
the total number of councils opposed to the government's civil
defence planning increases, so must the government be com-
pelled to abandon its proposals for the coercion, by financial
penalties or legislative force, of rebel councils.

The new wave of opposition to our nuclear policies is not a phenomenon unique to Britain, but part of an international rejection
of global nuclear politics and of the very real threat of total annihilation. In Britain, governments are not self-imposed, but the
outcome of democratic elections. Each of us has the power to
register our opinion, uniting as a collective force to be taken into
account. Every area of opposition open to us should be used – the
electoral procedures from local and county to national level, the
power of mass demonstration to influence government attitudes,
the various channels of media coverage, and the education of the
public to their responsibility for individual and collective survival.

We must not accept the possibility of being a statistic among the
millions likely to be sacrificed as an 'acceptable risk', or the possibility of being a surviving zombie – the walking dead.

DEFEND US AGAINST OUR DEFENDERS
Democracy and Security

> *Quis custodiet ipsos custodes?*
> (Who guards the guards themselves?)
>
> *Juvenal*

Just about the time I began the first draft of this chapter, a few Argentinian scrap merchants had moved into South Georgia to dismantle some old whaling station gear. By the time I had got an outline ready to circulate, I pencilled a note in the margin to suggest that reactions to events in the Falkland Islands might be mentioned as modification to my first paragraph, in which I had asserted that British society is not a militaristic one. Then I went for ten days to a country where I didn't see newspapers or hear broadcasts in a language I could understand.

When I got back, I found our government involved in a game of bluff and counter-bluff which was already getting out of hand. Within days it had escalated into a war − a war which has shown, if nothing else, how easily the game of bluff by adversaries with dangerous weapons in their hands can lead to full-scale armed conflict. The weapons used in this case were not nuclear. But the Argentine *fait accompli* of armed occupation did not deter the British task force, nor did the approach of that task force deter the Argentinians from continuing their occupation. In the game of deterrence, postures led to conflict. In the immortal phrase of a tabloid newspaper, 'What is the use of a deterrent if you don't use it?' the whole concept of deterrence as a force for peace was blown sky-high. A momentarily perceived advantage, a calculated risk based on a miscalculation, and blood is shed out of all proportion to the seriousness of the issues involved. Politicians on all sides fear loss of face more than they fear the loss of (other people's) lives. The events of 1982 have reminded us afresh of all these truisms about war. The gung-ho jingoism of a section of our people and the majority of our media has also been brought home to us in a salutary way. A longing for violence, adventure (by proxy) and a simple, righteous cause for which to cheer lies all too near the surface in many citizens – as much in university common rooms as in saloon bars.

Does the 'Falklands experience' have things to teach us about our society and the dangers that threaten it? It has certainly illustrated the degree to which war, the preparation for and back-up of war, and the 'defence' and military sector as a whole are allowed first call on our resources. A government which argues in pennies and halfpennies against a wage increase for a hospital porter bringing up a family on a take-home wage of £50 a week, can miraculously find the resources to transport thousands of troops and supplies across thousands of miles of ocean, and can spend enough in a few days to have settled all the inhabitants of the disputed islands in comfort for the rest of their lives in places of their choice, entirely in the interests of political face-saving. But even more, this small war has demonstrated the dominance of the defence sector not only over the country's resources, but over the whole area of the media of communication. It was not only a question of the – very possibly legitimate – delay of actual war news. The rage expressed by members of the government and their supporters against the cautious expression on the public media of opposition to their policies, even by members of their own party, and the deferential way in which the media responded illustrated the increasing power of the state in the whole area of communications, rather than the direct control of the military.

For, in many not unimportant ways, ours is not a military country. We don't admire the military virtues; courage and self-sacrifice are not in fashion. Big occasions are not celebrated by large military parades, service men change into mufti immediately they go on leave and are rarely seen in our streets in uniform. We are one of the few countries left in the world which has no peace-time conscription, and the recruiting propaganda for our professional forces emphasises the trade or craft element in their training rather than the discipline or combatant. Contrasted with many parts of Eastern Europe, for instance, the military here has a low profile and a limited apparent influence. Thus, in attacking 'militarism', we may be in danger of missing much more influential and much more sinister influences on our daily lives. Peace activity must always be directed at the real dangers, as far as possible, and it is important to see how these vary in different countries.

The 'Berlin Appeal' issued to the people of East Germany from a Protestant Peace Group in 1982 includes an appeal against military toys and the teaching of war studies in schools. In a country in which the army is pushed down the throats of children in their comics and in the classroom, this appeal makes a great deal of sense, particularly when the state which controls the publications and the curricula preaches a doctrine of peace. But in Britain, I doubt whether the campaign against war toys and toy guns should be in the forefront of women's activities. In my own family I have watched this persuasion through three generations, and have seen children replace guns with sticks, or with fingers − shouting *bang bang* instead of firing off caps. Prohibitions and proscriptions can too easily take the place of positive teaching. Children act out fantasies at different ages, fantasies of dying and killing, reducing through acting and games the real terrors that beset them. They play at earthquakes, wars, funerals and disasters, jumping up again after their simulated deaths. French and English change sides in the ritual of capture and release, and if we as adults step in to regulate the games, they wait until we're out of the way to get going again in rituals which are much older than we are. It could well be that the arbitrary assertion of authority adds spice to the forbidden games, and may certainly increase their perception of adult authority as irrational and unjust.

The important lessons we have to teach our children are not as easily subsumed into symbols. It is more important to teach them to respect differences, to believe that they could be wrong, to resist the temptation to overtake the person ahead, and instead to help the person behind, than it is to try and dictate to them the games they may play. It is always difficult to avoid anecdotes when one gets on the subject of children; I want to tell one which is only marginally relevant. A colleague took his oldest child away from a rather posh private school at which the little boy had been miserable, and with some trepidation sent him to the local primary school. They lived in an area of very mixed social and racial occupation, and the parents gave the child a little lecture before he went off to school. They warned him that there would be all kinds of children in his class, in fact that all the children 'would be different'. That evening he came home from his first very happy day at school, beaming with the joy of discovery – 'Daddy,' he yelled, 'Daddy, I'm different too!'

The lessons of respect for other people, of respect for genuine authority, of awareness of differences and of common interests and common humanity are some of the hardest lessons to learn. Far more aggression is engendered by the misuse of authority in the home and the classroom than by playing at soldiers or cowboys and indians. It is the authoritarian nature of the state, the arbitrary invasion of civil rights and the increasing power of the 'security' sector of our society that represents the greatest danger to democratic society, not, in our country, overt militarism or respect for military authority. In fact, the 'civilian' nature of much of the defence establishment may well lull us into a sense of false security.

There are some parallels between public and private actions against authoritarianism and aggressiveness. To encourage in our children the qualities which make for cooperation and tolerance is a slower business than using the easy weapon of sharp authority. To run a country without submitting important decisions to the process of democratic decision-making is both quicker and more 'efficient'. We have to put up with slower actions, frequent changes of direction, mistakes and confusion which must inevitably arise if large numbers of people are brought into decision-making. In return we may hope for more fundamentally sound decisions and a greater commitment to solving the problems of our society from citizens who feel themselves responsible and concerned. There will always be a tension between participation and efficiency, in public life as in the home. Perhaps, if an atmosphere of genuine trust is established, certain routine matters may more easily be left to administrators to decide. There is certainly no easy formula which is going to produce efficient and open government at a stroke.

Nevertheless, what is most sinister and disturbing about our present society is the constant erosion of democratic processes, the encroachment by agencies of the state on civil liberties and freedom of expression. And by far the most important of the agencies which are destroying both existing freedoms and the possibility of extending our rights as citizens are those which come under the heading of 'defence' and 'security'.

Here in Britain we have one of the most secretive defence establishments in the Western world, and one least accessible to control by the democratic institutions of the country. The growth of this powerful sector in the years since 1945 has contributed to the decline of democratic practice in important areas, to restrictions on individual liberty, and to the development of a class of unaccountable 'directors', who have the power to investigate our lives, record and store information about us, and to transmit such information to potential employers or others in a position to exercise authority over us or affect our jobs or lives. And all this is without our knowledge, let alone consent. Any university teacher will tell you about the confidential enquiries that are made about students, the range of wholly irrelevant questions that are put by skilled interrogators. People in more sensitive professions will have even more experience of such practices.

No one denies, of course, that in an imperfect world there must be sectors of local and national government which are not open to every one. Nevertheless, even in the area of sensitive military information, such areas must, in a democracy, be subject to the political control of elected authorities. The very scale of modern weapons, and their differentiation from the ordinary processes and technology of the country have helped to build up the secret sector. In the days when wars were fought with weapons which were adaptations of more familiar techniques, the line between war and peace technologies was not so sharply drawn. The navy was made up to strength by the reserve from the merchant fleet, the guns fired by soldiers were not so different from those used in sport. A bayonet might need practising with, but its end could be envisaged by anyone who had watched a butcher at work in the village shop. Today's complex and sophisticated weapons bear no relation to the ordinary industrial technology of the country – and in areas of overlap the benefit of the doubt is given to mystification and secrecy. (Perhaps children who play at push-button Starwars are being indoctrinated with the ultimate Fantasy – the war without passion, the bombs without a bang.) The outstanding example of course, is the so-called 'peaceful' development of atomic energy. Because of the sensitive nature of the military uses, decisions to spend vast sums of our money on installations which put whole areas of our countryside at risk have been taken without any reference to us or to our elected representatives. At best we have been informed about some of them when they have already been built. This huge area of secrecy involves not only a small number of military experts, but a whole sector of the productive forces of the country; the workers, the scientists and engineers together with their families are subject to severe limitations on their freedom of movement and on their expression of opinion. If any of them are worried about their conditions at work, concerned about the effects of what they are doing, to express these doubts and worries can be treated as treason against the state.

But it is not just that the workers are sworn to secrecy – and literally so, since they are subject to the Official Secrets Act, and are required to accept its terms as a condition of employment, but very many of the most vital and expensive decisions about 'peaceful' as well as 'military' research, development and construction, are taken without reference to parliament or even to a full meeting of the Cabinet. The planning and spending involved in these massive programmes can be organised so much more easily over periods of ten or twenty years, that the comparative frequency of parliamentary elections and changes of government can be inconvenient. So we saw that the so-called Chevaline programme, the modernising of the Polaris missile, on which one thousand million pounds was to be spent, was carried out under three different governments – those of Heath, Wilson and Callaghan before parliament was given any firm information about it. The crucial decision to accept the Cruise missile programme was agreed by the British government in 1979 without reference to parliament, and had it not sparked off the revived peace movement in Europe and in Britain, one wonders how much concern members of the House of Commons would have shown at this omission. In the time-scale of such programmes, although the money is provided by taxation from us all, the obtaining of our approval for the expenditure of that money is an embarrassment and a hindrance. The very institutions we are supposed to be arming to defend are those which our self-appointed protectors are busy by-passing.

Let us not, moreover, pretend that we live in a state of emergency in which we can afford to suspend democratic procedures while we get on with our arms and 'defence' programmes, and then bring them back when we have defeated every non-democratic country in the world. Quite apart from the obvious facts that wars rarely influence ideologies, except to strengthen them, and that no one could emerge the victor from an atomic war anyway, there is still the crucial matter that democratic institutions take centuries to build. Every generation has had to fight the authoritarianism of the rich and the powerful; the achievements are fragile, they cannot be given up and claimed back at will. The only way to preserve both peace and freedom is to bring decision-making into the democratic process. Policy decisions affecting our whole future must not be left to self-appointed élites and experts. Some one must watch the watchers, some one must guard the guardians, and that some one can only be the elected representatives of the people.

Some of the first effective revolts against the encroachments of the state and the central authorities have been made in the field of local government. Right-wing journalists and politicians sneer at provincial councils who declare their areas to be nuclear-free zones, saying that such declarations are at best meaningless gestures. But the nuclear-free movement is a ray of hope in a darkening situation because it signals a change of attitude. More than half of us now live in nuclear-free zones, declared to be such by our elected representatives. We are not daft enough to think that we are safe from nuclear attack, or even that all the implication of such decisions about the siting of civil nuclear installations are enforceable at a local level. But what we do recognise is that our district has opted out of aspects of the nuclear game. We have declared that we will not play a 'survival' game of bunkers for top bureaucrats. We are not, either, in the game of 'civil defence', but have accepted the local authorities' admission, that they could not in any circumstances defend their citizens from a nuclear attack or provide them with medical aid or other services in the event of such an attack.

When radicals were elected to city authorities and revealed the 'secret' plans for action in the event of nuclear war — a few bomb-proof bunkers for the top brass and a circle of troops to prevent the ordinary people from fleeing into the countryside — the appalling nature of nuclear war was brought home to many people even more sharply than by actual descriptions of nuclear devastation. Every weapon from ridicule to coercion has been used against such local authorities by governments and media. As I am writing this, the Home Secretary has just announced that he has had to cancel the proposed civil defence exercise, 'Hard Rock', because too few local authorities are prepared to cooperate in it. He has threatened to introduce legislation which will compel them to do so in the future. The rights of local democratic institutions have been badly eroded in the past few years, and this is just another way in which freedom of expression will be limited, lessening the possibility of ordinary people making their views known through the processes of local government. We have to defend our local councillors, use every level of democratic procedure to elect members who will reject the atmosphere of secrecy and concealment, and who will bring the maximum possible number of the decisions which affect our future into the area of open debate.

All this will seem general and unspecific. Better writers than I have documented the relations between atomic power interests and the increasing power of the state in those countries with atomic programmes. What I am trying to suggest is that not only are we threatened by the danger of nuclear war, but the very processes of building a nuclear armoury are depriving us of material resources which should be spent on solving the real problems of the world – the problems of hunger, disease, ignorance and oppression in every country – and at the same time destroying those institutions in our country of which we are most proud. As the German writer Robert Jungk has put it: 'The atomic question has clearly sparked off a debate that is more far-reaching than it could have been imagined when the issues were first considered. What is at stake is the future, not only of our energy supply but of our form of government.'

Our form of government is threatened not by the dangers of military coup or the encroachments of military education into our schools. It is threatened by the interests of an immensely powerful defence sector, backed by political interests which reach into all aspects of our lives.

At least half the people in this country are seriously worried about our commitment to atomic arms, atomic bases and atomic energy. Yet the point of view that expresses these worries is treated by those in authority as an extremist position which must be kept away from any form of public expression. Since it cuts across parties, it has no part in the farcical attempts by programme controllers in the wireless and television services to maintain a 'balance' between political positions. A single lecture on the dangers of nuclear war has to be countered by a series of eight explaining and justifying the government's nuclear arms policies. The single Bronowski lecture given by Dr Nicholas Humphrey in

1981 had to be preceded by a dismissive introduction, and succeeded in killing off the series in which it took place. Only our ability to publish and broadcast outside the official networks has kept the arguments alive, and here the enormous sales of literature, journals and pamphlets testifies to the widespread concern. The challenge to the complacent controllers has to be deafening before a whisper reaches them.

We must take back the language of freedom and the practices of democracy from the people who are perverting them. Who but ourselves can defend us against these defenders? Their policies impoverish us materially and oppress us politically. We have to take our country back, and defend it in our own way. The survival of our civilisation depends on the elimination of the worst forms of destruction, but also on the encouragement and extension of the values of mutuality, cooperation, toleration, so that the most basic problems of the world can be solved by the joint exploitation of the world's resources and not frittered away in mutual destruction. These values have to be taught and encouraged in the home as well as in the schoolroom, in our organisations as well as in our propaganda. Every one of us is involved, and we are the only people who can do it — and in the short time we have left, we are accepting the challenge.

JANET DUBÉ

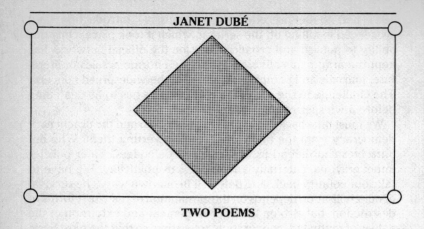

TWO POEMS

dry bamboo leaves jostle;
a yellow shirt shudders
wetly on the line:

a whisper catches trees together;
the dry hedge braces itself: wind.

the sound of Chopin
from the radio:
sheep graze steadily
in the field beyond.

we meet, or we pass
and neither is the easy way.

we see and we are seen
but it is hard to see
as we are seen;

teachers cannot teach us,
for they do not know;

doctors cannot heal us
for they cannot heal themselves:

preachers cannot save our souls
for they do not know our god
and we know their god is dead,

and the beginnings of the fathers
are visited on the beginnings
of their children, and the parents
have eaten sour grapes and
the children's teeth are set on edge.

the radio on the table
the news on the radio

and still we remain ambitious for our children

that they may survive
that they may inherit
that they may transcend

the children of our bodies
are not the children of our world;

they are the children
of what we do not see;

into what fearful certainty
will grow the children
of our uncertainty?

what meaning, hidden now?,
will seek out the children
of unmeaning?

what god will find the children
whose parents have killed god?

compassion, children, have compassion
on your parents, who also hoped.

our fathers used their strength
to crack open the grain of mustard seed
and they found dust;

we are the children of dust
you are the children of what
we do not see
beyond the dust

unable to pull ourselves together
we pull ourselves apart;
unable to put down roots
we put down you;

unable to send forth messages
to our sisters in the dust
and our brothers in the dust

we send forth you
When you see, children,
what we do not see

have compassion on us
blind children of the dust.

We too wished
not to leave the world
as we have found it.

A VOICE FROM THE PEACE CAMPS
Greenham Common and Upper Heyford

On Sunday, 21 March 1982, coaches sped to Greenham Common from far and wide in eager anticipation of a festival 'to celebrate the unity of all life', organised by the Women's Peace Camp. The festival was to precede the twenty-four hours of direct action beginning at seven that evening. After a great festival, enjoyed by all the family, more than 150 women chained themselves in groups to each of the eight main gates of the air base, and began the first ever twenty-four-hour women's blockade of a military base in the history of CND.

Huddling under the stars in the dark, on the edge of a devastatingly bleak military base, guarded constantly by US Army personnel, might have been a daunting experience, but the women were sustained by their convictions, and unified by a fervent desire to forward the cause of peace by resisting the installation of Cruise missiles on our soil. Throughout the night, the discomfort of the cold ground, the weight of the heavy chains shackling us to the fence were forgotten as support groups rallied round with hot food and drink. Theatre and music groups provided entertainment, and in between we sang peace songs, watched the smouldering camp fire and talked — waiting for the dawn and the response which would follow from the authorities. With the daylight came floods of film crews and reporters from local, national and international sections of the media, but the welcome publicity they represented was overshadowed by a massive police presence, and by the anger of car drivers protesting against the total blockade of the roads surrounding the air base. We joined in singing 'We shall not be moved', greeted the military police as they approached, and answered the many questions from journalists until the continuous drone of army trucks behind us drowned out all conversation. Sixteen hours into the protest, the Ministry of Defence, the Military Police and the United States Airforce conceded moral defeat, having been prevented from gaining access to the site. So far we had achieved total victory and had halted all work inside the fence. In a mood of euphoria we tucked into well-cooked porridge – difficult to eat with both arms shackled!

Suddenly police numbers doubled, and three vanloads of protestors were swept off to the local police station to face a charge of 'obstruction'. In the meantime, a hole had been cut in a section of the fence to give access to the base. Thirty-nine brave women raced to fill the gap, and were promptly arrested while traffic carrying base personnel and supplies queued up to drive in. Frightened but determined, a group of us unchained ourselves from the fence and hurried through police barricades to refill the gap and prevent them from getting in. We joined five other women and sat in front of the gap, facing some forty to fifty policemen. We attempted to explain the reasons for our protest to the police, and linking arms sang protest songs. Since the women who had already been arrested had filled the local magistrates' court to capacity that morning, orders arrived to make no more arrests. So what were the police to do? The answer seemed to be to remove us, and this they did, none too gently. Each time we were thrown aside, to the policemen's amazement, we picked ourselves up and rejoined the group in the gap. This pattern persisted until the twenty-four hours were up. We did not prevent all traffic from gaining access to the site, but we made its passage inconvenient and difficult by our presence. With forty of us at the gap and another hundred and more chained to the gates we had proved that women could cause a great deal of embarrassment to the authorities and could unite to make an effective protest against the increasing danger of nuclear war. Our parting words were – 'We'll be back soon!'

As I left the USAF base at Greenham Common at the end of the twenty-four-hour blockade, I felt a robust sense of strength and determination. The way I was living seemed inadequate to the needs of the time, I needed more time and freedom to continue the work of protest. I took the decision to leave my studies for a time, sold enough of my personal possessions to give me an income, and finally found myself at the USAF base at Upper Heyford in Oxfordshire. Perhaps because I was in at the very beginning of the camp here I feel an especial affection for it, but although it has grown and become stronger in the months that followed its establishment, there is no room for complacency at Upper Heyford.

Looking through the perimeter fence of the air base, listening to the roar of the F 1 ll's stationed there, I feel as if I am looking across a demarcation line between war and peace. As yet, peace has few victories to celebrate, but our protest continues. Our daily presence here is a permanent witness to our determination to work for peace, and it will be reinforced by action of many kinds in support. To begin with, we aim to make the American personnel think. This may sound condescending, but the fact is that military training discourages independent thinking or any questioning of their individual responsibility. We are here because we are afraid – afraid of the mindless commitment to destruction that these bases represent. We intend by our presence to remind ordinary people of the need to protest, to gain strength through cooperation, and to achieve the ending of the threat of nuclear war.

People often ask me what we do all day at the camp. Much time is spent in publicising our activities – our first month was devoted to attracting people to come and visit us, holding children's parties, folk evenings and so on. This brought together the network of support which now helps to sustain us morally and practically. We cherish the support and friendship of so many beautiful people. We also direct our focus at the base itself, for example by holding an all-night picket of the main gates on the night during the Falklands war when so many lives were needlessly destroyed by the sinking of the Belgrano. The hardest part of our work is winning acceptance by the local people, so many of whom are employed by the base at administrative and other ancillary jobs. We are seen as outsiders and regarded with some animosity. We work hard to overcome this, and to enlighten people as to the real nature of the base. 'The boys helping the boys' describes many of the locals' feelings towards the US airforce, coupled with a sense of powerlessness to alter things. We have not given up trying to change attitudes.

There is plenty of other interest, however. As I write, a group of German pacifists arrive, then an Anglican preacher. Yesterday an

American radio producer was here. Many different people come, all of them enjoy a cup of tea with us and express their support for what we are doing. At night time we know it will be different as the American service men, filled with liquor and feeling threatened by us, drive by and shout obscenities. We are saddened by this – people must learn to talk and not to hurl abuse, throw stones or discharge guns.

I am here not just because I don't want my children to grow up threatened with a nuclear holocaust, nor for the opportunity of sheltering from the flagrant sexism I used to confront in the streets of a busy city. I am here because my heart weeps over the great folly of men planning for war throughout the ages. Just as there is no time to ponder endlessly on the enormity of the task before us, there is no time for women to feel powerless. Women, we are strong! Every man, woman and child must unite, and as we work for the day when we share a truly peaceful world, we look forward to a new age and a new dawn. We have a very powerful weapon. Truth is on our side.

After the CND demonstration in London on 6 June 1982, a group of the Upper Heyford contingent went to the Russian Embassy and staged a sit-down protest against Soviet nuclear weapons and nuclear testing. They were arrested and kept overnight in the cells, charged with obstruction. Below is a short extract from the notes Maggie jotted down in the cell:

As we lay down, I felt enormous strength.
The police looked down from above. The traffic stopped.
The embassy traffic stared in disbelief.
Anxiously, we awaited the press,
But we sang and sang and believed.
Then, everyone was to be arrested!
Too late to opt out now,
A tree looks down, sheltering us from the sun.
Truth glistens through the trees,
We're off to court
This will be cut off at any time
The men have gone.
'Stubborn bitch,' one shouted.
Everything was pandemonium;
'Do this' 'sit here', 'where were you born?'
'Why – Why don't you tell us?'

Labelled a ringleader, inciting political protest.
We were not to be beaten.
We've learnt a lot, and hopefully these scribbles witness only a
beginning
No more time . . . no more paper.

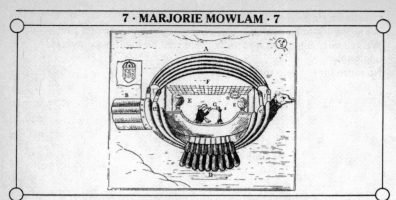

FUEL FOR THE NUCLEAR ARMS RACE
Nuclear Power and Nuclear Weapons

Oddly enough, it was not the fear of living with the threat of nuclear war, the illogicality of deterrence or the horrors of a nuclear holocaust which first made me a nuclear disarmer. It was the realisation that I was opposed to the nuclear society in which I already lived. The creation of nuclear technology for weapons and energy has come from a society whose values I cannot support; a society which sacrifices the possibility of high employment by diverting investment into capital-intensive industries, like the nuclear industry, which results in few jobs for the amount of money expended. Huge investment in that industry means resources are being diverted away from education, housing and health. The existence of nuclear technology is incompatible with democracy. In civil nuclear plants, workers' statutory rights to information on collective bargaining, vital health and safety precautions and unfair dismissal protection are severely restricted. The nuclear industry is an industry in which the Offical Secrets Act applies and armed police are used to combat the threat of terrorism. Such secrecy and security conflicts directly with the need for greater democracy and accountability. The long lead time (the time between the placement of the order and the delivery of the goods in working order) for investment in nuclear technology means that a newly elected parliament cannot reverse decisions that have already been taken and which will last for the whole of that parliament's term. Parliamentarians are expected to consider the serious implications of a crack in a nuclear reactor in a short debate sandwiched between school meals and the future of Belize. This is not the kind of democracy in which I want to live. Decisions about nuclear power and weapons involve choices about how we want to live our lives. Decisions everyone must make.

This may sound rather depressing. To stop nuclear war by working for unilateral nuclear disarmament in Europe is a tough enough struggle: the additional necessity of halting the nuclear energy programme and changing the identity of the decision-makers and the way we share resources is an enormous task. But is nuclear energy inevitably linked to nuclear weapons? Is the structure of our decision-making processes so crucial? To create the kind of society in which I want to live don't we *need* nuclear energy as a cheap energy source? I will attempt to answer these questions.

One apparently convincing argument for retaining civilian nuclear energy despite the dangers of nuclear proliferation is that if we do not use such a cheap energy source there will be another energy crisis; the resulting conflict and turmoil will at best create internal strife and at worse produce the nuclear holocaust we are so keen to avoid.

The argument for cheap electricity as the major inducement for nuclear power is not simply misleading; it is a lie based on the assumption that although the initial capital costs for nuclear energy are higher than for other fuels, the cost of energy production would be so cheap as to be negligible. This claim has not been borne out by nuclear history. Capital costs are not only higher than other fuel sources but much higher than the original estimates. In Britain, for example, the building of four advanced gas-cooled reactors was initially costed at £418 million. As yet unfinished, costs are now running at about £1,300 million, a 350 per cent increase over the original estimates. These cost increases were not specific to the British industry. The US Atomic Energy Commission estimated in 1974 that capital costs had risen 500 per cent in the last five years.

According to the figures from the nuclear industry, nuclear fuel production costs have increased twice as fast as fuel costs per unit of output in coal-fired stations. The idea of cheap nuclear-fuelled electricity is even less credible if the costs of replacing plant machinery and the closure of a reactor at the end of its thirty-year life are added into production costs. With inflation, the cost of new machinery is expensive, while estimates for decommissioning a reactor are, in the USA, thought to be about equivalent to the cost of building it in the first place. In England, no reactor has yet lived its full life and we are clearly unsure as to the costs involved.

Nuclear energy is not only uneconomic but also unsafe. Figures on safety records are not easy to obtain. The deaths of one-fifth to one-third of uranium miners in America, Canada and South Africa from radiation-induced cancer are acknowledged by the industry, but not included in their figures. The shockingly low compensation paid to Windscale workers' families makes radiation-induced deaths difficult to ignore. And the surveys showing the increase in leukemias and cancers around nuclear installations are also difficult to refute. Many of the potential health risks to nuclear workers are hard to trace because of the short-term nature of much of the employment in nuclear facilities. In the USA, for example, 54,675 people left jobs in the state-owned industry between February 1969 and December 1972, 16,000 of whom had worked in it for less than three years. This short-term employment is not limited to the USA but is also found in Britain and West Germany. In *Science* magazine the head of a plant in Buffalo explained his understanding of the figures: 'When there is a fairly radioactive machine to repair or move, it would be stupid to use qualified personnel and expose them to radiation which would hasten the time when they would have got their dose and had to retire . . . So we use outside staff.' The effects of radiation leaks from a nuclear plant or nuclear waste will not show up for many years after the plant has been in operation just as some of the deaths from a nuclear war will occur only years later.

The nuclear industry has created additional problems which it has not been able to solve. The most frightening of these is the inability to dispose of highly radioactive nuclear waste. It has tried many different methods of disposal but finally acknowledged in 1982 that waste will continue to be stored until at least the year 2000. Storage vessels were built for short-term use only and already leaks have been monitored in the USA and Britain.

Nuclear power is, in its own right, uneconomic, unsafe and a bad bet for the future. It is argued, however, that when compared with other risks we face in society, nuclear risks are worth chancing to avoid a future energy crisis. Future energy demand is not just a question of estimating demand, supply, availability and the balance of different types of energy. It is not solely an economic or statistical problem, but a political question, about the kind of society we want to create. Energy demand *is* high if more pollution, increased private transport and more centralised industries with little worker participation are all taken as imperatives. But if energy demand is looked at in the broader context of jobs and extensive energy conservation then non-nuclear energy alternatives seem more suitable. In the USA, for example, about 40 per cent of energy production is wasted. An increase in the efficient use of energy could contribute enormously to economic growth.

Nuclear energy should not have a future in its own right as an energy source. The links between nuclear energy and weapons make the case against nuclear energy even stronger but also show clearly how their futures are indivisible.

Nuclear technology was developed first for nuclear weapons. The civilian uses of nuclear energy were emphasised some ten years later to justify the costs, both in economic and moral terms, of a programme which culminated in Nagasaki and Hiroshima. The demands of the Cold War, the costs of nuclear technology and vested interests in the nuclear industry were of primary importance to the civilian development of nuclear technology. The reasons given at the time, however, were very different. President Eisenhower in his famous 'Atoms for Peace' speech at the United Nations in 1953 emphasised the importance of using nuclear technology to provide abundant electricity for the developing world. In opening the first nuclear reactor built for peaceful purposes at Calder Hall in England, the Queen emphasised that 'it may well prove to have been among the greatest of our contributions to human welfare that we led the way in demonstrating the peaceful uses of this new technology.'

The United States' hypocrisy in the 'Atoms for Peace' programme was finally exposed in a 1976 Senate study which concluded that 'Atoms for Peace' was an essential part of the US Cold War strategy. Eisenhower was shocked by the speed with which the Soviets exploded a hydrogen bomb. In order to appear before the United Nations and the world as 'good guys' in the Cold War, Eisenhower wanted to be seen to provide technical and financial resources to develop nuclear energy for peaceful, rather than aggressive, purposes.

The backing of a war economy and the secrecy of decision-making that war allows permitted the initial high costs of developing nuclear weapons. Attlee, for example, did not inform his own Labour cabinet of the existence, let alone the costs, of Britain's military programme. War made it possible to develop nuclear weapons very quickly. Less than three years elapsed between the establishing of the technical knowledge for an atomic reactor and the first explosion in 1945. The progression from war to peace made it increasingly difficult to hide the scale of costs involved in the nuclear programme. By 1956 the nuclear plant and equipment owned by the USA was of greater value than three of the United States' largest companies — American Telephone and Telegraph Company, General Motors and U.S. Steel — put together.

The huge investment of human and economic resources in the atomic industry weighed heavily in favour of continuing with a large nuclear programme. There was no going back. In Britain, before the development of civilian nuclear power there were already two reactors, as well as a uranium factory at Springfields in Lancashire, an enrichment plant at Capenhurst and a plutonium reprocessing plant at Windscale in Cumbria. Many of the buildings and equipment of today's nuclear programme owe their existence to the military programme. Nuclear power was not developed in Britain immediately after the Second World War, when a fuel shortage resulted in extensive power cuts and several industries had to stop production, but in the late 1950s when no energy shortage existed.

Thus civilian nuclear energy had a military birth. It was born for political and economic reasons rather than as an energy source. Such roots are difficult but not impossible to break. There are other bonds which make it difficult for nuclear energy to stand independently from its origins. These bonds that continue to link nuclear energy and weapons are the technical process, the raw materials and the nuclear installations.

The technical process is the same for both the civilian and military uses of nuclear power: nuclear fission occurs in a nuclear reactor and in a nuclear bomb. The only difference is that in a reactor the fission process is *controlled* by the use of control rods halting an ever-expanding chain reaction. That chain reaction is *uncontrolled* in the process at work in a nuclear bomb. The fission process in a chain reaction occurs when the atoms of an element such as uranium change by breaking in two. The result is the emission of radiation, the formation of different atoms known as fission products and the release of large amounts of energy. Nuclear weapons and nuclear power reactors work on the basis of the release of energy.

There are only two raw materials at present which can undergo a number of fissions to produce a chain reaction: one of them is uranium-235, the other is plutonium-239. Both these substances are essential for the production of nuclear energy *and* nuclear weapons. Neither of these substances can be used in nuclear fission in the form in which they are found in nature. The process and equipment necessary to make them viable to produce energy or explosions are identical. Only 0.7 per cent of uranium ore found naturally is suitable for the nuclear fission process. The usable uranium-235 must be separated from the unusable by an expensive process known as enrichment. There are two main methods of enrichment: gaseous diffusion and gaseous centrifuge. Both methods are based on using the uranium in a gaseous form. In the diffusion method, the gas is sieved through fine filters. The smaller molecules of uranium-235 pass through more easily than the other uranium molecules. When this process has been repeated hundreds of times, uranium-235 has been produced in a concentrated form. The newer method, gas centrifuge, consists of feeding the gas into a centrifuge. The fast rotations cause the slightly lighter uranium-235 to settle near the centre with the rest of the uranium remaining near the walls of the chamber. This is much the same principle as that used in separating plasma from blood. Passing the uranium-235 from one centrifuge to another, each time repeating the process, produces uranium-235 in an enriched form. It is possible to make a dirty bomb (high level of fallout) with the degree of enrichment necessary for the commercial production of energy. For a clean bomb (high radiation, less fallout) the degree of enrichment has to be higher. People not hit directly by a clean bomb have a greater chance of survival. In technical terms, this means reducing the size of the holes in the sieves in the diffusion process and increasing the speed of the rotations in the centrifuge process.

The other element for nuclear technology is plutonium-239. This does not occur naturally but is a by-product of the chain reaction which takes place in a nuclear reactor fuelled by uranium. It is therefore necessary to control the chain reaction before nuclear

before nuclear energy or bombs can be manufactured from plutonium. The spent fuel from a nuclear reactor is taken to a reprocessing plant and separated into three main elements: uranium,
plutonium and other fission products. The uranium and plutonium
are individually separated and purified by leaching them out in a
strong nitric-acid solution. The plutonium thus produced in a
reprocessing plant can be used *either* to fuel a nuclear reactor or to
make a bomb.

It is impossible to generate electricity in a peaceful nuclear
reactor without at the same time using or manufacturing materials
which can be used for nuclear weapons. The reprocessing plants
at Windscale in Britain produce materials for both nuclear
reactors and weapons. There are at present reprocessing facilities
at La Hague in France, Windscale in Britain, Tokai-Mura in Japan
and, presumably, plants in the USSR and China. It is from these
plants that waste from nuclear reactors around the world is repro-
cessed to produce plutonium as a reactor fuel or as a fuel for
atomic bombs.

From this evidence, there can be little disagreement about the
historical, technical, institutional and financial interdependence of
the civilian and military nuclear programmes. Differences exist
only in the *degree* of interdependence. But can a country have
nuclear power and no nuclear weapons or vice versa?

A country can certainly have nuclear weapons without having
nuclear power. The necessary components for bomb-making can
be purchased or stolen. (Libya has for some time been trying to
buy nuclear hardware on the open market. And in the early 1970s
a shipment of uranium disappeared in Europe which later turned
up in Israel.) Or a country can slowly build up its reserves of
uranium or plutonium bought for research purposes until sufficient has been accumulated to construct a bomb. According to
figures provided by the International Atomic Energy Authority
the USA has shipped enough weapons-grade material for bomb-
making to Australia, Belgium, Canada, West Germany, Italy and
Japan. India exploded a relatively weak 15-kiloton bomb in
Rajasthan in May 1974; despite all agreements and assurances to
the contrary, India had developed a bomb, code-named 'Buddha
smiles', by extracting plutonium from an experimental reactor of
Canadian design, a CANDU reactor. Pakistan, threatened by its
neighbour's success, tried to buy a reprocessing plant from France

which would have provided an easy route to bomb-making. US pressure halted the sale. In 1979 it became known that Pakistan had stolen the plans from the URENCO enrichment plant at Almelo in the Netherlands to build her own enrichment plant and was trying to buy the components on the open market.

The proliferation of nuclear weapons can therefore take place without having civilian nuclear energy. However, without that energy all nuclear facilities would be *clearly* military. There would be no civilian shield for military machinery or military costs to hide behind. Without nuclear energy, the proliferation of weapons, both within one country and across countries, would doubtless happen less quickly. Nuclear energy is the driving force behind proliferation because it spreads nuclear knowledge, hardware and expectations. Nuclear weapons make it possible to turn latent political dreams of power into a political reality.

Conversely can nuclear power exist without nuclear weapons? The answer is *no*, not only because of the technical links already outlined but also because of the problems of limiting the use of nuclear power to peaceful purposes. If civilian nuclear power could be controlled then it would not lead to the proliferation of nuclear weapons. The failure of efforts to control nuclear technology in the past thirty years is sufficient evidence to conclude that such control is not possible. In international politics nuclear know-how means political power and status. Controlling nuclear power and weapons is more than just controlling technology; it is also controlling power and international conflict.

The first significant effort at control was the International Atomic Energy Authority (IAEA) created in 1956 to promote the peaceful uses of nuclear energy and halt the production of nuclear weapons. If the arguments established above on the links between nuclear energy and proliferation are accepted, then it follows that the IAEA was doomed from the start, since it was based on an insurmountable contradiction: to promote nuclear activities at the same time as working to avoid proliferation. As seventy-five per cent of its annual budget is used to promote nuclear activities, it is clear how it overcomes the contradiction. In the two years after signing the IAEA Treaty the USA had also signed bilateral agreements involving trade and cooperation with forty-three countries. Under these agreements the USA exported research reactors with the necessary fuel and the training of technicians to such countries as Argentina, Brazil, Taiwan, Iran, Korea, Pakistan and Israel. All of these countries were known to be interested in developing nuclear weapons and a majority of them have been involved in regional power struggles. As one commentator stated, this list of nuclear-oriented military dictatorships looks like a Who's Who from Amnesty International.

There are only eighty IAEA staff who inspect approximately 400 nuclear reactors in over a hundred countries spread over several continents. Such a ridiculously small staff lends credence to the Australian government's Fox report (1976) on the IAEA, that its defects 'are so serious that existing safeguards may provide only an illusion of protection'.

The IAEA lacks the teeth to enforce its own decisions. Breaches of the treaty are reported to the authorities in the country in which they have occurred, and are recorded secretly at IAEA headquarters in Vienna. Thus irregularities in a nuclear plant result in no sanctions, not even the sanction of world public opinion. Critics argue that IAEA safeguards are like burglar alarms rather than locks, a totally unsatisfactory check when the impact of a nuclear accident is considered. The impotence of the IAEA was seen recently in the Israeli bombing of the Iraqi nuclear power station at Tamuz in June 1981. The IAEA had no authority to rebuke the Israelis for their attack. Asking permission from the Iraqis to investigate the accusations that the Tamuz plant was being used for weapons rather than energy production, the IAEA were informed that international agreements were not applicable in time of war. In moments of political crisis the USA has ignored the mandate of the IAEA. In July 1978, for example, President Carter, supported by Congress, decided to send large amounts of enriched uranium to India despite the fact that the Indian government had exploded a 'nuclear device' and refused to sign the Non-Proliferation Treaty (NPT). The US State Department's justification was that US-Indian relations were more important than implementing the IAEA regulations.

Other attempts to curb the development of nuclear weapons include the Limited Test Ban Treaty (1963), the Treaty of Tlateloloc (1968), and the NPT (1970). The more than one hundred non-nuclear weapons' nations who signed the NPT agreed not to acquire weapons and to permit their civil nuclear power programmes to be inspected by the IAEA. Britain, USA and the USSR, the nuclear powers who signed, promised not to transfer nuclear weapons to other nations and to work for disarmament. The peaceful application of nuclear power under international safeguards was agreed to by all signatories of the Treaty. But the NPT has failed on several grounds: the superpowers have not worked for disarmament; one-third of the world's countries did not sign the Treaty; two nuclear powers, France and China, did not ratify it and nations who are trying to obtain nuclear weapon status – Egypt, Argentina, Brazil, Israel, Pakistan and South Africa – refused to sign in order to 'keep their nuclear options open'.

Many non-nuclear nations who signed the NPT do not allow inspection and the superpowers have not made any noticeable steps towards disarmament: in fact the exact opposite. The NPT has faced the same fundamental problems that the IAEA ran into, and which later agreements, such as the International Fuel Cycle Evaluation Report and the London Club, have faced since: the lack of power to achieve two contradictory goals – halting the spread of nuclear weapons while increasing the use of nuclear power. Even if their goals were achievable and they had the power necessary to implement better control of nuclear technology, the state of affairs would still be far from satisfactory. Such controls would of necessity include an international police force, with powers of search and seizure and no clear method of accountability.

The links between nuclear energy and nuclear weapons are conclusive enough – we cannot do away with one and keep the other. A country will suffer greater devastation in a nuclear war if it gets its energy from nuclear reactors. No differentiation would be made between civilian and military nuclear sites in a war – both would be targets. The fallout from a bombed nuclear reactor is identical in its effects to the fallout from a nuclear bomb. The irradiation of people and land would be greatly increased in countries with large numbers of nuclear reactors because of the presence of radio-isotopes with a long half-life which would increase the longterm fallout hazard. In Britain, for example, the distribution of nuclear reactors around the coastline would mean that a coordinated attack would produce devasting effects, regardless of which way the wind was blowing. A country can avoid, or lower the probability, of a nuclear attack by removing nuclear weapons from its territory. If civilian nuclear installations are not also removed, the consequences of nuclear devastation can still result from conventional war or terrorist activities aimed at nuclear reactors.

As an energy source, nuclear energy is neither cheap nor safe nor clean. Its main function is as a stepping stone in the nuclear proliferation war game. The development of nuclear energy does not make any sense unless it is seen as an integral part of the nuclear weapons programme. To my mind, the links between nuclear energy and nuclear weapons are sufficient to halt the nuclear energy programme. But an equally important reason for halting it is to stop the creation of a nuclear society. The longer we live with nuclear energy, the more we begin to accept the need for secrecy, the need for an armed police force and the development of a small technical élite with minimal public accountability. Stopping nuclear energy and weapons means more than changing our concept of war or our means of energy production; it means changing the values and structure of our society.

Ann Pettitt

LETTER TO MY NEIGHBOUR
Nuclear War and the Countryside

Dear Susan,

About a year ago in the course of a conversation in which I tried to convince you that we would be safer without a nuclear 'deterrent', you said to me: 'But I don't think a nuclear war would be all that bad, anyway.'

Since then I have not felt able to broach the subject with you again. I am waiting for the day when the mere thought of trying to explain doesn't make my breath quicken. You, like me, have a degree from a university, you can read, you are aware of global problems because you worry about the world's growing population. Like me, you believe that for the good of the whole earth we should look after our own little corner of it, and not pour poisonous chemicals onto our gardens.

I know it sounds over-dramatic but my breath quickens because in a way I feel as if my life is in your hands, because as long as you and millions of people like you continue to think in the way that you do about nuclear weapons, we will inexorably move towards a war that *will* be that bad, and that can only be prevented from happening by you, and me, and millions of other people like us.

I've also been waiting for the day when I can give you a better reply than I did then. I remember looking out over your field, and up at the hill and the wood and at your goats, and saying, 'Well yes, we're not in a direct target area, we might not even get any immediate blast effects. I suppose it would all look roughly as it does now, only, it would all be radioactive, you see ...' I remember tailing off helplessly before your sceptical eyes, and realising that if I were ever to show you that I wasn't just scare-mongering, I would have to find out exactly what *would* happen as far as we can confidently predict, so that you would know what all the fuss was about; and I could begin to get at the truth behind a rhetoric about holocausts and Armageddons that begins to irritate me as much as I dare say it does you.

Here is a map showing some of the targets in England and Wales. These are the places where bombs were assumed to have been 'dropped' for the last Home Defence exercise, 'Square Leg', in 1980. This is if anything an underestimate of the bombs we would be likely to receive: wounding but not destroying our country's military capability would hardly be worth Russia's while.

'Square Leg' target map of Britain with circles showing extent of blast damage.

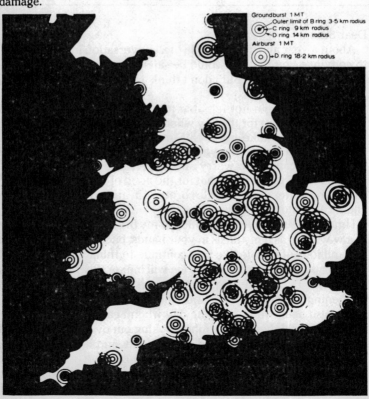

Groundburst 1 MT
Outer limit of B ring 3·5 km radius
C ring 9 km radius
D ring 14 km radius
Airburst 1 MT
D ring 18·2 km radius

The Russians have stated that they would never initiate a nuclear war, but that once under nuclear attack they will retaliate with everything they've got. Once we have Cruise missiles here in a year's time, they will have to drop far more bombs over us than this map shows to make sure we are no longer a threat.

You can see that we are relatively well off here. Our nearest targets are an RAF airfield and missile testing ground at Aberporth, about twenty-five miles away, and a US Base at Brawdy in Pembrokeshire, about forty miles away, which is to track Soviet submarines. The submarines are important to the Russians, and this makes Brawdy an important target; more than one bomb might be earmarked for it, to make sure of hitting it. The Milford Haven oil terminal, also about forty miles away, although not shown on this map, is also a potential target, both for its industry and deep water docking facilities.

If you and I and the other people living round here die as a result of the bombs aimed at these targets, that is not deliberate: it is called 'collateral damage'. The targets of these bombs would be military and industrial installations, communications and government centres rather than people. It just so happens we live in a crowded island, and you can see from this map that most of the population, in the grey areas, live close enough to targets to have their houses damaged or destroyed completely by 'blast'.

Jeanette Buirski's article looks at what would happen to city-dwellers in target areas. If we are lucky and 'our' bombs land on target, we might well escape the worst effects of blast, and only have some roof damage, windows broken and so on, from the nearest bomb. What might happen after that would depend on the scale of the war.

I'm not going to look at the very worst that would happen, because that would be if all the nuclear weapons that exist were exploded. I have not found any detailed studies of the possible results of such an event. Perhaps it is very unlikely to happen. But it is certainly likely that if we are attacked, bombs will soon also be going off all over the Northern Hemisphere. Perhaps if we wait long enough and lots of other countries get nuclear weapons, the Southern Hemisphere would be included also. But there has already been a detailed look at the likely repercussions of a large-scale war in the Northern Hemisphere. The Swedish Academy of Sciences commissioned and published in the journal *Ambio*, just such a study from a team of international scientists, specialists in environmental science and radiation effects, as well as in global economics and food production. The scientists were given a 'reference scenario' to work from which assumed that less than half the total megatonnage of weapons that will exist by 1985 — that is, 5,750 megatons out of a total 12,000 — would be detonated; the explosions would be mostly in the 200 kiloton to one megaton range on known targets in Europe, USSR and North America. In attempting to assess the fate of you and me as survivors of such a war, I am assuming we shall be trying to live in an environment which has received such an impact.

I suppose it is possible that a nuclear war could come right out of the blue — as a mistake no one could stop in time. But a war involving deliberate decisions would be preceded by a preparation period in which our government puts into action its pre-nuclear war plans.

That 'Square Leg' Home Defence exercise they held in 1980 began a week before the supposed attack started. What they did in that week was to shut down the telephones, give everybody leaflets about building shelters in their homes, and close to civilian traffic what are called 'Essential Service Routes' (ESR). These were main roads for the exclusive use of Army and government officials, unhindered by people ignoring 'stay-put' advice and trying to get away from the main cities and target areas. Civil servants, designated as regional governers, took up positions in blast-proof shelters all over the country.

The A40 road near us is an ESR, which would make stocking up on seed, potatoes, flour, animal feed etc. from our local Farmer's Co-op a bit difficult, as that's on the A40. The best thing would be to start stocking up at the first sign of any tension, to avoid the rush.

The other thing that happened in that week was that the army was meant to go round arresting people who might cause unrest. Presumably they would be taken to internment camps of some sort. Such people would include trade union leaders, members of the Communist Party and so on, but I've a horrible feeling it might also include people like me, who are well-known as disarmament campaigners, because the government knows very well that even at the last minute we would be trying to persuade people like you not to accept that war would be inevitable, but to protest and try to stop it happening. They would also know that people like me would be using our free speech to put across a rather different picture of the likely outcome of a war than the reassuring anti-panic noises emanating from official broadcasts.

I don't know what they would do with our children — whether they would go with us, or what. You can't tell if your name is on that sort of list, or what you would have to do to get it taken off. So it is possible that you'd be around to see the after-effects of a nuclear war, and to try your hand at surviving but I and my family might not.

'Still,' I can hear you say, 'millions would survive even a bigger attack than Square Leg, and more so in other countries, and I know it sounds a bit hard, but there are too many people in the world as it is.'

You'd be quite right, millions would survive; to start off with at least. It would actually be very difficult, even with nuclear weapons, to kill everybody even in a crowded country like ours by crushing, burning or irradiating them to death. Although shelters close to targets (an area that encompasses many thousand square miles of dense population) would simply become ovens or tombs beneath collapsed buildings, people whose only danger was from radioactive fallout could lower their dose by staying indoors, so long as their houses were not damaged at all. (Since fallout is air-borne, if your windows had blown in you would not be protected.)

What would it be like? I guess we'd be cowering in the cupboard under the stairs so I don't know whether we'd see a violet flash of light. Perhaps we wouldn't see the fireballs which would rise in the first few minutes. We're talking about something a kilometre across with a temperature hotter than the inside of the sun, and even here we're close enough for the retina of the eyes to be burnt which means blindness. The blinding might be permanent or temporary — you wouldn't know. Must remember to warn the children, anyway, not to look at a nuclear bomb.

I don't know what we would hear but even if the pressure wave did not reach us, two or three areas of 800 kilometre an hour winds, created by the pressure waves, within a fifty-mile radius of us would scarcely leave us untouched. The electricity and the mains water supply would go off. The telephone would be off already, of course, but it would probably be unusable even by the authorities because so many power lines would be down. It is very likely that the radio would not transmit messages either. This is because of something called 'EMP'.

'EMP' stands for 'Electro-Magnetic Pulse'. When nuclear weapons are exploded at heights above forty kilometres the 'EMP' they give off disrupts and damages electronic equipment. If the radio was switched on at the time this happened, it would not work again. It seems to me doubtful that an attacker would ignore such a simple way of compounding chaos. The modern targeting systems are electronic, too. The prospect is that missiles that are in the air will go haywire and land off target all over the place.

When the winds died down, there would then be an odd kind of silence.

For the people nearer the blasts, on huge outer rings of target areas all over the country, that silence would be broken by cries, whimpers, moans and screams. But the last thing the radio would have said was, 'Stay put. On no account leave your homes. Your only protection against fallout is to stay indoors'. In those areas, many would be frantically trying to dig children, friends, parents out of shattered buildings; many millions would be trying to run away – carrying injured children, friends, parents – from the huge fires that would have started. Half an hour after the first bombs had dropped, millions of people would be in the open as the fallout clouds began to descend.

In our area, farmers would be out too. They always are, seeing to their animals; the animals would be going berserk, because their world was breaking up and they were blinded by the fireballs.

The first fallout from the bombs might even be visible as a cloud of fine dust and ash, which would settle on everything. What you wouldn't see would be the radioactive isotopes which had attached themselves to the particles.

These isotopes are literally the broken-up bits of the atoms whose tearing apart has released the energy that held them together. Einstein worked out that the energy released when atoms split would equal their mass multiplied by the speed of light itself – '$E = mc^2$'. So you take a grapefruit-sized lump of plutonium, and you get a wave of blast and heat that pulverizes a city in a second. The broken pieces of atoms that are left are called 'fission products'. There are thousands of them, all trying to reach a stable level of balance between the electrical forces in their atoms, and doing so by off-loading energy and particles. So they shoot out gamma rays, which is the most penetrating form of radiation and goes through reinforced concrete, and particles which are beta and alpha radiation which cause most damage when they are inside your body, although beta radiation to the skin can cause 'beta burn'. Some isotopes decay to stability in a fraction of a second — a quick burst of gamma rays and that's it — others take thousands of years, such as plutonium itself. The two main fission products which are around during the fifty years following atomic explosions are ^{90}strontium and ^{137}caesium.

The radioactivity does not just come from the broken-up atoms of the bomb. When bombs are burst near enough to the ground, the neutrons shot out during the explosion turn many of the elements on the ground — the metals in buildings for instance — into isotopes also. A hydrogen bomb has such a huge fireball that this would be bound to happen even with a bomb exploded quite high up. So the fallout from groundbursts, and from H-bombs exploded in the atmosphere, contains additional radioactive iron, cobalt, zinc, etc., in the huge cloud of debris sucked up into the sky.

The radiation levels would be going down all the time (assuming no more bombs were dropped); but the damage radiation does to living cells, in our bodies and those of animals and plants, is mostly permanent and therefore accumulates, so however well you avoided direct contact with fallout dust, you would inexorably accumulate an increasing dose of radiation damage.

Whether we received fallout from Brawdy, or from any of the other targets which surround us, would depend on the wind. Our prevailing winds are westerly, and it is likely that the main fallout cloud from Brawdy would come towards us. With a SW wind blowing, we would fall within the area that receives a dose of more that 900 Rads, if the bomb dropped on Brawdy is one megaton. Such a bomb would cover about 1,170 square miles (the area of a plume approx. 1,390) with fallout heavy enough to give a dose of 450 Rads to anyone in the open.

You can see from the diagram on p. 97 what this sort of dose would do to you. You can also see the map on p. 98 the areas in Europe covered by the 450 Rad dose — enough to kill half the people within a month. They die because the cells that make the blood inside their bone marrow don't work: their blood won't clot, and they haven't enough white blood cells to stop them getting overrun by bacterial infections. The same effects are produced in children by a lower dose of radiation.

The fallout map (p. 99) does not take into account rain, which can bring down much heavier fallout, or the nuclear power stations and waste storage sites which are also likely targets.

The map on p. 98 gives some idea of how much more fallout

there would be if these places are also hit. The shaded area shows a dose to the air of 100 Rads at *one year* after detonation.

I see it just misses us out — but I wouldn't count on it. It all depends which way the wind's blowing, whether we would get all the crud from the French reprocessing plant at Cap de la Hague or not.

The point about fallout from reactors and especially waste storage places is that most of these isotopes are very long-lived. Direct hits on these places would spread their radioactive contents quickly throughout the air, the seas, the earth, the plants, and the bodies of creatures which together we call 'the food chain'. But even if they are left alone, loss of electricity, not to mention loss of the workforce would result in accidents and leaks which would also, more spasmodically, ensure eventual distribution throughout the environment of these indestructible man-made poisons, more carcinogenic and mutagenic than any substance known.

It is impossible to say what kind of a dose you and I and our families would receive if we stayed indoors, even with the doors and windows blocked up. We'd be safest under the stairs for a week at least, but simply breathing the air would give us enough of a dose to make us vomit and get diarrhoea, so I don't see a week under the stairs as really possible. We, and everybody else who had 'survived' would have no idea whether or not radiation had sentenced us to death in a few weeks' time anyway.

Somehow or other, farmers would (whilst staying indoors) have to keep up milking, or the cows would dry off. They would have to throw the milk all away because the levels of ^{131}iodine and ^{90}strontium would make the stuff lethal for weeks. Round here, only animals that were indoors would survive the early fallout, and if indoors means a dutch barn, many of those would die too. Eating heavily contaminated pasture, drinking water full of dissolved ^{127}caesium would mean they would quickly accumulate lethal doses. If you could look outside, you would maybe see cows and sheep eating grass, as usual; and you would know they, perhaps like you, were like plants whose roots have been eaten by maggots: they look normal for a bit, and then one day they turn yellow and die.

Let's assume we are still alive after a week. Perhaps lack of food, or water, or just wanting to meet someone else, will force us out. The radiation, as well as leaving the pastures littered with dead animals will have been sufficient to kill off the pine trees and

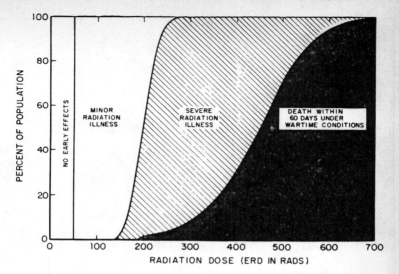

The expected early (within two months) outcome from radiation illness for populations exposed to various levels of radiation from fallout. This chart describes the development of severe radiation illness in the 100–700 rad dose range as follows:

'The initial symptoms are ᾳ . . . nausea, vomiting, diaorrhea, loss of appetite and malaise . . . After the first day or two the symptoms disappear and there may be a latent period of several days to two weeks . . . Subsequently there is a return of symptoms, including diaorrhea and a steplike rise in temperature which may·be due to accompanying infection . . . Commencing about two or three weeks after exposure, there is a tendency to bleed into various organs, and small haemorrhages under the skin . . . are observed . . . Particularly common are spontaneous bleeding in the mouth and from the lining of the intestinal tract. There may be blood in the urine due to bleeding in the kidney . . . [These effects are due to radiation induced] defects in the blood-clotting mechanism . . . Loss of hair, which is a prominent consequence of radiation exposure, also starts after about two weeks . . . Susceptibility to infection of wounds, burns, and other lesions, can be a serious complicating factor [due to] loss of the white blood cells, and a marked depression in the body's immunological process. For example ulceration about the lips may commence after the latent period and spread from the mouth through the entire gastro-intestinal tract in the terminal stage of the sickness . . .'

Fallout pattern if nuclear reactors and waste storage and reprocessing facilities are targeted. The shaded area shows 100 rad. dose at one year.

maybe some of the ashes and sycamores. The grass is fairly resistant but I doubt if it would look green, because it won't have seen the sun for a week.

An area of forest in the Northern Hemisphere totalling the combined size of Norway, Denmark and Sweden would be burning. This, say the writers of the *Ambio* report on the atmosphere after nuclear war, is almost certainly an underestimate. The fires would lead to the absorption of sunlight at noon by a factor between two and 150 over the whole Northern Hemisphere. That is from forest fires alone, for their smoke and dust is particularly light-absorbing. That is not counting the dust and ash from the burning cities and industry. That figure does not include, either, the smoke from all the oil and gas stores which would burn and the wells which would be uncapped, whether from blast or neglect and whose contents would spew out under great pressure and catch light.

The fine particles would remain suspended as an aerosol in the atmosphere for months. The effect on all green plants would be

Fallout patterns for population centers in Europe according to Ambio's scenario.

dramatic, and would be exacerbated by the dark sooty ash that would fall on to all vegetation, further reducing the light that reached its leaves. Some areas would already be suffering either complete sterilisation by radiation, or a reduction of varied plant communities to the few more radiation-resistant varieties.

To see how long plants could last out light deprivation, I potted up a flourishing young oat plant and a clump of grass in rich soil with plenty of water and left them in a darkened (not completely dark) shed. After five days they were a pale greeny-yellow with brown patches.

It is interesting to consider the latest theories about the disappearance of the dinosaurs, which suggest that dust arising from a meteor hitting the earth screened out the sun long enough to pull the vegetable mat out from under the larger animals.

We'll be very murky indeed if Milford Haven oil terminal is a target. I would imagine our little patchwork hills will look a sort of dirty yellow. The sky would look thick and the air would be smelly.

You can see now that timing could be crucial. We just have to hope that a nuclear war doesn't take place the same time of the year as I'm writing this — mid-June when you can almost hear the chorus of photosynthesis.

If, on the other hand, the war happens during the winter months, when there is less sunlight anyway, I would imagine sheer cold would become a major killer (you don't warm yourself by the heat from a blazing city, you run away from it) and the effect on plant life would be the more complete.

Nuclear weapons, by heating up oxygen and nitrogen in the air, making nitric oxide, produce the same sort of conditions of atmospheric pollution as happens in Los Angeles from all the car exhausts. More oxides of nitrogen will also be churned out by the fires and the burning or vaporising oil and gas wells. The result would be a severe and persistent photochemical smog and a build-up of ozone and other harmful pollutants, such as ethane and 'PAN' in the lower atmosphere.

The effect of ozone on crops grown in the Los Angeles area has been studied. At concentrations well below those which would result from a nuclear war, crop growth is inhibited and yield reduced, wheat for instance by thirty per cent.

The smog conditions would be sufficient to make the sky look brown.

If the green plants die, or the area covered by green is much reduced, so also is the oxygen output to the atmosphere. This would make eventual recovery of our normal air even less likely. A vicious circle would develop, in which the plants could not regulate the air and the air conditions would further damage the plants' possibility of recovery.

The thick, polluted, dark atmosphere would have other drastic effects as well. Rain would be less likely, but when it did fall, would be very acid, again inhibiting plant growth. But the greatest shock could be for the microscopic ocean life which is the basis of the marine food chain.

If the production of aerosol by fires is large enough to cause reductions in the penetration of sunlight to the ground by a factor of one hundred, which would be quite possible in the event of an all-out nuclear war, most of the phytoplankton and herbivorous zooplankton in more than half of the Northern Hemisphere oceans would die.

It is the phytoplankton which produce most of our oxygen.

If ozone in the lower atmosphere is a major pollutant, in the upper atmosphere it is vital to our planet because the 'ozone layer', which has gradually built up over the billions of years, protects life below from the harmful ultra-violet radiation from the sun.

If a war takes the form of many smaller explosions (200 kilotons, for example) with many ground-bursts, the main results would be the atmospheric darkening, thickening and polluting I have just described. However if fewer, larger, higher (airburst) explosions happened, then the nitric oxide production would be happening in the stratosphere (the upper atmosphere) and the result here would be a large-scale reduction in the ozone layer. The reduction could be as high as seventy per cent over the Northern Hemisphere, spreading to maybe forty per cent for the South. The ozone would take about three years to recover, but in that time the damage caused by the ultra-violet light could be as dramatic as that caused by the screening of the sun.

UV-B radiation depresses photosynthesis and cell division; causes skin cancer and 'snow blindness' (this would happen to animals as well as ourselves) and would kill off a large proportion of the smallest marine organisms, the plankton living in the warm layer of the sea close to the surface.

As for us, a simpler fate might befall you and me, if we had enough food and clean water stored to survive weeks of darkness and high radioactivity, and had perhaps decided to start sowing oats onto the brown tangle of dead grass, or to plant potatoes rather than eat them. Ten minutes in the sun would be all we could take before we'd be badly burned. Ever resourceful, we'd cover up like berber tribesmen and fashion goggles out of old plastic bags maybe.

We wouldn't know the earth was dying all around us. There would be a lot of flies around, and probably a smell as well. I remember walking through a wood once in which a game-keeper had hung perhaps a dozen dead crows. The smell of carrion was all-pervasive. That smell would be everywhere, inescapable.

You know the way greenfly and caterpillars will always attack a weak plant? All the plants that tried to grow, once light levels began to recover, would be weak.

The basis of terrestrial life, the plants, would have to struggle in feeble light against many other factors inhibiting growth: high world-wide levels of radiation; severe alterations of atmospheric chemistry leading to changes in climatic temperature and in the quality and quantity of rainfall; high concentrations of air pollutants such as ozone; increased ultra-violet radiation; and an increase in the numbers and strength of insects, particularly the plant-eating kinds. (These insects are many thousands of times more resistant to radiation than the higher animals and many plants.)

Some plants are very hardy, especially mosses and lichen and that ubiquitous inheritor of landscape disturbance, the willow-herb. But the food crops which we have spent thousands of years developing are not among them. The plants hold the soil, and also create it. Erosion, as a result of large-scale loss of forest and plant cover, would mean that an unknown amount of the world's thin living skin – the soil – would simply be washed down into the seas. Eventually, many green fertile valleys would be brown dusty deserts.

Meanwhile, on all the fringes of the devastated areas, two weeks to a month after the war, people would be dying. Bone marrow collapse from the radiation dose accumulated in the first few days would mean no resistance to the diseases which would be epidemic. Just about everybody, and certainly all children, will have absorbed enough radiation to make them vomit, feel ill and have diarrhoea. There would be no normal water supply for washing. The first rain, when it came, would be welcomed by survivors desperate for water, many of whom would be burned, or who would have burnt children. But it would be so radioactive it would cause direct burns to the skin, as well as delivering a deadly dose to the whole body. People would be dying of cholera, dysentary, typhoid, perhaps plague as well as directly from radiation damage: the choking atmosphere would make breathing difficult. Chesty people – a large chunk of the British population – would have little chance of survival beyond this point.

Nearly everybody who was still strong would be surrounded by people, especially children, who weren't. The more compassionate would stay with the dying, trying to help. The more callous who could ignore the injured and dying, would be heading this way – west, using whatever petrol and food they could find.

There would be stocks of food, yes, but these would be rationed (by regional controllers who had survived in bunkers) according to willingness to undertake the more dangerous clearing up jobs – cremating the bodies, clearing debris. Work like this would mean risking disease and further radiation. A young policeman told me recently that police were expected to keep going on an upper limit of 50 Rads dose a day. Apart from the sheer impossibility of measuring, in the circumstances, everybody's dose, this is a dose which would rapidly build up such permanent damage that death within weeks would be inevitable from bone marrow damage, gastro-intestinal collapse.

Ultimately, ours and anybody's survival beyond a few weeks and beyond existing food stocks would obviously depend on whether we could grow food crops. The countries which supply the bulk of the world's grain may well have suffered complete economic and agricultural collapse.

If the atmosphere and climate did, in a matter of months, return to conditions which would allow crops to be grown – and this seems very unlikely – there would be no question of massed ranks of combine harvesters moving across fields of wheat treated with pesticides and weedkillers. As the interdependent world economic order collapsed, and food supplies were cut off as well as the all-important supplies of hybrid seed and fertiliser, billions – not millions – of people in the Third World would die of starvation. So, I suspect, would we.

For the sake of continuing with our story, let us assume that the war happens in November, that we are somehow able to gather wood for fuel without accumulating enough radiation damage to kill us, and we stay indoors more or less continuously with sacks of barley and water piped up from the well all winter. By April the sun shines again but does not strike us with UV radiation because the bombs were mostly smaller ground bursts, generating massive dust and radioactive contamination but doing little damage to the upper atmosphere. Ever hopeful, we plant the potatoes we've carefully saved and we may even have some oat or barley seed still left. Unfortunately these crops, which will grow in our climate, are among the most radiosensitive of food crops.

How would you like to get pregnant? Sixty per cent of the radio-active mix of isotopes in the fallout would have reached the earth in the first weeks. The remaining, forty per cent of finer particles would be deposited during the next seven years. Much of the fallout would have decayed to safe levels, but the longer-lived isotopes, including many neutron-activated metals from ground-bursts on cities and military and industrial targets, would be in constant circulation in soil, plants, rivers, lakes, oceans and the air.

The calculation which estimates global fallout levels from a war as envisaged by *Ambio* to be twenty-three times that resulting from atmospheric testing, does not take into account the increased fallout from groundbursts. Professor Lindop of the Department of Radiobiology at Barts Hospital, has calculated that after twenty-five years, the whole of Europe will have received a dose of 100 Rads – enough in peace time to necessitate complete evacuation.

Such a dose would be enough to present a one in forty chance of developing cancer, and half of these cancers would be fatal. When looking at cancer risks to survivors, however, it is worth pointing out that such statistics are based on studies of healthy populations exposed to known doses of radiation. No one irradiated the inmates of a concentration camp to see how they would stand up to it. We would be in such an emaciated, broken state that cancer would not be the only disease to show the extent of our damage. Damaged eyesight, tiredness, depression, chronic digestive and skin problems, would be so common as to be seen as normal. There would be no vaccines: pneumonia, tuberculosis, meningitis, whooping cough, diptheria and polio would all be common.

The effect of a global nuclear war upon the human population would not simply be to reduce it in size; it would also sicken it, reducing its efficiency and its ability to recover.

So it is impossible to calculate exactly the risk to survivors of cancer, and to babies born to survivors of cancer and genetic defects, except to say that they would be much higher than at present. At the moment about one in thirty babies in the UK is born severely handicapped, and about one in 2,000 dies of cancer before the age of ten. A dose as low as 5 Rads can increase such expectation of childhood cancer and leukemia tenfold.

But the word 'dose' does not really convey the reality of radio-active elements spread right through whatever food chains will survive. Plutonium and caesium will concentrate in the coastal parts of the oceans and the estuaries, from which we would catch fish. Living things, including plants, cannot tell the difference between plutonium and iron, caesium and potassium or strontium and calcium. That gives you some idea of where these things end up in your body – plutonium in your lungs and sex organs, caesium everywhere, strontium in your bones. Each radioactive atom would pass through many creatures' bodies in its radioactive lifetime, leaving behind it damaged cells which would reproduce as cancers, and disordering the precise genetic architecture in the sex cells which would reproduce as damaged creatures.

As radioactive elements are passed up the food chains, they

increase in concentration. A study of the radioisotopes in the Columbia river, western United States, found insignificant levels of radioactivity emanating from a nuclear power plant in the water. But the radioactivity of the river plankton was 2,000 times greater; that of the fish and ducks feeding on the plankton was 15,000 and 40,000 times greater; the radioactivity of young swallows fed on insects caught by their parents in the river was 500,000 times greater; and the radioactivity of the egg yolks of water birds was more than a million times greater.

Notice that it is the largest creatures, at the top of the chain, that concentrate the most radioactivity. That is the group to which we belong.

All radiation causes some damage; growing cells are the most susceptible to damage. I simply do not see how any baby would be born undamaged, in some way or other, in such an environment. Many would be born with an already developing cancer; or with damaged immune systems which would make 'cot death' or death from simple infections in childhood, a common event. Many would inherit a susceptibility to cancer, to try their luck in a highly carcinogenic world.

We just wouldn't know. Pregnancy, childbirth, parenthood, would be a nightmare. We would not be able to look at any child and be sure that it was strong and healthy, and had a good chance.

I remember my mother telling me how she wanted to give me milk to drink when I was a child, but was worried because of the strontium in it from the atmospheric tests. That sort of dilemma would apply to everything there was to eat or drink.

The really big long-term question mark is genetic. Think for a minute of all the genes of any species, be it ours or humming-birds' or a 'flu virus, as if they existed independently of our bodies. This is called the gene pool of a species. Only a tiny fraction of the genes at any one time are actually playing out their dance of combining to reproduce the infinite variations on the theme of being people, or humming-birds, or 'flu virus. The rest are waiting their turn. One certain result of a higher level of radiaton is a higher number of genes that don't work properly − mutations.

Some of this damage would emerge as obvious deformities but much of it would remain hidden for generations, since a damaged gene has to meet another similarly damaged before it pairs up and emerges as a defective part of some creature's body. The chances of such genetic meetings increase down the generations, as the damaged genes themselves reproduce and proliferate. Creatures subject to natural selection and with a high turnover – like 'flu virus – can withstand and even benefit from this sort of genetic onslaught, but we might not. The result for us might be that each successive generation would be weaker.

So, if we survived this far, it would be by luck and callous ruthlessness, for we would have had to grab a lion's share of food stocks in the pre-attack period to last us months, and we would have had to refuse to share it with anyone. Even if we were alive, our children would be dead from radiation, infection, or both. We would be in a similar position to the plants. We would be weakened by starvation, radiation, air pollution and injury and our predators – the bacteria and viruses we fight with white blood cells and drugs – would be both stronger and far more numerous. So would their carriers, the flies and rats. We would have no drugs, and fewer white blood cells. We could not tell if things would get better, or worse, for fresh evidence of hidden damage would emerge with every month and year.

Not I nor anyone else has any idea whether the human race, not to mention many other animal species, would survive the destruction of our present environment which would follow any large-scale nuclear war. I think the most likely outcome for us would be a sort of irreversible decline, which would take several generations before a group of people either adapted to their unhealthy surroundings, or gave up. You see, we forget about the sheer numbers of sick people, handicapped people, people suffering from all sorts of chronic and progressive, incurable and mysterious illnesses. People would be under such a strain of fear and horror and sorrow and anger that they might destroy themselves; anybody reasonably able-bodied would be surrounded by those who were not, and we would all be competing for scarce and dwindling food supplies. The people with the best chance of surviving would be those who'd be prepared to kill others for food, people we would now think of as dangerous.

Animal species and people can tolerate a certain amount of disruption, depletion of numbers up to a certain point. Beyond that point, a vicious circle sets in and if they are to survive they have to be rescued and stuck in a zoo. When there seems no hope animal species, and human groups, and individual people give up and die.

˙Then you said, 'Anyway, nobody would be so stupid as to start a nuclear war.'

I'm afraid there's no guarantee that the people who make that kind of decision know the worst that could happen.

President Truman knew nothing of the new bomb when he took over from Roosevelt in early 1945. When they told him, he just thought it was a bigger kind of bomb that would make America all-powerful. Before he decided to drop it on Hiroshima, some of the scientists who had developed the thing tried to warn him and Churchill that such an act would start an arms race that would end the living world. There were other ways of getting Japan to surrender, and they wanted these other ways tried first. But they were ignored by short-sighted politicians who wanted to end up 'on top'; and they can be ignored again.

No one is going to *decide* to launch an all-out war and end the world: the 'big' decision won't look like a big decision, it'll be a little step, a decision to drop one 'save-our-boys' lives' bomb. The generals have been making it easier for the politicians to take that step by presenting them with smaller, not bigger, nuclear bombs, whose use need not seem so momentous. It's called 'flexible response'.

If you've read this far you probably know more about the possible outcome of such a step than does the Secretary of State for Defence.

Look — you and I, I'm sure, decided to move here because of an idea about health. When I look outside, today, this is what I see. I see a dazzling June day. There are cows lying down in silky fields steaming slightly from the recent rain. In the corner lie five new calves, brown and shiny. The children shout as they find the circles of white mushrooms, and swallows carve up the air. I see a khaki and lime patchwork of fields being cleared for winter silage. A phrase from a poem fills my mind: 'The little living hills.'

Can you imagine a dusty world in which everything was poisoned — in which you could trust no appearances, in which rain was poison, milk gave your children bone cancer, and peas had to be tested with a geiger counter?

But I keep forgetting. There would be no peas or swallows.

Think about it, will you?

Yours,
Ann

TAKE THE TOYS FROM THE BOYS
Competition and the Nuclear Arms Race

We're encouraged to think of the Russians as a crude, rather barbaric people who wear fur hats and are just waiting to stream across the Iron Curtain in their hordes. This is supposedly why we need nuclear weapons, to protect Us from Them. They are are also considered to be formidable adversaries, with nuclear weapons superior to our own. This is supposedly why we need *more* nuclear weapons. The two images of the Russians don't quite tally, but then the concept of deterrence means many things to many people.

It means so many things, in fact, that deterrence explains only a few aspects of the arms race. I'd like to look at the nuclear arms race in terms of rivalry and competition for power, status, and money, and to show how these values, rather than deterrence, have actually determined many events in the race so far. After I've briefly looked at various institutions, the British government, the US government, the US armed forces, science and business communities in those terms, I'd like to look at the terms themselves. They overwhelmingly belong to white, educated men, and more than just getting rid of nuclear weapons − imperative as that may be − it's vital to challenge both the men and the values that created them in the first place.

Only one country had the atom bomb in 1945, when Prime Minister Clement Attlee authorised the British atomic weapons programme. The Russian threat was only a possibility, but the desire to keep up with the Americans was all too real. 'The Government and the majority of the British people believed Britain to be a first-class power . . .' explains the official history of the British nuclear programme. 'It seemed axiomatic that first-class powers should have first-class weapons.' The Soviet Union managed to develop the second successful bomb programme, at which point the race became three-way. When Britain finally let off its first bomb, the official history states the effect in terms of Britain's competition with both superpowers: 'Britain had success-fully taken her place as the third nuclear power, believing herself to be close on the technological heels of the United States and Russia.' At least initially, it seems that nuclear bombs were developed in Britain more out of a sense of competition than from any worries about defending the isles.

This competition wasn't entirely one-sided. During the Second World War, British scientists had helped the Americans develop the first nuclear bombs, but in 1946 the Americans passed a law, the McMahon Act, which banned all foreigners from access to atomic secrets. As a result, Britain's only means of attaining nuclear status was through an entirely independent programme. 'Whatever the United States attitude had been,' rationalises the official history, 'it is unlikely that . . . the British Government would have surrendered the essential independence of their project. They wanted collaboration but would under no circum-stances accept subservience.' Prime Minister Attlee made the point in terms of male rivalry. 'That stupid McMahon Act,' he later complained, 'they (the Americans) were rather apt to think they were the big boys and we were the small boys; we'd just got to show them they didn't know everything.'

The latest symptom of Britain's competitive spirit is the decision to buy a fleet of Trident D-5 submarines from the Americans. The D-5 is supposed to replace the Polaris submarines which currently carry Britain's nuclear missiles. More than simply replacing, the Tridents will vastly upgrade Britain's nuclear capacity, carrying more warheads on missiles with greater accuracy and three times the reach of the Polaris missiles. Even for those who think deter-rence is necessary, the Trident is far more sophisticated than simple retaliation requires. But, if the Americans have got it, it seems that Britain must have it as well, albeit in smaller numbers – four versus a projected thirty.

Perhaps the most pathetic aspect of Britain's competitiveness is that the superpowers are never going to take Britain seriously. Britain has been a nuclear power for thirty years, yet neither the USA nor the USSR has ever bothered to invite it to disarmament negotiations. It hardly seems likely that all the thousands of millions to be spent on four Tridents will change that. What Britain wants out of its nuclear weapons policy is some degree of super-power status, not just the ability to deter a Soviet invasion.

Deterrence assumes that the USA and UK need their nuclear weapons to protect us against *Soviet* aggression. Yet at least as far back as 1960, America was planning on using nuclear weapons around the world. According to a *Times* report on the Davey Crockett (a nuclear 'gun' which could be carried by a single man), 'President Eisenhower saw a short range atomic gun which the Army said could be taken to any trouble spot in the world by small combat units within a matter of hours.'

Far from being reserved solely for defence against the Soviets, former defence analyst Daniel Ellsberg maintains that nuclear weapons are integrated into America's foreign policy as a whole, 'It is the reigning consensus in the government that there will continue to be wars threatening US strategic and community interests all over the world, particularly in the Third World. The wish is to be able to suppress these "native uprisings" with the use of nuclear weapons.'

What the US considers to be its 'strategic interests' was first determined by an elite group of American bankers, lawyers and businessmen and politicians. These men (women were barred) were all members of the Council on Foreign Relations. In 1940–41, while Hitler was taking over Europe, the Council undertook a comprehensive study of the world economy, monitoring ninety-five per cent of its trade. The Council wanted to know what economic impact the war would have on America, and, in the words of one of the Council's members, 'what "elbow room" the American economy needed to survive without major readjustments.' The Council's recommendations often become US foreign policy, and the 'elbow room', or, as they also called it, the Grand Area, consisted of the entire Western hemisphere, China, Japan, the Dutch East Indies, and the United Kingdom, including all of what was formerly the British Empire. But instead of playing the colonial role the Council intended for it, Japan was itself an imperial power encroaching on the Dutch East Indies, an area which contained essential raw materials. The Council was actually trying to devise a way of involve the US in a war with Japan to stop the encroachment when Japan made matters easy by attacking Pearl Harbour.

The atomic bomb was first used against an already devastated Japan at the end of the Second World War, when it was Soviet troops who were threatening to encroach on the Grand Area. This time Japan itself was the territory in question. Since then, America has considered using nuclear weapons in Korea, China, Laos, and Vietnam. America's nuclear weapons, then, are intended to put down revolts within the ranks as well as threats from outside them. The stated policy may be defensive, to deter the Russian threat. But the actual policy is aggressive, to maintain control over other countries.

Nuclear weapons such as atomic guns, canon shells, depth charges, and short- and medium-range missiles are intended to be used on the battlefield. Called tactical nuclear weapons they're mostly under the control of the US Army. Strategic nuclear weapons include long-range bombers and missiles; originally intended for use against Russian cities and industrial centres, they now have specifically military (counterforce) targets as well. The struggle between the armed forces for control over these weapons has had a determining impact on America's nuclear weapons policy.

Despite the horror and immorality of the Hiroshima and Nagasaki bombs, America continued to refine and build up its nuclear bomb programme after the Second World War. By 1948, it had built up an arsenal of about fifty bombs. These were under the control of the Air Force, whose 'Harrow' war plan involved dropping the bombs on targets in twenty Soviet cities. The Air Force's intention was to cause 'immediate paralysis of at least fifty per cent of Soviet industry,' thus continuing the policy of bombing cities developed during the war. The Air Force soon upped its bombing ambitions to include seventy Soviet cities.

At the same time as these war plans were being developed, President Truman announced very strict limits on the Federal budget in order to curb inflation. The armed forces were not excepted, but the atomic bomb programme was funded separately, as it was supposed to be under civilian control. So the armed forces, in order to expand their power to what they felt was a necessary degree without overstepping their budgets, turned to atomic weapons. In 1949, the Joint Chiefs of Staff asked for a major expansion of the atomic bomb programme in order to counter, as historian David Alan Rosenberg points out, the Soviet Union's *conventional* forces. At that time the first Soviet bomb had not been exploded, and no one had any idea how long it might take the USSR to develop a bomb. Superpower rivalry may explain the Air Force's plans, but deterrence had to wait until the Russians actually had a bomb to deter.

The Air Force's control over the bombs was very threatening to the Navy. It seemed as though the Air Force might be able to fight and win wars on its own, thus making almost the entire Navy obsolete. Accordingly, when the Air Force and Navy did a joint study of whether or not they wanted the hydrogen bomb to be developed, it was the Navy which could most clearly see the drawbacks. The new bomb would be literally thousands of times more powerful than the bombs that devastated Hiroshima and Nagasaki, and the joint report listed some very serious reservations about it. Among these were the fact that the bombs would not actually be able to stop armies advancing, and that their use on Soviet cities would vindicate Soviet propaganda about America, thus uniting the Soviet populace in the war effort. The report did recommend that the bomb be produced, but the Air Force considered the Navy's criticisms so dangerous that they prevented President Truman from ever seeing the report. Consequently when Navy admirals criticised atomic planning before a congressional committee, it was interpreted as simple hostility to the unification of the armed forces which was being attempted. The dissenting admirals were removed, and opposition to the Air Force's plans was basically eliminated.

In the 1950s it became clear that not all three of the forces were going to be allowed to develop intercontinental missiles, presumably because of the expense involved. The result was an interservice propaganda war. Each service asserted that it, and only it, was the right and proper home for nuclear weapons. In an official statement that went right over the top, the Air Force claimed that they would be 'derelict in their duty to the American people if they allowed citizens to be brainwashed by the claims of the other services that they, not the Air Force, are the true path to peace and security.' The feuding became so intense that a senator had to call on the President to stop the 'bickering' before it became a 'national scandal'.

Eventually both the Navy and the Air Force were allowed inter-continental missiles. The Army was left in control of the battlefield nuclear weapons, but it is still keen to maintain its nuclear pre-stige. One of the main reasons for developing the Pershing II medium-range missile is that the Army's Pershing I was becoming outdated and the Army was faced 'with the prospect of . . . losing the last vestiges of nuclear missile turf to the enemy: the US Air Force and US Navy', according to defence observers Alexander Cockburn, James Ridgeway, and Andrew Cockburn. They note that Pershing II was being developed *before* the Soviets announced the SS20, which had provided the excuse for the Army to actually produce the Pershing II. Pershing II will increase the Army's status, because, unlike Pershing I, it will be able to strike the Soviet Union directly (in five minutes, no less, from West Germany).

And so the major rivalry been between the two forces continues. By the early 1960s the Air Force was claiming that their missiles could devastate Soviet forces in an offensive, first-strike attack. Robert McNamara, Secretary of Defence under Presidents Kennedy and Johnson, describes the political impact of the Air Force's claims:

. . . the advantage in the US warhead inventory was so great (by 1962) vis-a-vis the Soviets that the Air Force was saying they felt we had a first-strike capability and could, and should, continue to have one. If the Air Force thought that, imagine what the Soviets thought . . . the way they reacted was by substantially expanding their strategic nuclear weapons pro-gramme . . . So you have the action-reaction phenomenon.

McNamara stresses that the US government was not pushing for a first-strike capability: 'We didn't have any thought of attaining it [a first-strike capability]. But they [the Soviets] probably thought we did.' Yet despite government policy the Air Force continued to push for programmes – more warheads on missiles with ever greater accuracy – that only made sense to the Russians in terms of preparations for a nuclear attack. The Air Force was able to do this in spite of government policy; and of course the result was a great acceleration of the arms race.

At least part of the answer can be found in the Air Force's rivalry with the Navy. After each side had actually obtained the intercon-tinental missiles, the focus of the competition shifted. The Air Force began to move towards doing one better than the Navy: while the Navy's submarine-fired missiles were indeed adequate for simple retaliation, the Air Force was attempting to bound ahead with war-fighting missiles.

The Navy has been making steady progress in developing missiles that match the Air Force's in accuracy, but inter-service rivalry means that even when the forces want more or less the same equipment, it is nearly always researched and developed separately. This is as true for conventional as it is for nuclear weapons, partly because of in-built competition, partly because of sheer unwillingness to cooperate. Each force has its own acquisition bureaucracy which has a closely linked role with the design and production of weapons. If one force has to take on weapons already designed and produced by another, its acquisitions organisations lose out. In the case of the Cruise missile, for example, the Air Force rejected the version developed by the Navy on the grounds that the Navy's Cruise was 'too big for their missile racks'. The government then authorised the Air Force to research an entire new Cruise (based on the same principles), which also turned out to be too big for their missile racks!

Aside from its relatively inane – though expensive – effects, such as duplicating weapons systems, inter-service rivalry has lent a momentum of its own to the nuclear arms race. As a result of this rivalry, the decision to authorise the hydrogen bomb was made without the benefit of important information. Navy admirals with dissenting opinions were posted elsewhere; and the Air Force has pursued a first-strike capability seemingly without the government's consent. The struggle to be top dog is clearly as important to each of the armed forces as their claim to be doing their patriotic duty in deterring the Russian aggressors.

Scientists like to think of themselves as noble seekers after truth, ever guided by the scientific method to a deeper understanding of the universe. In reality, however, scientists thrive on competition as much as any politician or soldier. 'In their relationships, scientists share many of the problems of other workers in the United States,' writes the Thiman Laboratory Group of the University of California. 'These problems are complex, but arise directly or indirectly from profit-seeking and competition among individuals and groups of individuals.' In their quest to make new discoveries, scientists are also questing to be the *first* discoverers, the Nobel prize winners, the heads of laboratories, the chief research assistants. In the case of nuclear weapons, this desire to be first has led scientists to push for weapons which the military and politicians would never have dreamed possible.

The hydrogen bomb, for example, was not a simple or inevitable step from the bombs that destroyed Hiroshima and Nagasaki. The hydrogen bomb works on the principle of fusion, in which energy is released when two small atoms join together. The Hiroshima and Nagasaki bombs, on the other hand, worked on the principle of fission. This involves splitting one very large atom into smaller bits. To make a bomb on the fusion principle would require a brand new research programme: 'We should make an intensive effort to get ahead with the Super (the hydrogen bomb),' wrote Atomic Energy Commissioner Lewis Strauss. 'I am thinking of an investment of talent and money comparable, if necessary, to that which produced the first atomic weapons.'

When that memorandum was written no politician or military officer had enough understanding of atomic physics to conceive of such a bomb without some help from the scientists. But J. Robert Oppenheimer, the man who had led the first atomic bomb project, opposed the development of hydrogen bombs. Oppenheimer believed the hydrogen bomb was immoral: it was so big that it could be used only against cities, and he thought it had little military value.

It's doubtful whether the effort to develop the bomb would have been made, at least at that time, without the driving ambition of physicist Edward Teller. Teller had become obsessed with the idea of making a fusion bomb while he was working under Oppenheimer on the Hiroshima and Nagasaki bombs. After the war, he got around other scientists' objections by enlisting the support of the Air Force, who were quite keen on the project, and he also lobbied men in influential positions, such as Commissioner Strauss.

Oppenheimer's influence was so great, however, that Teller believed him to be responsible when initially only twelve men came forward to work on the hydrogen bomb project. Believing that Oppenheimer was frustrating his ambitions, Teller helped to destroy Oppenheimer's career. During the McCarthy era, Oppenheimer was called before the House Committee on Un-American Activities and Edward Teller allowed himself to testify against his fellow scientist. The question before the committee was whether Oppenheimer could be trusted with atomic secrets, many of which he himself had helped to discover. Teller told the committee that, while he did not doubt Oppenheimer's loyalty, 'If it is a question of wisdom and judgement . . . then I would say one would be wiser not to grant clearance.' Later, he drove the point home, saying, 'I would personally feel more secure if public matters would rest in other hands.' Largely as a result of Teller's testimony, Oppenheimer was denied access to the work around which he had based his life. Oppenheimer was a broken man. His friend and co-worker Hans Bethe remembered that after the hearing, 'He was a a changed person and much of his previous spirit and liveliness had left him.'

Rivalry between scientists rarely results in such personal tragedy, but it nearly always plays a role in scientific achievement. Yet in the case of nuclear weapons, the Americans are so far ahead of the Russians in almost every aspect of the technological race that the competition isn't directly between the two. The Americans had solid-fueled nuclear missiles by the early 1960s, for example, which enabled them to fire their rockets much more quickly and safely. The Russians were still working on the problem in the early 1980s. The Russians may indeed be competing to catch up with the Americans, though internal power struggles have definitely shaped Soviet science – for years classical genetics was not allowed to be researched because a few powerful scientists didn't believe in it. American scientists don't really need to compete with the Russians – they've got each other.

Many scientists are as interested in plain old profit as they are in academic glory, and many of them play a key role in business. The President's Science Advisory Committee, for example, is the US government's highest ranking source of scientific advice. Of the fifty-five 'academics' who served on the committee up to 1974, two-thirds were directors or consultants to corporations worth ten million dollars or more, and half were directors of corporations worth 100 million or more. To these men, defending the country against Soviet aggression is far less immediate than competing with other firms for contracts.

National defence seems to be so far from their minds, in fact, that the scientists and businessmen are willing to sell weapons that don't, and can't, do what they're claimed to do. The two new weapons that are slated for Western Europe both fall into this category. General Dynamics is developing the ground-launched model, while Boeing is working on an air-launched model. Both firms are struggling to solve some very fundamental problems of the Cruise missile. In particular, neither knows how to get the missile to read its computer map when the missile is flying over the sea or tundra, where every point looks just like every other point. The solution some weapons designers have come up with is to add details to the computer map from a ground survey. But the missile is intended for use against enemy territory, and it's hard to imagine the Russians allowing such maps to be made. A Congressional report admits that the Cruise can't be deployed against 'certain' tragets in the Soviet Union because the 'maps have not been made'. But then, how can they be? A Pentagon missile guidance designer has commented, 'One of the beauties of the Cruise . . . is that it is a weapon made for cheating. It works really very well if the memory map is based on an extensive ground survey as well as radar survey from a low-flying aircraft. Then everything works just dandy.' Not entirely surprisingly, the December 1983 delivery date for the European Cruises is almost certain to be put back.

With regard to Pershing II, Alexander Cockburn, James Ridgeway and Andrew Cockburn report that, 'Veterans of Pentagon procurement say that even by the usual relaxed standards the tests of the Pershing II guidance system were "outrageously faked". ' The three maintain that Martin Marietta Corporation desperately needed to sell the Pershing II – without the sale, the corporation would have been reduced to merely making parts for other companies' weapons. The need to sell the weapons neatly dovetails with the armed forces' need to buy them. Martin Marietta wanted the contracts, and the Army wanted the status. Whether the missile actually works or not is somewhat beside the point, provided no one makes a fuss.

The Soviets clearly have mirror military and scientific institutions, complete, most likely, with mirroring rivalries and power struggles. They also have their equivalents of weapons companies. Cockburn *et al*. point out that the Soviets created the Nadiradze Design Bureau in the early 1960s and that the SS-20, the Soviet counterpart to the Pershing II, is their first success in all that time. Without it, Nadiradze might well have 'gone out of business'.

To the arms manufacturers, then, self-preservation matters more than the preservation of the nation, not that any nuclear weapon ever could help preserve a country.

The Russian threat just doesn't explain a whole range of aspects of the arms race. These aspects, the super sophistication of Britain's Trident submarines, America's nuclear targets in the Third World, the report on the hydrogen bomb which the Air Force kept hidden from the President, Edward Teller's single-minded drive to develop the hydrogen bomb, and the fact that many of the weapons just don't work, all do share a common thread. They are the result of individuals competing to increase their own status, power, or wealth.

It's no coincidence that the overwhelming majority of these individuals are white, educated men, because the governments, military forces, scientific and business establishments involved in the nuclear arms race were created and are now maintained by white, educated men. The institutions they have created all share a common structure which is based on a pecking order, or hierarchy. The point is to peck up as high as possible – to become father of the H-bomb, or possessor of the deadliest bombs, or winner of the most lucrative contracts. At this point in time, any person or group could take on the competitiveness and ambition and climb the hierarchies. But white men as a whole do regard the power structures as their property, and they tend to systematically exclude outsiders.

The white men who run the arms race are so overwhelmed with their ambition that they dismiss or choose not to think about simple questions that might bring their structures falling down. If they ever have doubts about what the bombs do to the earth, or to people, or think about the vast resources in money and intelligence that the bombs suck up, then the Russian 'threat' does make a bizarre kind of sense. It's the security blanket these men use to cover up their guilt, if they feel it, about the violence their actions could do to the world.

These men *could* kill us all with their nuclear weapons, but they are killing us right now by other means. In many parts of the world they are practising non-nuclear warfare, organised torture, and genocide. In Britain this direct sort of violence is limited mainly to police brutality, rape, incest, beating and individual murder by individual men. And from their fantasies, from the unavoidable beat-'em-up cops and robbers series on television, the war comics produced just for boys and the phenomenal amounts of sadistic pornography produced for men, it seems that men don't feel at all guilty about their violence. Rather, they seem to revel in it.

This violence is at the core of the hierarchies that produce and maintain the bomb. It provides an affirmation and a reinforcement of the more subtle methods that the men in the nuclear arms race use – the seeking to control through status, wealth, and the power of nuclear weapons.

Urgent as it may be, nuclear disarmament alone does not fundamentally challenge the men, the values or the institutions that created the bombs. Unless we also challenge these, violence in all its forms will continue.

ALTERNATIVE DEFENCE
The Search for Non-nuclear Alternatives

No form of defence, no weapon no matter how sophisticated or costly, can guarantee victory. This is especially true of nuclear war: losses would be so staggering on both sides — except if it were a successful first-strike attack — that it would be more like mutual surrender than winning. So it is reasonable to question whether nuclear weapons are capable of defending at all.

Most countries do not rely on nuclear weapons for their defence. Some countries who have had the means during the past few decades to manufacture the bomb have decisively rejected the concept of nuclear defence. Sweden, with its long history of armed neutrality, chose non-nuclear defence as the surest way of avoiding entanglements, or confrontations, with the superpowers. In 1966 in the spirit of détente, Prime Minister Trudeau opted to dissolve all Canadian nuclear weapons. Canada is today an ex-nuclear power: it remains loyal to NATO, as always, but favours non-nuclear defence because it found nuclear bases to be impinging upon national sovereignty. Now that Canada has gone non-nuclear the Americans could not launch a nuclear attack from Canadian territory unless the Canadian Government gave them express permission. Canada and Sweden, among other countries, have illustrated that nuclear weapons are superfluous to their national defence requirements.

Many other countries have been prevented from stockpiling nuclear weapons or other weapons of mass destruction by the cost. Little by little, however, some of the poorer countries are beginning to declare their 'need' for a nuclear 'deterrent'. Nigeria and Argentina, for example, see themselves as leading developing nations: this, they feel, gives them the right to become nuclear powers.

Britain, as the first non-superpower to go nuclear, must take its share of the blame for nuclear proliferation. If Britain developed and advocated through its foreign policy a non-nuclear, non-offensive defence strategy, it could encourage some states to think twice before rushing into the nuclear rat race, thus reversing the tide of proliferation. All states — with the exception of Costa Rica — perceive the need to defend themselves from outside aggression through constructing a military defence system of some sort. Wouldn't it be preferable for developing nations to import non-nuclear strategies and strategists instead of uranium and nuclear scientists? It would clearly be much easier to convince countries of the advantages of non-nuclear defence *before* they went nuclear.

While some developing nations are beginning to manufacture their own A-bombs, Britain and other militarily aligned nations are expanding the breadth of the arms race. The two nuclear alliances rely on a wide assortment of weapons of mass destruction. Current NATO and Warsaw Pact planning is known to include preparations for chemical warfare. I find this aspect of the nuclear arms race most horrific because chemical warfare means actually fighting, not deterring. What is more, if a chemical war did break out, more civilians would die relative to soldiers than with any other type of weapon, including battlefield nuclear weapons. These days troops are trained to fight while wearing the gas masks and protective suits necessary to survive chemical warfare. Medical teams would dole out antidotes (drugs to counteract the effects of the poisons) to those soldiers who were unable to put on their protective clothing in time. The effectiveness of such protective measures could mean that the chemicals would kill relatively few soldiers. But the rest of the population would not be protected. People living in the area would by no means receive the same medical attention as the soldiers; in NATO countries the people would not even be equipped with protective clothing. Their sole 'protection' would be staying indoors with the doors and windows sealed. It is estimated that if a chemical attack did occur, twenty times more civilians than soldiers would die — and this is a conservative estimate.

The stockpiling of chemical weapons is a good example of an

inappropriate response to the problems of preventing chemical warfare: stockpiling escalates the original danger, making the situation far more threatening than it was in the first place. A more logical and humane approach would be, first, to seek genuinely to minimise threats and conflicts, secondly to expand and improve protective measures for soldiers and civilians alike and, most important, to develop a less escalatory yet more effective defence strategy which would not so appallingly harm the people, the way of life, and the territory it was seeking to protect.

But the key question is: do we need defence at all? Without doubt, there are valid reasons for advocating non-resistance to all aggression or for supporting a pacifist over a military response. (This case is argued in the next chapter.) However, there are those of us concerned with disarmament who feel we must deal with today's political realities; we must compromise absolute principles if that enhances our chances of survival.

Some would welcome a move from nuclear to non-nuclear defence as a significant step in the direction of total disarmament. Others would welcome it because it could prove to be a cheaper method of defence; a saving of three per cent annually could be skimmed off the defence budget to help create full employment, for example. The main objection I have to the twin non-military policies of non-resistance (surrendering without fighting) or non-violent resistance (using persuasion, pressure tactics, and obstruction to thwart enemy objectives) is that neither provides a particularly sound deterrent to invasion, although the latter approach could wear down the enemy in the end. It seems to me that to rely on military forms of *defensive deterrence* would be the safest bet.

Advocates of defensive deterrence do not consider nuclear weapons to be deterrents: the threat to use them necessarily implies possible use, which must mean a failure to deter in the end. The non-nuclear forces of defensive deterrence could conceivably be the same as they are now in Britain, or preferably they could be designed and moulded into an inherently defensive approach.

In proposing conventional defence strategies, I do so without the conventional military perspectives. I recognise that using conventional weapons would undoubtedly be devastating, but I accept that greater destruction might in some circumstances be avoided through their use. To mount an effective conventional deterrent, a nation would need to make serious military preparations; it could not wait until the last minute, when invasion appeared imminent, to set up the deterrent structure. Therefore, it is important to evaluate the various kinds of advance preparations.

A wide range of non-nuclear options exists in national defence policies which, although not exactly comparable to Britain's situation, could provide valuable alternative models. Territorial defence, for example, is an inherently defensive method. It seeks to defend home territory, and that alone, in depth, by mobilising troops in a chequerboard pattern over the entire land. Territorial fighters are equipped to fight on their own soil, exploiting their familiarity with the terrain. They are not prepared to launch an attack elsewhere and they would not be equipped with air force bombers since they would not wish to bomb their own territory.

Guerrilla tactics can be employed to harass and wear down invading enemy soldiers. The Viet Cong and Tito's Partisans, for instance, used guerrilla tactics effectively to tie up technically superior forces over a long period of time. It is believed by guerrilla strategists, like Mao and Régis Debray, the French political writer, that guerrillas must be supported by regular soldiers in order to inflict the final defeat. Guerrilla tactics on their own could not be expected to bring military victory; what they can do is add to the overall deterrent, making invasion of that country appear too costly in lives and equipment.

Frontier defence means defending the borders from invasion. In the case of an island like Britain, this would be the same as coastal defence. Economic defence would defend the country against economic sanctions, embargoes, blockades, or general wartime shortages by stockpiling those key raw materials which are imported and critical to the economy. Psychological defence can be used to boost the morale of the home population, meanwhile lowering that of the enemy, through propaganda. Civil defence aims to protect the population from the dangers of nuclear and conventional attack; although it can also of course be set up as a system to control the populace when the normal structures of government break down.

These various defence approaches have their drawbacks as well as their strong points. Nevertheless, they do show that defensive deterrence goes beyond guns and ammunition, though some would not necessarily be suitable for a non-nuclear Britain.

Yet a crucial element in any successful deterrent strategy would be the actual weaponry. A large amount of defence theorising is about weapons and how they work. While it would be ridiculous to fall into the trap of advocating one weapon system over another, one general point should be made: the more complex and 'perfected' the weapon, the less reliable it is. In the words of Mary Kaldor:

Modern military technology is not advanced; it is decadent. Over the years, more and more resources have been spent on perfecting military technology of a previous era. As a consequence, modern armaments have become increasingly sophisticated and elaborate; and they can inflict unimaginable destruction. But they are incapable of achieving limited military objectives . . .

In other words, the weapons are not well suited to the job; if they were workers, they would have been sacked long ago. Any good, cost-effective defence strategy must take into account that these weapons are ultra-sophisticated, gold-plated, and superfluous. The defensive non-nuclear strategies I am proposing would depend on weapons which are primarily used to defend rather than attack. Long-range bombers capable of striking the heart of Russia would be ruled out, while relatively cheap and effective missiles like Exocet, and Precision Guided Munitions would be recommended because they can destroy armaments such as battleships and tanks that are far bigger and costlier. For example, HMS Sheffield, valued at £85 million in 1980, was sunk by one Argentine Exocet missile costing 'only' £100,000.

The rest of the chapter will examine the possibilities of restructuring the British Armed Forces to make them more capable of defending us properly. The first step would be to de-nuclearise Britain's forces. This would automatically mean scrapping the Polaris and Lance systems and getting rid of all American nuclear bases. The government would then have several options to choose from. I will discuss three broad choices, but of course there could be endless variations of each.

The first choice is non-nuclear membership of NATO. In this scenario, Britain's nuclear forces would be dissolved and the American nuclear bases would be removed. But because Britain still participated in NATO, it would probably have no choice but to cooperate in NATO nuclear strategy by maintaining all or some of the surveillance outposts based here. Brawdy, situated on the coast of Wales, provides crucial services for NATO by monitoring the movements of Soviet submarines. Bases like Brawdy which facilitate NATO nuclear planning would be difficult for Britain to dissolve while remaining a member of NATO. Because it is difficult to say exactly where nuclear cooperation begins or ends, a non-nuclear Britain in NATO could be nearly as vulnerable to Warsaw Pact attack as it was before giving up its nuclear status.

The non-nuclear position described here would be comparable to Norway's or Canada's present status. The Norwegians refuse to allow the Americans to base nuclear weapons on their territory during peacetime. In war, however, they would permit them. The Norwegian coast continually provides monitoring facilities valuable to NATO; since these bases could become strategic Soviet targets, Norway's position remains ambiguous.

Nevertheless, if Britain were to choose this option, it would be a move in the right direction. Britain, like non-nuclear Canada, would continue to contribute to the defence of West Germany, but not to its nuclear system. This would mean maintaining the 55,000 British troops permanently based in Germany, but de-nuclearising their aircraft and arms. A non-nuclear Britain in NATO would also be obliged to maintain its contribution to the NATO Navy. A sudden withdrawal of British support could cause enormous alarm, since approximately seventy per cent of the NATO Navy is British.

While this option could prove slightly less expensive and escalative than our present policy, it would have substantial drawbacks. It would not, strictly speaking, be an entirely non-nuclear policy: Britain would still be cowering under the NATO nuclear umbrella. Another drawback would be that NATO could expect Britain to make up for the loss of nuclear force by contributing more troops, more aircraft, and so on than before. This option would definitely not be a radical break from our present policy, nor would it significantly decrease the chance of a war between the two blocs.

A second option would be taking up an oppositional membership of NATO. This option starts where the first leaves off. Britain would take the same de-nuclearising steps, but in addition be determined to advance the process of nuclear disarmament within NATO. She would remain a member of NATO in order to change it from within. Britain could draw up a list of conditions for NATO to meet if she were to continue contributing to the NATO Navy. The conditions that Britain should focus on are ones which would unite all European disarmament campaigners. The most basic might be these three: that NATO should agree never to use nuclear weapons *first*; remove all battlefield nuclear weapons from Western Europe; remove all tactical nuclear weapons from Western Europe. Once these three conditions were met, more could be proposed. Such conditions offer incentives for European states to unite in opposition to the most controversial aspects of NATO nuclear strategy – such as threatening to use battlefield nuclear weapons to repel an invasion by conventional forces into West Germany, which would certainly be at the expense of the Germans living nearby. The conditions would seek to make all of Europe more secure, not just Britain. In this scenario it would be hoped that several other European members would support the conditions, and pressure NATO to fulfil them.

Difficulties would arise if any of the basic conditions were not met. Because oppositional membership is rooted in the belief that the NATO nuclear alliance, as it stands, is unsatisfactory, if no changes took place, then Britain would have to pull out. Perhaps other European members would leave too. It is possible that internal dissent and general dissatisfaction with NATO's inflexibility would cause NATO to collapse.

The third scenario is non-alignment. If Britain did leave NATO, it could join the ranks of the non-aligned and be seen to be unequivocally refusing to rely on the balance of terror. This option would be similar to Sweden's position as a non-aligned, non-nuclear nation dedicated to promoting disarmament. Sweden has had a policy of armed neutrality for over 160 years. It has set up a formidable defence network, known as a high entry cost policy, which tries to deter the enemy by making the country too risky and too costly to invade. Because this policy combines a variety of other forms of defence with military force, the Swedes call it 'total defence'. To defend the country from blockade or economic embargoes, Sweden stockpiles critical raw materials such as oil. And in order to increase the chances of surviving radiation fallout caused by nuclear explosions in other countries, civil defence has been seriously undertaken. Unlike the members of the two blocs, Swedish defence is based on the premise that it would only be attacked by non-nuclear weapons, and that the enemy would not commit its entire military might against it. Not being a primary target of attack in itself would enhance its chances of survival.

Could the Swedish model be applied to Britain? Many pro-NATO spokespeople say that Sweden's approach is very costly – too costly for Britain. The debate about who spends most on defence can be presented in several ways. One is the ratio of defence spending to Gross National Product (GNP). Using this method, according to the Stockholm International Peace Research Institute (SIPRI) Sweden spends just 3.4 per cent of its GNP on defence, while Britain spends 4.9 per cent. Or alternatively, if the costs are presented in absolute terms, nuclear Britain spends five times more than Sweden, six times more than Yugoslavia (another non-aligned, non-nuclear state) and eight times more than Switzerland (also non-aligned and non-nuclear). Figures from the International Institute for Strategic Studies in London cite even greater disparity between Britain's current defence expenditure and that of the non-aligned countries. Thus it would appear that we could not discount this third option on economic grounds.

The main worry that some might have about this option is the possibility of American retaliation for British withdrawal from NATO. No NATO ally has to date completely left the alliance. France under de Gaulle in 1966 merely rejected military membership of NATO. Ever since it has continued to cooperate on a political level and to participate informally in NATO exercises. Greece in the 1970s and again in the 1980s has announced its desire to remove all American bases and leave NATO altogether. But as yet no firm commitments have been made. In brief, there are *no* precedents of an American government's taking revenge on fellow NATO allies, but this cannot be ruled out.

If the Americans did decide to retaliate, it might be in the form of propaganda campaigns, CIA destabilisation and subversion, or economic sanctions. The chance of attacks on British airfields does seem extraordinarily remote. But these possibilities would have to be weighed against the risks of staying in NATO and giving the Americans tacit permission to wage nuclear war on Britain's behalf or using Britain as a base for their own military adventures.

If Britain chose the third option, defence priorities would have to be radically altered. The emphasis would become much more defensive than it is today. The Navy and Air Force would need to be scaled down since Britain would no longer attempt to defend outposts thousands of miles away. A task force or a rapid deployment force would be out of the question. The army might be strictly territorial as it is in Sweden, or it could be a combination of regular, territorial and frontier fighters. The possibility of a mix of regular soldiers and guerrillas, similar to the Yugoslav Peoples'

Army would not be appropriate for Britain: guerrilla tactics are best suited for rural areas, shrouded in greenery in mountainous or hilly terrain. In theory *urban* guerrilla warfare might seem a splendid option for Britain to develop, except for the fact that this type of defence would probably result in much more destruction than any foreign occupation: the purpose of defence is not to win the war, but rather to protect as many people as possible, especially civilians, from war.

The dramatic policy changes which would accompany the third option might force Britain to re-evaluate the need for national conscription. In Yugoslavia everyone takes part in the defence effort. Children of both sexes are given military training in school and adults are called up for retraining every so often. Yugoslavia's defence planners believe that a high level of military readiness is necessary to make their defensive deterrent work. They have accepted greater security at the cost of a more militarised society. Whether Britain would 'need' conscription is a particularly controversial issue.

Many other aspects, which are beyond the scope of this chapter, need further study. Proponents of British disarmament must explore the range of defence alternatives so that they can present their own models. The purpose of my discussion has been to provoke our side to draw its own conclusions. The options I have suggested are meant, above all, to open up debate.

In sum, it should be clear that each type of defence has its own risks. Each country should assess the likelihood of external threat and decide what, and how much, needs to be allocated to the defence sector. Ideally it should be feasible for foreign policy, in conjunction with defence policy, to 'wither away' the need for defence. If enough nations adopted strategies of defensive deterrence, gradually security threats would fade away. The withering away of defence through developing alternative defence strategies is one of many routes to disarmament.

Changes in British defence policy must start from where the world stands today; and any step away from the precipice of disaster should be welcomed.

ALTERNATIVE DEFENCE
Nonviolent Struggle and Peace Building

The theory and practice of nonviolence has been discussed and used throughout history and increasingly in this century. It may well be a response to the growing fear of, and revulsion from war, and the ever-growing sense of helplessness and hopelessness experienced by so many people today.

Nonviolent resistance to bad laws or to oppression is essentially a 'do-it yourself' tool. It carries no guarantee of success in every situation, but it must be remembered that at least as much uncertainty goes with methods of war and violence. The successes and failures gained by warlike action in the past have had little to do with the justice or moral strength of the victorious cause. Usually the more cunning or stronger side has overcome the weaker or less prepared, but in many cases justice has been on the side of the loser, and in many cases, too, the problems that were fought over could have been solved without violence or bloodshed – and indeed still remained to be solved after the war and bloodshed were over.

The pacifist has liberated him or herself from the tradition of war, by renouncing the whole concept of war as a means either of defence, or of effecting change, or even of throwing off an oppressive military or dictatorial regime.

Nonviolent struggle is not, however, exclusively a pacifist approach. It may be seen as a tactic for meeting conflict and even military strength without armed action. The reasons for using it may be those of expedience – there may be no arms available, or morality — a desire to avoid the taking of life, or simply pragmatic — the recognition of the fact that violence simply begets further violence and rarely leads to a permanent solution of any problem.

Nonviolence is natural to every one of us in our daily lives; very few women — or men — solve their personal problems by injuring or murdering the person with whom they are in disagreement. Nonviolent resistance has been used many times, in collective struggles against oppression, even against armed aggression. The most recent example has been in Poland, where a sustained non-violent campaign was undertaken by the workers, rebelling against intolerable economic conditions and an incompetent and repressive government. Methods used in this and other such struggles in the past, included non-cooperation with authority, strikes, boycotts, alternative systems within neighbourhoods and other forms of unarmed resistance. Even armed invasion and military or militarily-backed occupation have been met with non-violent resistance, as in Norway and Holland under the Nazis or in British India. The Gandhian movement against British domination helped to inspire the civil rights movement in the United States, led by Martin Luther King. During the Vietnam war the Buddhists practised similar nonviolent tactics with great effect, on world opinion as well as on the occupying forces.

All these nonviolent responses to threats and oppression offer experiences and material which could have been more widely used and studied and might well have prevented other wars and saved many lives.

It is, of course, doubtful whether an unarmed nation, using nonviolent methods, could prevent an invasion or guarantee adequate defence against a full-scale armed attack. Nonviolent resistance can certainly, in the end, make an oppressive regime disintegrate and could seriously disrupt a military invasion. The point of this chapter, however, is to indicate why the pacifist has no faith in even limited armed resistance, and does not believe that partial or selective disarmament will avert the threat or practice of war, or offer the defence or security we are all indoctrinated to believe is essential to our survival.

A pacifist believes that a lasting solution to the problems of the world can only be found once the decision has been made to refuse to use the method of war. Once this last-resort threat (which may, indeed on occasion be a first-response on impulse to an imagined danger) has been renounced, the skills of the human race will find new ways to develop their ideologies and will learn to live without using killing and destruction as a means of imposing these ideologies on others. The ultimate goal must be to remove the words 'peace' and 'war' from our vocabularies and to build a society based on justice and reverence for life.

This century has seen an escalation in the quality and quantity of armaments, in nuclear weapons and all other instruments of death, on a scale hitherto unknown. It has seen two world wars and hundreds of more limited conflicts, resulting in the deaths of tens of millions of citizens, some fully armed, some unarmed, many incapable of bearing arms. The terrible consequences have been seen throughout the world – homelessness, disease, crippled and distorted bodies, the disruption of anything approaching a 'normal' life, changes of regime, sometimes for the better but often towards even more repressive and militarist systems.

After the nuclear bomb was used against Japan, a sense of shock slowly spread through the world as more and more knowledge of its power seeped, almost like radiation after-effects, into the minds of men and women. Had our masters at last gone too far by inventing a weapon capable of destroying life on earth? Had they in fact invented a weapon which by its very nature would make the Second World War the last? In 1945 this seemed possible, but we ignored the warnings or we were too unaware of the implications. The chance of building a sane world during the first few years after the ending of World War II was lost, and nation followed nation down the slippery slope towards disaster. Today, we who live, live on the edge of the greatest danger ever faced by the human race, and one of the symptoms of our disease is the highly infectious ability to create enemies and then fear what that enemy could do to us. Former enemies become allies, old allies become enemies. Armaments increasingly control the relationships between states, and have been used again and again in the many wars suffered, since 1945, in the third world countries under the patronage of Britain, the US and the Soviet Union. Over all our heads hangs the ever-nearing cloud of the H-bomb. With the increase of this threat has come a growing awareness that our leaders, be they military 'experts', 'responsible politicians' or ministers of state, are no longer in control of the armaments they have helped to invent and manufacture. Caught up in the spiral of the arms race, we have not found the way to a breakthrough.

It is precisely because we live in a world where political leaders so easily resort to military solutions, and where those military solutions today could result in nuclear conflict, that the institution of war itself must be challenged and abolished. Over thirty years have been wasted and all efforts between states to improve the situation have failed. Although some will apportion blame for this failure to the USA and others to the USSR, such analysis gets us nowhere, indeed it serves to stimulate the fear which in turn permits the arms race to accelerate. All we have to recognise is that both major powers and their allies have stockpiled weapons of mass destruction to the point at which they threaten all humankind. Therefore they have to be stopped. We, the people of the world, can no longer trust any government to decide who is our enemy, nor trust their judgement as to when diplomacy and negotiation can be said to have failed. On their judgements war is declared, but it is we, the people, who are ordered to do the killing, and to 'lay down our lives' at their call.

Too many people today are obsessed by the need for 'defence' and look only to armaments for their security. This is one of several reasons for the lack of progress in disarmament, and yet still no one feels 'secure'. The disarmament movement stumbles at the same hurdle. There are many movements working actively in different parts of the world. Their approaches differ. Some are more cautious than others, some put their faith in the United Nations, others in unilateral initiatives; but *all* are calling for a halt and trying to bring the world to its senses. Common to many is the call for the banning of the use and ownership of nuclear weapons. It is not too difficult to prove that such weapons cannot be included in the category of 'defence purposes only' items – nor indeed that a country without nuclear weapons, being less of a threat to the superpowers, might in fact be safer for that reason and a less likely target for destruction. But so deep-seated are fears of attack or invasion that, in order to prove that their position is both desirable and practical, or perhaps in the hope of being taken more seriously by those in power, the search for alternative defence methods plays an important part in the programmes of many of these movements. A great deal of energy, research and thought has, for example, been put into what is usually called 'popular civilian defence' – the idea of a people's armed force, trained to defend in an emergency but not to be used outside the nation's territory. Those who advocate this position believe it to be both practicable and possible but they can no more prove that a partially disarmed country could survive a nuclear attack or armed invasion from a superior force, than the military strategists have been able to prove that their vast nuclear arsenals can guarantee a future without war or survival after a war. My main objection to this position is that the *conception* of armed defence remains, the training for war continues, the know-how for the manufacture of nuclear weapons still exists and new weapons can still be invented and quietly stored 'at home' or put on the market for others to use.

The pacifist's position is totally different because she or he is not concerned with defence and, in fact, has renounced armed defence of any kind. Nor has he or she ever felt secure or protected whilst living in a society that relies on war to solve its problems or to meet an attack from another country.

It is necessary to emphasise the extreme peril we are facing today in order to put the pacifist position in its proper perspective, and to suggest that disarmament trends that concentrate on alternative forms of defence are not only moving too cautiously but in the wrong direction. We have seen that if we continue to rely on nuclear weapons under the myth of deterrence that some time — possibly in this century — we are doomed to die and to kill millions of others in the process. If we refuse to make or to use these nuclear weapons, but retain and perfect other means of so-called defence, we continue to sanction war and not one step towards peace-building will have been made. Pacifists have no proven plans for unarmed defence. They do not believe that humanity can reverse the course of history simply by abolishing the more advanced weapons, nor that it would be desirable to revert to the use of the so-called 'conventional weapons' that have been the cause of death to nearly thirty million people since 1945.

The third approach, that of total disarmament, backed by a revolutionary foreign policy and a refusal to sanction the method of war is a step that carries risks, but the risks we face daily are far greater, and meeting them with caution and compromise has not lessened the danger. Therefore a great leap into the unknown has to be made. Some would call it a leap into the dark, but those who believe that war is both immoral and outmoded see a light in the distance.

Although it is impossible to guarantee security through non-violent civilian defence — and it is recognised that nonviolent resistance is unlikely to prevent an armed invasion — training and practising nonviolence is a way of changing our whole society and of protecting values in a way that no war or armed revolution has ever achieved. The power of nonviolence is not to be seen as an alternative to war but as a new and different way of bringing peace and justice into the world. Nonviolent resistance has to be matched with peace education and learning how to deal with conflict, whether in our own neighbourhood or under threat of oppression or aggression, without the response of physical violence. The purpose of nonviolent action is related not so much to the absence of violence as such, as to the need to achieve *change*. To change a situation without violence means that opponents have to understand one another's viewpoints instead of killing or defeating each other. An opponent has to be disarmed in both senses of the word. Being unarmed yourself is already one step ahead in the process of negotiation because you pose no immediate threat. Your opponent can, of course, kill you, just as you might have killed him had you been armed, but short of this there are innumerable ways in which military strength can be undermined and thwarted by sustained nonviolence and non-cooperation. Anyone already committed to a programme of disarmament and protest should add to his or her duties the study and practice of nonviolent resistance. No people are more fitted than women to take a leading role in the nonviolent struggle for peace. This is not to suggest support for the view of women as 'the weaker sex'; on the contrary, it is to recognise the peculiar resilience and courage which they share, perhaps just because they have not, as yet, got into the *habit* of using the gun as a means of attack or defence. The human addiction to violence has to be challenged and curbed, not by sermons or theoretical tomes, but by action and by the practice of nonviolent alternatives.

There is nothing passive in this conception of a new attitude towards conflict and war. Nor is it a dream outside reality; it is a way of saying 'give peace a chance', that moving call to open doors on a new world which would concentrate less on the balance of weaponry or the debate on defence, and more on learning to live. The pacifist cannot offer a blueprint for a solution to our predicament, but neither can the militarists who have brought us into it. Those who decide that, under certain circumstances, they would be prepared to wage war must face the fact that it is then logical to maintain the most powerful weapons available. Those who have renounced the whole method of war are committed to resist every form of its preparation and should be prepared to train for nonviolent responses with a dedication that few in the armed services are called to give. It is wrong to liken nonviolence to passivity or neutralism. Of course there have been failures and set-backs, but the main weakness to date in the experience of non-violence has been the failure to sustain confidence in its power in the face of opposition.

If the human race could put the same courage and faith in non-violence that it has put into war, constantly seeking to improve techniques and adapting methods to suit new needs, the tools for building peace would become increasingly creative and effective. It has taken two thousand years to bring us to a situation in which, demonstrably, war must be removed from society or society must perish. Nonviolence is not an alternative to war, but a way of living positively. Nonviolent resistance and nonviolent defence are only steps towards this totality, which must start from within the indi-vidual. No government can order its people to disarm or conscript them into nonviolent training as it can order them into war. The movement must start from the will of the people, from their refusal to bear arms or to prepare for war. Nor must we wait for other nations, allies or enemies, to take the initiative, but must start here and now for ourselves; the smaller nations are best fitted to take the lead, representing as they do links in the chain of power held by the superpowers. Let us snap those links before it is too late.

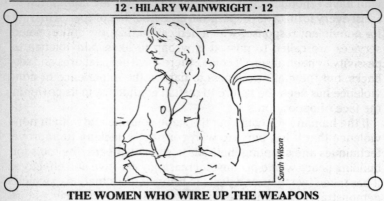

Sarah Wilson

THE WOMEN WHO WIRE UP THE WEAPONS
Workers in Armaments Factories

In *Three Guineas*, Virginia Woolf argues that women are well placed to prevent war. The emotions of aggressive pride and arrogant patriotism which lead to war, do not, she argues, take hold of women to the same extent as they do the majority of men. The rallying cries to defend 'our country' do not have the same resonance among women. Women have too little stake in the country's wealth and power to consider the sacrifice of lives to be justified. She goes on, however, to say that women can only develop and express this scepticism about the excitement and glories of war if they are financially independent of men. Yet such financial independence requires education, and the education system is dominated by values and ambitions which, in the past, have led to war – as are the majority of professions through which financial independence might be gained. So, argues Virginia Woolf, women need to seek means of financial independence, while at the same time remaining distant from the corrupting centres of power and status. And from that distance they should create a culture and a movement able to subvert the vested interests and misplaced pride that lead to war.

Virginia Woolf was thinking mainly of 'middle-class' women. She referred briefly to the women who make munitions, but her call to action was aimed primarily at 'the daughters of educated men' who, in her view, could challenge all the ceremonies, rewards and cultural praise which encourage the desire to impose 'our civilisation' on others. With hindsight – Virginia Woolf was writing in the late 1930s – we can say that she overestimated the power of a predominantly cultural challenge to imperial and militaristic values, a challenge coming solely from within 'the educated' classes. The daughters of 'educated' men need to make common cause with the daughters of 'working' men, especially those daughters who have gained their financial independence by making arms. But how well placed are this latter group of women to prevent war?

These women too, are faced with a division of labour which distances them from wealth and power, even more so than the majority of their brothers in arms production. The vast majority of women in arms production are in clerical, unskilled or semi-skilled manufacturing work. Their numbers in the industry have grown as electronics, with all its 'fine' delicate circuitry, has become the technological basis for modern weaponry. But women form a ghetto within that industry, a ghetto of wirers, winders, and circuit assemblers.

In Lucas Aerospace, for example, over eighty per cent of the workforce are highly skilled, both on the shop floor and in the drawing offices and design rooms. This eighty per cent is almost entirely male. Among the remaining twenty per cent of unskilled or semi-skilled workers are two groups of women: thirty or so in Bradford and around 350 in Birmingham. In Bradford, they are in a section of their own, winding wires for electrical systems on military aircraft. In Birmingham, they are in a factory on their own, making electronic circuits for bomber aeroplanes. Tina Mackay from the Birmingham factory describes their work:

We sit in rows like a classroom, though the foremen sit at the back. They can overlook us better that way. We are separated by such large gaps that we cannot talk unless we shout. Some of the jobs are extremely uncomfortable and tedious. For example 'lidding' the circuits involves sitting in front of a six-foot machine and working with rubber gloves up to your armpits in a vacuum case. You have to put the circuits, the electrodes and the 'lid' together for automatic welding. While the welding is going on you cannot move. Your just sit there, your arms sweating, your legs not being able to fit under the table properly and your head going bonkers!

There are a few men in these ghettoes, but even the women say 'they are not real men, you know', reflecting the low esteem with which women regard their own work. The men too feel that their work is somehow beneath them. Tina describes how:

The men are always trying to do extra technical bits, completely unnecessary to the job, to prove they are different from us. I keep telling them they are giving their time free to the company. It's ridiculous to me, but it's important to them.

Women's restriction to these ghettoes of the semi-skilled makes them outsiders, uninterested in the status and even satisfaction that skilled men gain from working on highly sophisticated weapons systems. Joan Jenkins from an EMI factory doing Ministry of Defence work in West London describes the approach of some of the men towards the job and the product:

Some men brag about how sophisticated is what they are working on now, compared with what was used in the last war. They are boasting about the cleverness of what they are doing. The technical people are even more extreme. They design the weapons and they do not seem to have any qualms about it. Though they do drink a lot, maybe that's why!

This commitment to the job, especially the skilled content of the job is contradictory, though. In Lucas Aerospace it led men to be so determined to save their jobs that they drew up a list of alternative products on which they could use their skills for the social good rather than face the dole. But even at Lucas, the shop stewards who drew up this alternative plan for socially useful work, had to overcome a strong feeling that, as Dave Newton a technician from Wolverhampton put it:

Aerospace work, especially on prestige military projects is considered high status. Some designers rather looked down on the idea of working on products for hospitals.

At least these designers are aware of what they are working on. The other side of women's lack of interest in the job, is ignorance of the product, an ignorance reinforced by the extreme fragmentation of the production process in the arms industry. For a group of women at British Aerospace in Stevenage, it was the Falklands war which revealed to them the lethal nature of their work. One of them from a wiring section put it like this:

Until the Falklands it was just another job to me. That's when it really came home to me that the things I'm making are going to kill someone; and it might be our own people. The job we do is so far removed from the actual thing, that you do not think of it as a lethal occupation. Even when you see the actual thing (a missile), on an open day, it does not really register.

Interestingly, it was the Falklands experience which also jolted the women working on explosive devices at the EMI factory at Hayes; Betty Jones, an EMI shop steward described the impact:

We talked about it [the issue of working on arms] for the first time during the Falklands. One of the women said to me, 'Did you see that mine on telly? Wasn't it one of ours?' I said it wasn't but, my God, it could have been.

However, none of these women felt that they could do anything about this realisation. Betty describes how she copes with this:

You start making excuses, you think, well, someone could be attacking our blokes and there's got to be something that can stop them. I never dwell on it, because I am the sort of person whose conscience would say — 'That's it, I'll look for another job.' If I sat and actually thought about it constantly, I could not work here, and I think that applies to most of the women here.

Most of these women cannot follow through their thoughts or their conscience. Leaving their job is not an option. The reasons seem particular and personal but they follow a pattern. Betty again:

It's a bit personal, but at one point I did volunteer for redundancy, and then things began going wrong with my husband. I couldn't stand much more of him so I began thinking about a divorce. For that I would need the money for the kids, even though it's a pittance. So I went and pleaded for my job back.

Ironically, selling her soul as well as her labour at work, was the only means of gaining her independence at home.

It was the same for Margaret Smith who works on contracts for repairs for guided weapons at Ferrantis in Oldham. She got the job in order to keep her husband while he was at college (she gave up her college course). At first she thought it was just another clerical job and did not fully realise that she was working on lethal weapons. She was promoted within the contracts department and began handling the repair contracts at source. With the contracts referring to names like 'Bloodhound', she soon realised what she was working on. She complained to management because she felt she should have been told:

I felt bitter because they assumed that as I was a mere clerk I was not important enough to have any opinions on this. But in fact I was working on something I objected to strongly.

Logically then, her next step would have been to leave Ferrantis and find other work. After all she had only come to Ferrantis for two or three years. But the position most women are in is not logical. Certainly Margaret's was not. She wanted to leave, but:

Unfortunately my 'beloved' had sorted himself out, got a job, and gone off with another woman. I was left with two kids. I could not pack in my job. The work at Ferrantis brings in regular money, even though it is not a lot. So there I was, stuck at Ferrantis for the next eight years, in spite of my feeling about the work I was doing.

For the women who wire or repair the weapons, then, financial independence is not enough for them to help prevent war. Their situation is very different from that of the literary daughters of 'educated men'. For these latter women, financial independence also meant work over which they had some control; work which they could direct towards the prevention of war. The daughters of 'working men' have no control whatsoever over their work. In fact their attempts to exert such control could itself be a contribution to preventing war.

What strategies for control are open to them? What strategies have they considered?

Margaret Smith started by taking control of the office walls!

I've got this tiny little office. I covered the walls with CND posters. Fellas would come and say they liked a particular sticker, and could they have one. I realised that there were people in Ferrantis who had doubts about nuclear weapons. They felt they could talk to me because I was sympathetic. Rather than feeling two-faced and hypocritical about working here, I felt I was reaching people who I would not have had the opportunity to reach before.

Not surprisingly management kept asking her to take them down. And had she not been a union representative and likely to get support if management had moved against her, they would have succeeded. However, it was not just management who were hostile. Many of Margaret's co-workers felt that CND would take their livelihood away. It was particularly the women who felt threatened in this way. Margaret explains:

It was fairly easy for fellas to get jobs elsewhere in Ferrantis, on commercial orders. Because of their skilled position the fellas knew they could move around. Whereas the ladies, who are kept in low positions, are vulnerable. They do not have the same sense of mobility and usefulness.

So, propaganda, posters and leaflets are not enough either. Maybe they give the activist a great sense of influence, but they are not sufficient to give the majority of women workers the sense of control they need before they can give open expression to their feelings about their work. Strong moral arguments are of little comfort when their implications would throw you on to the dole queue or back into a state of financial dependence.

Several groups of well organised, highly skilled trade unionists in the arms industry have found a way out of this dilemma, or at least they have sketched out a credible strategy for workers' control over the purpose and content of their work. I have already mentioned one such group, the shop stewards at Lucas Aerospace, who campaigned for Lucas management and the government to switch production away from arms to socially useful products for medical, transport and energy conversion purposes. Several other groups of arms workers have taken similar initiatives, for instance, in the Vickers' tank and warship divisions and in the British Aerospace factories involved in the Tornado, a military aircraft project. The preconditions for workers developing alternative plans in these companies included two features which are usually absent amongst women in arms production. First, the plans required the kind of political and industrial confidence which comes from strong shop floor and company wide trade union organisation. Secondly, workers motivation to be involved in suggesting alternative products developed from the familiarity and confidence with the design and production process which comes from being highly skilled – that is, experienced and trained in the skills which are valued within industrial production.

It is not surprising that women have not been very involved in developing these plans, in spite of their moral doubts about the end product of their work. One reason why many women arms workers suppress their doubts about their work is because they do not feel they could possibly influence decisions about war and peace, about arms production and the arms trade. They believe that whatever decision they might individually take, the momentum of the arms race will go on. Any individual protest of theirs will be futile. Jean Byrne from Marconis at Chelmsford expressed this sense of powerlessness:

I worked on the Chieftain tank, making cable for the radios inside. When I sat at home and thought about it, I came to the conclusion that if we did not do it, someone else would, so there's not much point in refusing. It's very nice having all these ideas about wars being wrong but I don't think that by refusing to work on armaments you can change anything. I mean I've got a son and when the Falklands began, I was scared stiff that it would go on long enough for him to be called up. And I didn't have a son to go out and fight and be killed. But you cannot do anything about it.

In part, this feeling of powerlessness reflects a weak trade unionism; the women do not feel part of any collective force. More often than not they are formally in the union but they receive little communication from union officers, have few meetings with fellow members and consequently gain little sense of the union as anything more than an occasional channel for individual complaints. The women's lack of skill, or at least lack of the label 'skilled' — some of them are, in fact, very skilled from experience — also deprives them of a sense of their own potential usefulness for anything but their present work.

In Lucas Aerospace, these divisions between skilled and unskilled were to some extent overcome through an organisation which brought together representatives of all unions, staff and shop floor, skilled and unskilled at a factory and a company level. At its best, this organisation — a shop stewards combine committee — enabled workers to gain an overview of the production process, a view that is normally the monopoly of management. At the Birmingham Lucas Aerospace factory, the alternative plan itself helped to draw the shop floor women and the drawing office men together in the face of redundancies. Anne Caudwell, a shop steward at the Birmingham factory, points to the importance of the plan in this respect:

It brought the staff and the shop floor together as a team. A fine team we were then. We had something to fight for. Management had put all their eggs into one basket: we were saying we needn't be in that situation. Yes, the plan was important, what else did we have?

So far such alternative plans have been drawn up in response to the threat of redundancy, rather than out of a commitment to disarmament — though of course the two are connected. There is a strong case, however, for such plans being a central part of the disarmament movement, and for a special effort being made to involve women arms workers more centrally in developing these plans. Until recently, conversion of arms production to civilian production has usually been seen as the responsibility of government. Even disarmament campaigners have often seen conversion as something which is thought about *after* they have successfully exerted pressure on the government to disarm. Yet many thousands, if not millions of people, depend for their livelihood either directly or indirectly on arms production. We have seen, in the ambiguous responses of women arms workers, that people working in the arms industry, whatever their innermost personal doubts, will always be a powerful popular ally for the arms lobby so long as the disarmament movement does not concern itself in detail with alternative employment. Viv Clements from British Aerospace put this clearly:

Every time there is talk of defence cuts, my members' jobs are on the line. So we lobby our MP's for more orders, to buy British and to save our jobs. We have to, don't we? We're shop stewards and our job is to look after our members' jobs.

Conversion plans are not only a way of getting beyond the false dilemma of jobs versus disarmament; the drawing up of plans which show in vivid, specific ways how the resources at present locked up in arms production can be used to meet current social needs, contributes to the *positive* case for disarmament. Through this process people develop a vested interest in disarmament. People begin to imagine how industry could be organised under popular control. Margaret from Ferrantis was recently involved in discussions about alternative products:

At present the company here are using sound things and long waves — no, I can't really tell you about them (because of the Official Secrets Act) — for early warning systems. We, that's our ASTMS branch, started talking about using the same technology for communications with ambulances. There were other ideas too. It made me think, if we were running this place, it would be smashing.

The discussion also made her feel she could do something about it. This is an important feature of workers' alternative plans. For although decisions about war and peace concern so-called 'ordinary' people intimately, these decisions seem totally out of our control. How they are taken, the forces leading to the build up of war production, seem opaque and unstoppable. Even massive demonstrations of popular feeling seem to have little impact. The process of drawing up alternative plans within the arms industry is one important way of overcoming a sense of powerlessness, and of revealing the workings of militarism. This could be true both for the workers directly involved and also for all those in the community who would benefit from the alternative plans and the improvement in social services which they imply.

We have seen in the responses of almost all the women

interviewed, deep ambiguities in their feelings about their work. We have seen how conversion plans provide an important way out of a moral and material problem facing women workers in the arms industry, especially those involved in nuclear weapon systems (who include the women in Marconis, British Aerospace, Ferrantis and Lucas Aerospace). We have seen some of the obstacles to women becoming involved in such conversion plans and thereby contributing to the prevention of nuclear war.

A very basic issue we have not explored explicity, is how the position of women in arms production, straddling both the work of destruction and the work of reproduction, influences their consciousness. I found in discussion with these women, that once conversation moved beyond their initial doubts about their work and into discussion of the fundamental questions of war, they expressed both extremes of patriotism and of humanitarian revulsion from war. And both extremes were connected in their minds with their children. Both sometimes came up in the same conversation; Marjorie Brown from British Aerospace talked about the funds women in her section organised for 'our boys' in the Falklands:

Our attitude was that although it was unfortunate we were involved [in the war], once it was upon us we had to get on and do everything to back our boys. People were very willing to work overtime and do whatever was necessary, whether you've got a son involved or not, when it's the English, it's your boys, isn't it? I mean it could be your boy next time. I've got two sons and one of them would have been prepared to go. So you look at them as if they were your boys.

Betty Jones from EMI made a different connection between a woman's commitment to her children and her attitude to war.

In my opinion women are more worried about the working here. I think this is because women's instinct towards their children makes them think that way. I mean, men can go off and leave a wife and six kids. That happened to me when I was ten; to me they are hard. Not many of them have those feelings of protection. I think that affects their attitudes to working here.

The first view gains official encouragement under the present government; there are plenty of channels through which it can be expressed from the South Atlantic Fund to support for the Thatcher government. And it is a view which implies that wiring up missiles and assembling circuits, however uncomfortable and tedious, is valued and important. The second view, however, remains vague, without a focus. Moreover, it is a view which increases the worker's sense of alienation from her work, without any hope of resolution. This is where conversion plans could be so important: they could provide an industrial and political focus for these humane instincts; they could value these woman's insights and tacit skills; and they could provide a means of control over the purpose of their work.

Conversion plans alone, however, cannot achieve nuclear disarmament, any more than could the cultural influence which Virginia Woolf advocated. Coordinated political action on an international scale will finally be necessary. But professional politicians rarely follow through a serious challenge to the status quo, especially to the military foundations of that status quo unless they are under truly momentous pressure. Proposals drawn up, campaigned and bargained for by workers in the arms industry, supported by local communities and public sector unions will generate the vested interest in disarmament needed to give backbone to this pressure. Moreover, this process will prepare people to take action themselves when politicians flinch from the implications of their promises.

[Thanks to Sue Plummer, Lesley Merrfinch and Meg Beresford for their help with this article, and thanks especially to all the women arms workers whose real names I cannot use for fear of their victimisation, but who talked to me fully during their lunch hours and after work].

ANGER IN A BLACK LANDSCAPE

I am no expert in anything, not history, not psychology, not medicine nor peace studies neither (least of all) strategic planning. I am, simply, a child of the nuclear age. I was five years old when they, or, rather, the Allies — that is, we — dropped an atomic bomb on Hiroshima, a small city of no strategic importance in Southern Japan whose name, together with that of Auschwitz, has now entered our vocabulary, the most tragic legacies of the last war, names synonymous with horror that, hitherto, was unimaginable. Before Hiroshima, however, it might have been possible to predicate a future time in which people, savagely rendered sane by experience, would look back on the century of Auschwitz as the blackest period of human history; since Hiroshima, the possibility of that kind of hope for the future diminishes in direct ratio to the growth of the nuclear arsenal.

That act of warfare, the dropping of the A-bomb, perpetrated — obviously — without either my knowledge or consent, although they said it was for the sake of my future, changed irrevocably the circumstances in which that future life would be passed. Let me not be sorry for myself about this; it changed them less than if I'd been five in Hiroshima. But change them it did, and may well inexorably dictate the manner of my life's ending. For to plan for your old age, these days, seems an act of high optimism, of outrageous gallantry, even. I am, therefore, a child of irony and the absurd; of black humour, of guilt and of anger. These are my credentials for contributing to this book. I believe they are sufficient.

And, over the years, I've grown rather tired of rational, objective arguments against nuclear weapons. To approach rampant unreason with the tools of rational discourse is something of a waste of time. On the other hand, to pose the question: 'Do you really want you and your loved ones to be fried alive?' will always, even, presumably, from Thatcher, procure the answer: 'No.' Which isn't much help, either, even when it *is*, finally, as simple as that, since one way of forestalling this grisly fate might be to fry the Russkies first, mightn't it . . . well, then. Another way might be to build oneself a personalised bunker, in which to sweat out the thermonuclear blast. Terrific.

One of the most curious phenomena of the post-war period has been the growth of fictions about the blissfully anarchic, tribal lives the lucky fifteen million survivors are going to lead in a Britain miraculously free of corpses, in which the Man with the Biggest Shot-Gun holes up in some barbed-wire enclave and picks off all comers. (Polygamous marital arrangements are often part of these fantasies.) The post-nuclear catastrophe novel has become a science fiction genre all of its own, sometimes as warning – more often as the saddest and most irresponsible kind of whistling in the dark.

Have you seen Goya's 'black' pictures in the Prado, in Madrid? You go through several rooms full of sunlit, happy paintings – children at play, beautiful young men and women dancing, picking grapes, a world of sensual delight – and, then, suddenly . . . paintings in black and ghastly grey and all the colours of mud, where swollen, deformed faces emerge from landscapes incoherent with devastation. The most awful one, that most expressive of a world of nothingness, shows a dog's head peering over the side of a mound of slurry. The sky, if you can call it a sky, is the colour of a bruise. And you know, from the infinite desolation of the scene, he is the last dog left, and, from the look of him, *he*'s not going to last much longer.

Impossible, in that appalling room, to escape the notion, that Goya, in his famous despair, in *his* hatred of war and human folly, saw further than most people; there is something prophetic in these pictures, that have the look, not so much of paintings, but of photographs taken with some time-warped, heat-warped camera, of a Europe in a future that remains unimaginable . . . a wreckage of humanity, a landscape from which all life has been violently expelled . . . unimaginable; but not impossible.

We think people who sell heroin are very evil and, if we catch them at it, send them to prison for a very long time. The men who deal in instruments of infinitely greater destruction acquire great wealth and respect.

Yet the iconography of such catastrophe is, surely, familiar to us all, by now! Anyone who reads this book will have her or his own private nightmare of pain, loss, annihilation; my own private image is not a violent one. It is of a child crying in the dark, and there will be nobody to come, not ever. Which is the worst I can possibly imagine.

Yet somehow the hideous poetry of the *terminal* nature of nuclear warfare can exist almost in a dimension of its own, that deforms thought. As if we still saw war itself as a metaphysical scourge, one of the four horsemen of the Apocalypse, arriving from nowhere and dominating the world, our real masters. Not as war really is, the product of an interlocked tissue of political and economic causes, of human actions and decisions. But as if nuclear weapons themselves – symbolised by the Bomb – were the very transcendental essence of war, and, more than that, an external-isation of all our notions of the ultimate evil. The Bomb has become a very potent, perhaps *the* most potent, symbol of Original Sin.

Well, I've always thought the notion of original sin was pretty silly, anyway; and it certainly gets horribly in the way of any attempts to persuade human beings to behave better than they generally do. Because to deny that people are inherently evil isn't to say that the world isn't full of freaks, zombies and loonies, nor that such as they, with their limited imaginations and atrophied hearts, do not tend to rise to the top in the military or in those places where men and women (but mostly, I'm proud to say, men) sit down with a cup of coffee and systematically design bigger and better ways of causing pain. It is no good saying, 'Think of the children, crying alone in the dark!' to a person who hates children, and, given the opportunity, will beat and torture his own. Most people, on the whole, enjoy being alive but a significant number feel they have the right to deny this privilege to other people, for a whole complex of reasons. We live in a country where a good number of British citizens may not sleep easy in their beds due to the murderous activities of white racist thugs and it might even be possible to argue that such a country deserves the visitation of fire from heaven. (You see how easy it is to slip into biblical language, here.)

But such fire will fall upon both the just and the unjust, and upon the innocent, the helpless and the deluded, and some of the latter, alas, are just those with the kind of emotional limitations who can kill in cold blood, and who can certainly contemplate the use of nuclear weapons — on somebody else, that is.

However, demystifying the Bomb — that is, stopping thinking about it as the product of a Faustian bargain, infinite knowledge for infinite destruction, as if it were all somehow tragically fated, and also *trying* to stop thinking about it as a full stop in human history, certainly doesn't make the Bomb a friendly beast. Far from it, because, of course, it *is* just such a full stop. But not a necessary or inevitable full stop. The horrid poetry of it, that mankind was the species that Knew Too Much, doesn't help us understand how, for example, the idea of strategic bombing — that is, wiping out civilians — became so fashionable in the twentieth century. Nor does it help us try to do our best to prevent the circumstances in which nuclear weapons might be used. It certainly increases one's personal sense of impotence. And it doesn't help us to get *out* of this mess.

So. Let's start again, from another angle. How has it come to pass that this overcrowded, relatively poor, relatively insignificant little island of ours fairly bristles with nuclear installations? (I'm not being historic about this. I'm speaking out of blind prejudice.)

Surely you must have noticed what an exceedingly law-abiding race the British are? (Or, rather, we *like* to look law-abiding, whilst privately criminal. But, in practice, appearance is reality.) This was made very apparent in 1981, when a widescale attempt at civil disobedience was mooted after the Law Lords countermanded the fares cuts made by the Greater London Council on what is the most expensive, as well as the least efficient, public transport system of any capital city in the civilised world. One would have thought, considering how unpopular the fares increases were, that it would have been the simplest thing in the world to organise London transport users to revolt. All the revolt was supposed to entail, after all, was a simple refusal to pay. But did we? Did we, hell. And I include myself in this, because I didn't want to make any fuss — another British characteristic.

Admittedly, a speedy bit of legal sleight of hand meant all kinds of nasty and humiliating things could happen if you didn't pay up and play the game. But I don't think it was fear that made us put our hands in our pockets. No. We paid up out of simple, ingrained obedience. Desire to please the powers-that-be.

In Florence, when they put up the bus fares a few years ago, enraged Florentines torched the buses. And, more magnificently — for the British can torch things when they feel inclined, but usually only when there's no point to it, in a hobbyish way — far more magnificently, ordinary Japanese people contrived to halt the building of the new airport in Tokyo for *fifteen years* by systematic sabotage and vociferous civil disobedience. Peasants attacked the construction teams with rice flails. And this from a race the British are accustomed to regard as besottedly compliant with authority. At last, when all was lost and the runways built, overnight the protesters put up a large tower on the biggest runway, effectively halting proceedings for a few more weeks, as a final gesture. Admittedly, the fares in Florence went up — from a massive ten pence flat fare to a staggering twenty pence. And Narita Airport is now in operation, although the peasants on whose land it was built ended up with a fair bit of compensation.

Okay. So you *can't* win. Although it is possible to negotiate the terms of defeat from a position of strength and so end up ahead of the game. Concerted and passionate protest against nuclear weapons in these islands may not achieve a global ban, and a universal end to war; but we might, just might, achieve a nuclear-free Europe, or, at least, a Britain cleansed of the diabolical things ... Perhaps it is just that we aren't used to public protest doing any good, these days. We are most lugubriously accustomed to our own democratic absence from vital decision-making in this country. Why is that?

How *did* it happen that this island has become a moored aircraft carrier for instruments of destruction? The primary decisions about Britain's relationship with NATO were taken out of our hands long ago and all was accomplished with such a degree of secrecy that most people in these islands, if they think about it at all, think that British membership of NATO is a very good thing. Most of us also think that the British Army is a Good Thing and now, basking in the glory of our famous victory in the Falklands — at this time of writing — it is probably the worst possible time to suggest it is *not* a fine thing to kill or to die for one's country. That, instead, it is a profoundly monstrous and obscene thing.

There, almost certainly, isn't enough time left to us to set about those long processes of altering public consciousness in an island that has, hitherto, housed one of the most bellicose nations in the world. The British have an exceedingly long history of militarism and of compliance with authority and are reluctant to lose the residual conviction that to be British involves some kind of guarantee against destruction. ('Britons never shall be slaves.') After all, we haven't been invaded by a foreign army for a thousand years! No. Nowadays, we invite the buggers in and call it NATO.

But we don't know whether or not anything can be done about changing things unless we try. As women, perhaps we are more used than man to living with a real sense of personal powerlessness and that may give us, as a lobby, a kind of extra anger. Agitating for a bit less public secrecy – *as well* as against nuclear weapons – might be a start.

But let me, again, begin at *my* beginning – for a personal history of how this particular person, five years old in 1945, learned to live with the bomb for all my adult life is relevant to us all, since our present impasse springs from a mass of personal accommodations to an intolerable situation.

Twenty years ago, yes, and more, I was in CND. And, truly, those long gone days of the marches from Aldermaston were some of the most moving and beautiful memories of my girlhood. It seemed, then, that in the face of those immense shows of serene public indignation – exhibitions of mass sanity, as they were – that, as had, after all, happened occasionally before, mass protest might change things.

I remember the Cuban missile crisis, as near the edge as we ever got. (As far as we know; much is concealed from us.) And, of course, it didn't happen. The weapons, so it seemed, *were* too terrible to be used. Just kept to frighten people with.

And, like most of us, after the emotional crisis of the Cuban missile crisis, I drifted away from CND. For, primarily, two reasons, neither of them anything to do with the comforting idea that, since the things hadn't been used, they'd *never* be used. No. One was:

Despair. It occurred to me that the reason why arms limitation talks and such were suddenly *on* was because those who enjoyed plotting ways of wiping us all out had decided to put nuclear weapons by for a while and concentrate on things that made less mess. Such as biological weapons, nerve gases and various other areas of research that were, from time to time, hinted at vaguely in *Scientific American*. It occurred to me that the superpowers were, far from learning to love one another, busily at work on instruments of warfare compared to which the thermonuclear flash might seem positively benign.

In other words, that the Bomb would indeed be banned — just as soon as they thought up something worse.

The second was:

Rationality. Applying my reason to the case in hand, I could see no qualitative difference between nuclear weapons and conventional weapons. (And the argument that we don't need nuclear weapons if we are armed to the teeth with the other kind still seems to me one of the most morally abhorrent, if one of the most commonsensical, in the anti-Bomb case.) Nuclear weapons were only the logical extension of the kind of warfare I'd been born into; the kind that unleashed its full fury against the civilian population. And, indeed, the next war will be the first in history in which those in the armed forces will stand a higher chance of survival than their loved ones at home. Maybe we should all sign on, now, as a mass gesture.

Although Tamburlaine the Great enjoyed reducing cities to rubble and slaughtering women and children, he usually did this after his band of paid killers had put down an opposing band of paid killers rather than before. The deaths of thousands, indeed, millions of non-combatants has never, hitherto, been a positive prerequisite for victory in armed conflict and it is this, rather than the nature of the weapons which inflict those deaths, that constitutes the moral difference between war in our time and old-fashioned kinds of wars. In *The Nuclear Barons*, Peter Pringle and James Spigelman suggest that strategic bombing was invented almost on the spur of the moment by Bomber Command, to save face when they found their target bombing was so lousy they'd deposited bombs on housing complexes instead of railheads and munitions factories. When I lived in Japan, people would tell me how the fire raids on Tokyo in 1944 had killed more people just as horribly as the Bomb on Hiroshima but nobody in the West seemed to have noticed, perhaps because John Hershey wasn't available to write it up. (Don't think the Japanese don't make jokes just because they don't smile, much.) Nuclear weapons are simply the most efficient way of 'bombing a country back into the Stone Age,' to quote an American president's plan for another Asian country some time later. (The New Stone Age seems the next plan on the agenda for us all.)

It came to me, then, that the only way to stop nations periodically going to war with one another in this new and morally indefensible way was a concerted impulse towards a federation constructed along humanitarian and egalitarian lines. Given my particular background and bias, this could only mean one thing – international socialism. (Note the absence of capital letters.)

Having reasoned myself into Utopianism, always the only rational stance, I asked myself: will it come in my lifetime?

After some thought, I reluctantly answered myself: no.

So, like most of my peers, I decided to put these heavy problems aside for a while and get on with living, for I was young, still, and it was the 1960s and, well, it was fun to be alive. Then – the Vietnam War, a focus for anger. And, increasingly engaged with the women's movement, there now seemed within that the possibility for actually creating a new heaven and a new earth, that this might even be within my own grasp, *as* a woman. For the private and public struggle of sexual politics was something that operated on terms I could more easily grasp than the one against the faceless enemy of militarism whose tentacles stretched everywhere. For *this* enemy had a face, a familiar and, indeed, often a beloved face, and I could understand the power system of sexual oppression because I had spent my whole life within it. Indeed, it was possible, in those heady days of the early '70s, to lump all the oppressive, life-denying systems together under one label – Patriarchy – and ascribe all the blame to men. Capitalism is a patriarchal plot. *And* war. It was easy, then – it still is, dammit! – to make jokes about the presidents of the superpowers opening their raincoats and flashing their weaponry at one another ('Mine is bigger than yours,' 'It's not!' ' 'tis so!' and so on.)

Women have always had a tendency to despise men for their emotional impoverishment. Men feel superior to women for the same reason. Impasse.

I really don't know if it would be a better world if women ran it. My natural prejudice suggests it might, although Mrs Thatcher and Mrs Ghandhi are *not* good advertisements for women in command. But this is no argument at all against women taking their fair share of policy and decision-making, and, since it hasn't been tried, before, it might well make a difference, in the long term. If there *is* a long term.

It is certainly no argument against asking all women, all normal, everyday women who tend and nurture children, make them clean their teeth and eat up their greens so they'll grow up big and strong, to appreciate that such activity might well be futile. If.

That such activity probably *is* futile. Because.

But my forties began, as my twenties had done, in a fury of rage. Driving across East Anglia shortly after the Soviet invasion of Afghanistan, under a sky black with bombers 'exercising', listening on the radio to a selection of freaks, zombies and loonies from the Pentagon threatening the USSR with nuclear reprisals, it was easy to forget it was all a publicity stunt ... as it, surely, has proved. Did the USA truly have the intention of teaching the Soviets a lesson by lobbing a warhead or two at the harmless population of the city of Kiev? Would that not have persuaded the beleaguered Afghans only of what they already thought, that the Infidel was as brutal, as foolish and as irrational as the imam had always said? It was all an exercise in frightening and I don't know what it did to the Kremlin, but, by god, it frightened me.

For I realised that, while my back had been turned, during those twenty odd years, the busy little bees in both the West *and* the East, the highly paid technocrats who live off the fat of the land and scribble away on their drawing-boards secure in the knowledge of those mink-lined bunkers to which they can retreat, if necessary ... these criminal lunatics had been dreaming up, not only non-nuclear weapons of a kind to make the mind reel, but also infinitely more powerful nuclear weapons, more and more infinitely powerful nuclear weapons, as if, once they'd got the knack of it, they couldn't stop.

And something else became apparent, too. In all the threatening and frightening that went on over the invasion of Afghanistan (to no avail; the Soviets are still there), the idea of a 'weapon too terrible to be used' was still there. But this seemed to apply only to the very biggest and most devastating bangs. A whole new class of nuclear weapons that might be 'too terrible to use', but certainly weren't too terrible to contemplate using, had sprung into being. Maybe what has happened is this: since they keep on inventing bigger and better bangs, the one that is 'too terrible to use' is no more than the one they thought of most recently. So, in a sliding scale, *last* year's ultimate and unthinkable weapon becomes second in line *this* year, and, next year, will be perfectly all right.

I get dizzy, and lose count, and lose heart, but the formula, 'containing n warheads each one with n times the capacity of the bomb dropped on Hiroshima', now haunts my dreams. Notice, too, how this formula contrives to negate the reality of the Hiroshima devastation ... as you might say, you ain't seen nothing yet.

We have, indeed, learned to live with the unthinkable and to think it. Last spring, I saw people, British people, not superficially psychotic-looking, wearing T-shirts with 'Nuke Buenos Aires' on the front. A new verb, 'to nuke'. So easily, in such an unacknowledged way, has the unthinkable slipped into our vocabulary. Note, too, how 'to nuke' is an active verb; it is easier to think of killing than of being killed, for obvious reasons. Can such atrocious garments be donned on Albion's shore without an enraged populace tearing them from the wearer's backs? They can.

The rational, objective arguments against Britain's participation in the scenario for blasting non-combatants off the earth in the name of military strategy and for subsequently rendering the planet uninhabitable have been deployed again and again, with increasing force, over the last three decades. And this is the result of it; the Argies had only to so much as tweak the lion's tail and, pow! How easily the final solution slips out! That the British do not have the capacity to unilaterally 'nuke' Buenos Aires is beside the point. The ease with which this neologism springs to the lips of the pro-nuclear lobby is unnerving in itself. There is a little man walks up and down the airport lobby in Boston, Massachussetts, carrying a hand-painted sign: 'Nuke Jane Fonda'. Useless to tell him you can nuke an individual only if she or he is standing alone in a very remote spot. I know. I've tried it. I didn't try snatching hold of his placard, throwing it to the ground and jumping up and down on it. Perhaps I should have.

As I said, I am no expert, although I possess a hereditary facility for vituperation. In the old days in my father's country, Scotland, the tribal chieftains deployed their poets in territorial disputes; they made them stand on ridges above the combatants, hurling abuse at the foe, until one or other was humiliated enough to leave the scene. Those were the days. Perhaps the time has come again to utilise these ancient skills − this time, against *both* sides.

It's sad but true that the 'irrational, subjective' arguments against nuclear weaponry, and, indeed, against militarism itself, are the moral and emotional ones − and morals and emotions might be more or less the same thing, at that. I've been engaged, here, in below-the-belt arguments, because these are, perhaps, the only ones left. We must plead, harangue, protest, demand − all kinds of things! A lot more democracy; a lot less secrecy; make (oh, horrors! oh, embarrassment!) a fuss, then a bigger fuss, then a bigger fuss again. The peace movement in the USA didn't rationally argue US troops out of Vietnam. It harangued. It shouted. It screamed. It took to the streets.

If the peace movement in Britain *cannot* persuade our (demo-cratically elected) government, this one or the next, to review our position vis-à-vis NATO, the establishment of Cruise missiles in this country and our whole relationship with the obscene farce of modern warfare, then perhaps, morally, we do not deserve to survive and, almost assuredly, we will not.

One thing more. As women of this island, our traditional role in warfare has been to wave goodbye to our loved ones and then either to grieve, or else, at last, after an agony of anxiety, to welcome them home, when, perhaps, they have been physically mutilated, certainly psychologically damaged and when we had to hide from ourselves the dreadful knowledge that they had killed other women's lovers and sons. This role has been eroded in modern warfare, which offers a wide range of clerical and admin-istrative roles to women and even, oh, thrilling! will let them into the combat zone if they are very, very good. It has, of course, never been true for, for example, the women of continental Europe, who, during wars, tend to trudge the roads as homeless refugees and be repeatedly raped by invading or victorious armies. It is always important to see our social roles not as universals but as relative to different situations, and a war with conventional weapons in the European theatre, of which we are a part, may well procure such a different situation.

Traditionally, we, as British women, are the loved ones for whom the boys fight, for whom they will return. But what − if we have been blown away? In the last war, those at home stood a good chance of violent death and, in a nuclear war, there will be scarcely any point in mobilising the troops except to keep down by force the sick and starving remnants of the civilian population. Non-combatants we might still be, but we will be on the front line and then, in a real sense, behind the lines, should we be unlucky enough to survive.

War is no longer the province of men and, as its most vulnerable potential victims, we *must* arm ourselves − not with weapons, but with rage, rage as if against the dying of the light.

BUILDING ON THE POSITIVES
The USSR

Never before has war threatened man with such dreadful devastations and calamities, and such massacres of whole populations, as it does at the present time. And never before have those feelings of unity and good-will among nations owing to which war appears to be something dreadful, immoral, senseless and fratricidal, been so widely spread. But above all never before was the deceit so evident by which some people compel others to prepare for war, burdensome, unnecessary and abhorrent to all.

This was Tolstoy, writing in 1897 to refuse the Nobel Peace Prize. His inspiring writings on disarmament on nonviolent resistance, which were so popular in the first wave of the peace movement here, have been reprinted in the new ninety-volume Soviet edition of his works, and are becoming increasingly popular amongst intellectuals there.

I hoped to be able to find here connections with my own work on Countess Tolstaya when I went to the Soviet Union, in, so I thought, September 1981. It was, in fact, January 1982 by the time my visa arrived. It takes just six hours to fly to Moscow. That year, though, it was taking British Council Exchange students rather longer. As detente crumbled, before our eyes both sides blamed each other for the delay: *their* cultural attaché had been expelled from London for KGB work, *our* cultural attaché wasn't allowed back in retaliation, our visas were apparently locked inside the Soviet Foreign Ministry building ... Rumours proliferated, both sides dug in their heels, the Cold War deepened. It's so much quicker by Cruise − only thirty minutes from Greenham Common to Moscow.

It was a strange four months' waiting, bag packed at the door. One foot already in Russia, I now began to read our newspapers through Russian eyes, wondering if the people I knew there would recognise themselves in the picture we get of them here. Most of them are hurt and puzzled by their 'Ivan the blockhead' image in the West. But it's probably a grimmer image than most of them imagine, an image formed in the first phase of the Cold War − of a peasant society, terrorised by cunning and coercion, tyrannised by Marxist dogma, implacably convinced that a world without war will come about only when the socialist mode of production rules the earth, a society ruled without mandate, tradition or legitimate political status, in which military policy is formulated on the basis of a 'war-winning' strategy of victory, superiority and first-strike capacity.

This, at any rate, was the place I was reading about when I studied Russian at university and was first exposed to the writings of influential Cold War historians like Richard Pipes. He was the one who introduced the Western world to the novel proposition that an all-out nuclear attack would actually *benefit* the Russian people − since every major war in which Russia has been involved (the Napoleonic, the Crimean, the wars with Turkey and Japan, the First and Second World Wars) brought major social reforms in its wake.

This version of the Soviet Union, mad and extreme though it is, nevertheless informs so much of what we read and hear about the place. It trains us to fear a people whose lives and history few of us know anything about, and habituates us to the idea of killing them − and ourselves − in a war to end all wars. It appeals to our worst fears and paralyses our will and perceptions, so that even if we do visit the Soviet Union we often see what propaganda has trained us to see. So that on at least two occasions when I got there I was reduced to a state of clammy unreasoning terror − by a massive unsmiling soldier running towards me on the street, greatcoat flapping, and by a midnight telephone call in my hotel room. Until it turned out that the soldier was asking me if I wanted him to cross me over the road (I then noticed that in fact he was smiling), and the phone call was from a friend and it was in fact seven a.m.

There are a number of cultural differences about the place, however, which I find deeply and immediately reassuring. I found

I was breathing more easily when I stepped off the plane to this place so remote from our own violent culture with its glorification of death, rape and pornography. (Several people blushed and couldn't listen when I told them about young men in leather and chains beating each other up on the streets.) It's a relief to be able to walk about free of the fears that pursue us on the streets here, free of the advertisements that degrade women and reduce us all to consumers.

One's immediate impression is of a peaceful society. There are huge peace posters everywhere. (The words for 'peace' and 'world' are the same in Russian — a highly significant and effective connection.) And *Pravda* and *Izvestia* carry daily leader articles and editorials on disarmament in which nuclear weapons are described without euphemisms, acronyms or macho bravado, and presented as what they are: monstrous weapons of destruction. The Russian language is direct, expressive, unanalytical, unironic. They don't go in for hearsay or innuendo about the West, as we do about them.

It's a highly ordered society too, an order whose roots lie deep in pre-revolutionary peasant culture and resistance. The old are honoured, women are not insulted, children are cherished. Russians have a sense of social responsibility and self-discipline which we may find quite alien. The Tolstoy Museum, where I spent a great deal of time working, was easily the friendliest and most sensible library I have ever worked in, with librarians, students, research workers and lovers of Tolstoy all piled into a small hot room together and with a real sense of shared purpose and excitement. The librarians involved themselves in what we were doing, and would bring relevant books to our desk. At two o'clock the books were put aside, the samovar was put on, tea was offered round, people put newspapers over their books and ate their sandwiches quietly.

And going home on Moscow's quiet and spotless underground one noticed how many people were immersed in thick books or magazines. The great radical writers of the nineteenth century — Tolstoy, Turgenev, Dostoyevsky and Chekhov — are printed and distributed in astronomical quantities and read eagerly by everyone. I liked the attitude to Tolstoy amongst people I talked to — friendly, respectful, yet not uncritical. I was moved by the Tolstoyan values of honesty and simplicity which are so evident amongst intellectuals. I even discussed with workers at the Tolstoy workers at the Tolstoy estate the idea of an exhibition in Britain on the theme of Tolstoy and peace — a joint venture that would get us away from official versions of war and peace.

None of what one observes squares with the widely held fear in the West of Russia's reportedly vast civil defence programme, and I was anxious to talk to people about this. From what they said and from reading a couple of Soviet civil defence handbooks, it seems far more probable that a mass of rules and regulations have been enunciated without any likelihood of their being remotely realistic. It's certainly true that the authorities boast a well-worked-out civil defence programme of blast and radiation shelters. The only hitch to this is that there don't actually seem to be any shelters. In fact their general invisibility is by now a well-worn Soviet joke, like this one,

'What's the way to the nearest fallout shelter?'
'Walk slowly to the nearest cemetery.'

One manual I read might have been a treatise on the unwinnability of nuclear and chemical warfare. If you find yourself in the centre of an attack, just 'look for the arrows', to direct you out of it. 'In the absence of arrows . . . follow the wind'. And 'in the absence of wind', lie down on the ground. If you're at home, keep the radio switched on, ascertain the whereabouts of the nearest shelter, 'in the absence of a shelter' improvise one, proceed to the hermetic sealing of your home, turn off gas, water, electricity — and so on, *Protect and Survive* style.

It's unclear why this sort of rubbish is put out. All Russians without exception are haunted by fears of the American menace. Is civil defence propaganda intended to reassure, or meant to convince people of the unwinnability of nuclear war? I have certainly never encountered any Soviet equivalent of the insane 'survivalist' mentality that has gripped two million United States citizens. There is something hopeful about this yearning for peace, a feeling that life is worth living and could be beautiful.

Now, more than at any other time since the last war, Russian people are aware of the crippling cost, social and economic, of the arms race. To a visitor, its effects are only too tragically visible in the shops, for it is inevitably consumer goods, rather than civilian investment, that are sacrificed to the arms industry. And it is inevitably women who must bear the burden of this, queuing for hours for scarce provisions.

Russia's recent approach to parity with the United States is not reflected in the way people there speak and write about war. Many older people are haunted by memories of the 1950s, when Americans boasted of 'massive retaliation' and 'more basic security at less cost'. My Russian friends were bewildered and desperate about talk in the West of their 'war-winning' strategy, and feel they are still paying the price for winning the last one and becoming a world power: twenty million dead, a further twenty million crippled, 1,710 towns, 70,000 villages and 32,000 industrial centres destroyed.

I came back feeling that between us we may be able to work out some level at which we can talk peace together which is both feasible for them and congenial for us. And it seems to me that as women we're in an excellent position to take some imaginative initiatives in this direction. In Russia and most other East European countries, women's organisations were formed just after the last war with the purpose of preventing another one and of fighting fascism, so that peace is traditionally seen as a 'woman's province'.

Perhaps we can now begin to discuss ways of using this already existing interconnection between the peace and women's movements to learn the particular ways in which the arms race affects women both here and there, and to make new links, including new use of existing town twinning schemes. One suggestion, for instance, has been to use the status of women town councillors here to contact local Soviet women's groups, which are always deeply involved in campaigning for the Soviet Peace Fund. This is a real practical possibility, one that may well beget further, bolder initiatives. The Soviet press has written admiringly and at some length about the Greenham Common Women's Peace Camp, and obviously appreciates women's campaigning work in the West. It even seems likely that they will follow the example of the German Democratic Republic, where increased threats of war have raised the status of peace campaigning to the point where it is now thought 'too important to be left to the women'.

FLOORED!!

BUILDING ON THE POSITIVES
The USA

If we are ever going to lessen the tensions in the world, to end the
war mentalities which interested politicians rely on to support and
carry out their policies, it is essential for ordinary people throughout the world to get to know more about each other, to meet, to
understand differences, to share problems. This sounds like a
sentimental truism, but it is, in fact, an expression of the most
starkly realistic self-interest. If we accept that a state of war is the
natural state between nations, then the world is already lost, since
modern weapons undoubtedly could bring about the end of our
civilisation if world war were to be let loose again. We, in Britain,
live in a country that was once a world power, part of a continent
that was once the centre of the civilised world. Today our country
and our continent are to some extent peripheral, and perhaps the
fact of our past importance makes our present subservience to the
superpowers even more frustrating. Nearly every one must at
times be depressed by the distance we feel from the two world
powers on whose decisions our future depends.

The peace movement today is, and must be, a world movement.
In every country including the two great powers, millions of
people are as desperately anxious to live in peace, to see their
children grow up, to make a more pleasant environment and a
more just society as any of us. If governments often don't seem to
represent the wishes of these people, it is up to us to try and see
behind the actions of governments, to break down barriers of

clichés and stereotypes, to reach out towards the positive peace needs and desires of our contemporaries in all countries, to try and make these needs felt by all governments.

To many of us, the Soviet Union appears monolithic and paranoid, and we can easily forget the enormous contribution that the east of our continent has always made to the history and culture of Europe. The United States, on the other hand, seems neurotic and febrile, aggressive, unpredictable, self-righteous and self-interested. The finger on the button seems to be potentially that of some Forrestal or Strangelove figure who has lost sight of the real problems of the world in some private power fantasy. It is too easy to identify the whole nation with its politicians and to despair of ever achieving disarmament or even a lessening of world tension by rational discussion.

There is a lot about life in modern American cities that Europeans find unpleasant and disturbing. Nevertheless, I am among the very many people who go back again and again, and find the experience rewarding and refreshing. If I suggest some positives that strike me, I know many people will disagree. Even a few years spent in such a huge nation can give one only the slightest idea of its life as a whole. And since this is a piece about positives, I know I shall offend some by largely ignoring negatives. So perhaps I should start off with one that will be familiar to many people. Americans, (I will use the term here, as there is, curiously, no short and easy word for 'citizens of the United States'.) when they get keen on something, lose no time. A 'new' idea which hits them, be it flower power or women's liberation must immediately be acted on and spread abroad. Many of us in Europe have had the experience of being lectured by eager transatlantic friends on how to suck eggs, and many of our own movements have suffered by the injection of language and methods of work from across the Atlantic which were inappropriate or even damaging. But this is the negative aspect of one of America's greatest virtues. Americans get on with things.

In spite of its size, in spite of its cumbersome political processes, America seems to be capable of bringing about changes in attitudes, in laws and in actual life at a rate which is quite remarkable. The changes in the position of blacks and women, for example, which I have seen since I first spent any time in the States in 1968, have been extraordinary. Not that either group has arrived at an ideal position, but the speed of change, the extent to which the changes have been embodied in laws and regulations, the extent to which such laws and regulations are observed, is astonishing. Imagine, to take a small example, an English university being under a legal injunction to employ more women on its staff. All right, such things don't happen in every state, they affect professional and middle-class people more than the generality. But they do happen; whilst in my own university and in my own department, for all the talk of greater equality that has gone on here in the same period, the number of women generally and the number of women specifically in senior jobs had declined considerably. Many years ago the Soviet writers Ilf and Petrov noticed that when Americans say they will do something they do it. This happens at an individual level and at some levels of government and administration to a degree that still takes Europeans by surprise.

When they do get started on an idea, Americans bring wit, style and inventiveness to it in a refreshing and stimulating way. I don't like mass meetings particularly, but I'd really liked to have been in Central Park for the peace demonstration on 12 June 1982. Big events like that − even the much smaller one of a mere 100,000 people that I took part in in Washington not long ago, are colourful, cheerful and determined. And reading the banners can be a delight. At one anti-Reagan demonstration students carried a placard − JANE WYMAN WAS RIGHT. One of the placards in Central Park read A NUCLEAR EXPLOSION COULD SPOIL YOUR DAY. The land of the catch-phrase and the quick cliché, it is also a land in which self-mockery and wisecrack can provide the instant putdown. The peculiarly American humorous tradition, from Mark Twain to Joseph Heller, has almost always been on the side of humanity, against bureacracy, self-righteousness and pomposity. In Manhattan in 1976, when New York City was in serious financial trouble, the city was sacking teachers and closing schools on all sides. Coming out of my upper East Side apartment block one day I found the street filled with a colourful procession of teachers, students, adults and children, with improvised posters, striding down the centre of the road. As they passed the many banks in the district, they chanted

You've got the money,
  We're not fools −
Take it out of the banks
  And give it to the schools.

In the same period, at local schools threatened with total or partial closure, parents organised occupations by day and night to prevent the authorities from locking up the buildings. The local cops, whose children also attended the neighbourhood schools, kept a protective eye on the action in at least one school I know of, where the action was successful and the school kept open.

In 1981, the Electric Boat Company at Groton in New England launched its new Fast Attack Nuclear Submarine, and had the crass insensitivity to name it the *USS Corpus Christi*. (The Defence department later claimed that they had named it after a city in Texas and not after the body of Christ.) The New England peace people organised an anti-launch outside the boatyard. A thousand people stood on a cold and rainy day to hear a series of speakers, amongst them, nuns, priests, trade unionists, scientists, doctors and many others. A priest performed an anti-launching ceremony at the same time as the official launch inside the boatyard. The whole occasion was one of serious purpose and the assertion of human dignity, and the speeches were well-informed, moving and powerful. I remember saying in my contribution that if the clarity and conviction of these speakers could once begin to get through to the American people, nothing could stop the movement. It looks as though this has at last begun to happen.

Most Americans or their forebears went to that continent to escape from actual persecution or from repressive and stifling social and political environments. If they have set up their own restrictive structures in some areas, they remain sensitive to issues of personal freedom, and manage to enforce many of these. Press freedom is undoubtedly greater than in any other country, although this sometimes seems a theoretical matter when one reads particularly the local papers. But an incident like the Watergate affair can revive the concern. The freedom of information provisions, for all the limits which have been put on some sectors, nevertheless amaze anyone who has tried to get such information in other countries. Historians of Britain can get better information on some aspects of our own recent history from American archives than we can from our own carefully guarded official sources. Even if some parts of your personal dossier are blacked out for 'security' reasons, you can find out much more of what the state or any other agency has on record about you than is possible anywhere else in the world. Like the Soviet rhetoric of peace, the American rhetoric of freedom has deep historical roots, and is profoundly believed in by many citizens. Cynical statesmen may pervert the values which these ideas embody, but they cannot totally ignore them. These positive values form the basis on which links can be built. We can learn a lot from America in areas of civil rights, and I predict that the peace movement which is now taking off in that country will have a lot to teach us about organisation and propaganda as it gets into its stride.

I have always found Americans friendly, hospitable and generous. But these are qualities which I've found in almost every country I've visited. Most people, in most parts of the world, desperately want to make personal contacts, to be given the chance to make up their own minds about the people they may be asked to fight or to 'defend'. One of the most important jobs we have is to make easier the exchange of people, including women, young people, children, families. Part of the work of the peace movement must always be at this level of simple exchange as well as at the level of official delegations. Even below the level of town twinning – the exchange of school visits, holiday visits, social organisations, choirs, amateur theatres – all aspects of our lives can be given an international dimension, by which some, at least, of the suspicion and hostility generated at the level of high politics can be called into question. Exchanges with America have a great advantage in that we share a language. The disadvantage is the great distance and the cost of travelling. But ways can and must be found to relate to the many positive forces for peace on that side of the Atlantic. Our future may depend on it.

JANET DUBÉ

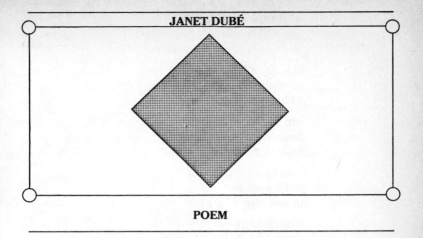

POEM

When it's a fine day
and the house is quiet
and I'm on my own

when the fire gets low
as the cat kills a bird
and the sun is blazing

on the daffodils, when
the chickens scratch
and cluck, scratch

and cluck, and the house
is quiet and the sun
is blazing on the daffodils;

when the pale mauve
anemones are open to the sun
and the blue green daffodils

unsheath to yellow
in the blazing sun
when the house is quiet

and the chickens scratch
and cluck and the lambs
learn to eat grass

when the blue green
daffodils unsheath to yellow
as the jets scream overhead

should I plant onions
or write a poem? Shall
I plant flowers or read

the paper? Would it
be better if I had a job,
or is that part of the war

machine? Is it better
to be certain
or uncertain? If I do

something for peace
does it help? if I do
something for peace

does it help me
or does it help peace?
if I do nothing
what does that mean?
Tell me, it's the one thing
I ever wanted to know, tell
me this one thing and I'll
never ask again, tell me
the truth, it's what I want
to know, I need to know,
tell me, how am I joined
to the war machine, tell me

can I get off?

CONTEMPLATING A NUCLEAR FUTURE
Nuclear War, Politics and the Individual

To recognise the truth about the immensity of the peril we face is not necessarily to be moved to do much about it, nor even to feel repelled by it. Many, perhaps most people, are aware in some sense that we may stand only a few years away from the end of human civilisation and possibly of the world itself. But few sense this as in contradiction with their being alive now, or feel responsible for its prevention. To speak of a lack of responsibility and not of the impotence of ordinary people may seem divisive and even élitist. I am not suggesting, however, that people are directly to blame, or that if it were not for a general apathy, the situation could change overnight. For the economic and political forces (and their concrete embodiments in the institutions and instruments of war) confront us as implacable givens of existence. They loom like mighty towers against which the assault of the individual will, however determined, seems in vain. The letter one sends to Brezhnev or Reagan or Thatcher telling of the agony of sleepless nights spent in fear, meets with a courteous reply reminding us of the crucial role of nuclear missiles in allowing us to rest sound in our beds. Those who control our lives do indeed appear to be beyond the reach of our control. I am therefore blaming no one for quailing before the combined forces of militarism, neo-imperialism, multinational capital and Soviet bureaucracy, and retreating instead to the more humane business of their private lives. The responsibility of which I am speaking, however, is an awareness and feeling of concern which in a way transcends politics, while at the same time being the source of our power and self-respect as individuals, and thus in the last analysis the support of all conventional authority. I am speaking of an interest in our own humanity, of a care for our own species and the world we inhabit.

This common sense of humanity cannot overcome the divisions of class or gender or race. It cannot alleviate the suffering of the Third World, nor any other form of oppression. But a concern for our own survival as a species must be the implicit assumption of all struggles for emancipation, for these struggles, in their various ways, aim to establish more harmonious forms of coexistence on earth.

In face of the global nuclear threat, we as individuals need to rediscover this common responsibility to ourselves. We have allowed our rulers, operating in the interests of 'capitalism' or 'socialism' or 'global stability' to transfuse this life-blood of political power into the bodies of their cherished institutions, the World Bank, the Pentagon, the Kremlin, NATO, the Warsaw Pact; and these now seem to animate our world and to be the heart upon which we depend for our existence. But if the heart is pumping towards its own destruction, then it is vital that we find ways of reversing this flow of power.

To do this, we must in the first place inform ourselves in as much detail as possible about what is going on in the name of our protection. We must equip ourselves with data about the effects of nuclear weapons and with the arguments used in the political debate surrounding nuclear arms and disarmament. In addition to providing ourselves with factual and political information, we need now, I think, to reflect more on what it is, psychologically, that has made the struggle for disarmament so urgent for us personally. And we need to try to communicate this without too many fears for its 'emotive' nature or its political naivety. We need to inspire others with our will to live. It is in this spirit that I offer my contribution and that much in this book, alongside the 'hard' facts should, I believe, be understood.

It is particularly relevant in this connection that women should speak. For by virtue of their role in human reproduction, their statements are given the authority of experiences that men do not have. Some of these experiences match in their crude biological vitality the crude wreck of biology that would be the experience of nuclear war. The starkness of contrast between the event of conception and the event which irradiates the womb, between the act of giving birth and the act which evaporates the child: this is something which women owe it to the world to talk about.

By thinking and speaking of these fundamental issues which the prospect of war brings us back to, but whose communication tends to be submerged beneath the more normal forms of political discourse, I believe that we can begin to regenerate ourselves as individual sources of power. We can begin to restore a sense of our own organic extension in the world, and thereby be shocked into responsibility. It has sometimes struck me that there is an odd paradox about the nuclear threat: for while, on the one hand, it presents itself as the most indomitable force that has ever confronted the individual, it is also a great political leveller. It took nuclear weapons to make me realise the full extent of the paltriness, the impoverished understanding and the sheer irrationality of most of those who govern me. I have not ever deferred readily to politicians, but I can no longer look on now in the same way while they are allowed to fumble around with the entire future of the world. It is almost as if I were a passenger in a storm-rocked boat who has suddenly realised that the captain is drunk. The feeling is: if they are going to behave like this, then I am going to have to do the job for them. After all, we have got to prevent nuclear holocaust.

Two years ago, I rejoined CND and have been active in it since. During that time I have not acquired any official political status I did not enjoy before: by all the formal criteria of power in our society, I am as powerless as I ever was. In reality I have acquired far more control over the destiny of world affairs than I held two years ago. In order to understand this, we have to understand that power of the kind I am talking about is not like natural energy, convertible but always quantitatively constant. It is more like love: we do not love the first child half as much in order to love the second. Likewise, to gain this power you do not have, to feel obliged *in the first instance*, to take power from somewhere else — from the Pentagon or the Kremlin or wherever. You need only to energise it within yourself through some process of realisation, of responsibility. This process will be different for different individuals. I want to describe the form it took for me.

Imagine human civilisation being blown apart within a few moments of your finishing reading this sentence. It seems an absurd suggestion. What spurred me into working for nuclear disarmament was a kind of conversion in my thoughts about war that made me realise that ideas of that kind were not nearly as absurd as they ought to be. I ceased viewing nuclear war as an indefinitely receding future possibility, moving away from us as we moved forward in time, and confronted it as an imminency. For the first time, I felt its menace as part of the fabric of our current existence.

What followed was a very frightening and depressing period in which I found myself placed imaginatively in various scenarios: I thought of myself going to work in a situation of mounting international tension; I thought of myself eating breakfast as the news came through that the country was on war alert; I thought of myself in bed with the children asleep as the sirens started wailing; I thought of myself huddled in some makeshift shelter whose corners had caught fire. I tried to think of myself coping with such moments, and could not: there were no psychological resources to draw upon.

I sensed also something of the shock of what it would be like for life in full swing to be suddenly arrested; and I began to think more fully about what it meant for us to live out our lives in the context of the possible total blackout of human civilisation. I was struck by the tension that the prospect of nuclear obliteration introduced between the importance of our lives and their possible vacuity. In thinking about my everyday activities, in the context of a possible abrupt ending to everything, I came to regard them in a fresh light: when I thought of each act as possibly the last of its kind that I was ever to undertake, the most mundane task seemed weighted down with an unnatural importance. At the same time, in that I was thinking of my activities as possibly cut off from the future into which they would otherwise have flowed, even the most major undertakings seemed utterly pointless. Because I was reflecting in this way upon the status of each present act and its relations with the future, I ceased for a time to act habitually. My life went on in all its activities just as before, but I was no longer immersed in it in the same way. The daily round of action temporarily lost its fluidity. Each moment in it seemed preceded by another moment of suspended action in which I questioned the purpose of what was being done if, in the next moment, I and the world I knew could cease to exist.

This was a period, then, in which the fear of nuclear war moved out of the background it had occupied throughout most of my life. I became aware in a way I had not been before of the horror that nuclear war would bring about. Above all, perhaps, what was new was a sense of contradiction; a sense of there being an impossibility about our current existence. It is a simple truth that we cannot live our lives as if the end of the world could occur. It is equally true that it is part of the reality of our lives that they have to be lived in the context of that possible occurrence. These truths are incompatible, but they come together now and will continue to do so, unless existing nuclear policies are reversed, for all the time of human history yet to come.

We have managed to place our lives within a dimension that is both so objectively real, and yet so inhuman, that it can only be thought about at the risk of a breakdown in normal living. Either we take on the prospect of possible global annihilation in all seriousness — and feel our hold on ordinary living slip; or, in the interests of remaining true to ourselves as authentic human beings possessed of our ordinary concerns, we deny the reality of that possible outcome. To live in minute-by-minute awareness that apocalypse is not the fabrication of a visionary but something that can be engineered concretely at the touch of a button — that, I suggest, is in fundamental conflict with what we mean by living.

It is this fact, I believe, which explains why even those who do confront the reality of our situation today, cannot dwell on it for long; and it is this which perhaps explains why so many people, possibly the majority, do not 'live' with the threat of nuclear war at all. What is important is not an analysis of this 'repression' but the attempt to lift it a little, however disturbing it may be to do so. Many people do seem to be doing that. There is no doubt that they are 'waking up', sometimes quite suddenly, to the horror of total death in nuclear war. And they are finding, as I did, that the only way out of the overriding sense of incapacity is to work for nuclear disarmament, often with consuming energy.

The threat to which we are subjected by the possible use of nuclear weapons has no exact parallel in earlier human experience. The fear it inspires is likewise without precedent, first because it is scientifically warranted, and secondly because it afflicts us all in some form. There have been isolated religious sects who have anticipated the end of the world, no doubt with absolute conviction that it would come on the appointed date. There has been superstitious dread of apocalypse. There has been the real fear of those who lived through the years of plague that human life was terminating. But never, I think, have people collectively, in the midst of life and health, been subject to the threat of sudden extinction we now face. The primitive watchers of the eclipse may have genuinely believed that the world *might* end at the point of total eclipse; and the victims of the plague may have felt that they were indeed experiencing its ending. But there is a great deal of difference between either the *uncertain* expectations of the former or the actual suffering of the latter, and our definite knowledge in anticipation that the world *will* end (at least in any form in which we currently know it as our world) if nuclear weapons are ever used on a large scale. Our experience differs from that of previous generations, in that we knowingly, but in a sense painlessly, live in history at a point where history could end tomorrow.

This sounds dramatic, but it is scarcely much of an exaggeration. The risk of nuclear war is increasing, and it is very unlikely to be limited. Even if nuclear war could be limited, the threat of its being total remains with us now and will do so as long as current arsenals are retained. It is this which I am claiming to be a unique form of terror — so terrifying that if we dwell on it seriously it is with paralysing consequences for our attempt to 'live'.

I have already linked our denial of the threat of war to our dependency on the prospect of the future to give content and meaning to the present. Our reliance in this respect goes beyond the span of time of our individual lives. To appreciate this we have only to look at our attitude to dying. This may seem a morbid theme to pursue, but in a climate where people are being daily conditioned into acceptance of the viability of conducting nuclear war, then any discussion, however disconcerting, that serves to alert us to what is being jeopardised by reliance on the fragile mechanism of deterrence, seems justified.

Now it may be said, in criticism of my points so far, that with or without the prospect of nuclear war, the fact remains (given the proverbial bus that each of us might at any moment walk under) that the end is always nigh for everyone. While this is true, it misses the point, for there is a crucial difference between living with the threat of the end of history and living with the threat of individual death. If it is only in the light of the future that we are able to go on living while we are alive, it is also only in the light of a future in which we, as individuals, will not be alive, that we can come to terms with dying. It is against the background of ongoing life that the prospect of death becomes tolerable and we can accept its possible imminency at any point. But to be faced with the prospect of collective death is to be disarmed of all the usual resources which allow us to come to terms with our individual mortality.

Should anyone doubt the contrast here, I ask her to consider those resources: the memories in which we are conserved by those who have known and loved us; our tangible bequests in the form of the things we made, the children we raised, the garden we planted, the poem we wrote . . . I ask her to consider dying in the context of all that, and then to consider a death without a heritage of that kind, a death coincident with the destruction of all memories and material embodiments of ourselves. It is not a prospect from which we can draw much solace.

To know our attitudes now to the prospect of collective death is not, of course, to know anything of what it would be like to go through it. Yet it is perhaps worth reflecting on the actual experience recorded by the victims of the Hiroshima and Nagasaki bombs. If we cannot now think 'realistically' about some future ending of the world, it is because we have glimpsed the truth that if we *were* to experience it, the experience would not be one to which we could react with any normal human sensibility. It could not be undergone as a *human* experience, eliciting feelings of despair, grief or compassion:

In Hiroshima, survivors not only expected that they too would soon die, they had a sense that *everyone* was dying, that 'the world is ending', Rather than panic, the scene was one of slow motion − of people moving away from the centre of destruction, but dully and almost without purpose. They were, as some among them put it, 'so broken and confused that they moved and behaved like automatons . . . a people who walked in the realm of dreams'. Some tried to do something to help others, but most felt themselves to be so much a part of the dead world that, as another remembered, they were 'not really alive'.

This numbing, or closing off of the mind by the victims of Hiroshima, 'so that no more horror could enter it', this was the reality then which seems to find a kind of reflection in our present repression of the prospect of collective death.

Now let me turn from death to life. Let me dwell instead on the role of the future in making our lives as we live them rich, meaningful and worth cherishing. Let me dwell on the role of a continuing history, and what it contributes in the way of language and culture and institutions of all kinds, to making us who we are — to giving us an 'objective' and non-biological dimension to existence without which we would simply not exist as human personalities. If we do not take account of this, we do not take account of the complexity of human life and of what distinguishes it from that of other species. Unlike other animals, our transmission of ourselves, the substance and continuity of our existence, is not confined to what we *in*herit genetically, but exists outside of ourselves, not being part of our biology at all. All of us, whether we like it or not, are born into an already existing world of material things (houses, parks, schools, churches), institutions (the family, government, the educational system) and modes of relating to each other (through language, forms of authority, behavioural conventions). This objectively existing world that we encounter at the moment of birth and have to live in thereafter, and to mould our personality within, is not something redundant to the person we become — as if, in its absence, we could remain as before in our true and singular existence. For while it is certainly true that we are *not* our language, or culture or our works of various kinds, it is equally true that we are not who we are without them. And it is largely through the differentiation that is allowed to us by the richness of this social world that we become as individual and unique as we do. All sparrows are much the same, give or take some minor differences in behaviour, health or feathering, precisely because they are confined to the limited individuation that is permitted by genetics. We, by contrast, acquire our individuality through what might be called a continuous 'extension' of ourselves in an objective realm — for example, in our children, friends, lovers, work, hobbies, pets and so on. Nothing, it seems to me, is more natural for human beings than to pursue this kind of 'self-extension' in various modes of loving, reproducing, creating and working; and it is this which gives human existence its specificity.

Nuclear war will destroy most, if not all, of the social bases that allow us to acquire an objective dimension of personality, even if it leaves a number of bodies unscathed. Even now the threat of war is eroding this dimension to the extent that it is curbing a spontaneous process of self-extension. I am thinking here of all those who have felt, in contemplating nuclear war, something of the pain expressed in Shakespeare's sonnet:

That time will come and take my love away,
This thought is as a death, which cannot choose,
But weep to have that which it fears to lose

I am thinking, for example, of those who have been deterred from having children (or at least felt more pangs about doing so) by the horror of what may lie in store for them. I am thinking of the way in which the prospect of an absolute 'coming to dust' of all our projects can make us doubt the ultimate value of any long-term undertaking. For in these ways, creation of all kind can seem blighted in the bud by the question that puts its future in question.

At the same time, the threat of nuclear war can lead to a simple refusal to look towards the future at all. The 'live for the day' attitude has, of course, always been a component (and by no means a wholly negative one) in our attitudes to the transience of human life and its unpredictability. If it is pervasive now, however, it reflects not so much a joyous irresponsibility as a rather sombre and reasoned estimation of the chances of having a normal life span. If young people tend to nihilism today, who is to blame them? It is, in fact, the height of hypocrisy for them to be condemned for improvidence and instability by 'elders and betters' who have never raised a voice in criticism of the nuclear policies that have made providence seem pointless and allowed stability to be identified with a balance of terror. In any case, against the disdain for permanence must be set the fact that many young people *are* planning for the future with CND if not with the Prudential.

There is hope, too, in the fact that not all reactions to the nuclear threat tend to solipsism or nihilism. In many people it seems to inspire an almost defiant kind of forward-lookingness. Instead of the cautious retreat from life or unconcern for its future, there is a sense that we must show confidence in its continuity in order, precisely, to secure it, and that by placing some 'stake' in the human race (most obviously and materially by having children) you help to guarantee its survival.

There is no doubt, however, that we invest in the future in this way only at the cost of complicating and intensifying our fear of nuclear war. This, at any rate, is my experience, for it is when I think about children — my own and children in general — that I feel most despairing. The despair is not so much to do with some possible future holocaust which they might have to suffer and die in. It is more to do with a society that can allow such a total contradiction between the tender, patient, day-to-day care that parents and nurses and teachers bestow on children, and the callousness of nuclear decision-making. Perhaps it is here, if anywhere, that there are connections to be made between militarism and a sexual division of labour. Why, on the one hand, should I be able to see in nuclear weapons things that melt eyeballs, blast bodies to bloody fragments and burn the flesh to the bone of living people, while military strategists see in them only counters in a game? Why is it that while I flinch at every euphemism they produce, these experts continue to computate their equations of terror and to offer their dispassionate appraisals of 'lethality factors' and 'collateral damage'? Some part of the answer, I suspect, must lie in the fact that this largely masculine body of personnel has never had to attend to children, intimately, day after day, ministering to their simplest physical needs.

These, of course, will be dismissed as emotive and feminine arguments. Or it will be said, perhaps, that *everyone* agrees that nuclear war would be more hellish than any other hell unleashed by war; the point is how to prevent it. I will argue through the irrationality of deterrence and current nuclear policy with anyone who cares to take me on: I will do so in detail, coldly and even clinically. But in a final moment of feminine intuition, I might well want to add that much of the 'rationality' of those who offer their 'realistic' scenarios is utterly and completely out of touch with the reality of what nuclear weapons can do – and thus in turn with a significant part of the reason for not wanting to have them.

If our lives as human beings owe so much to what is not a mere matter of biology, then we cannot identify survival simply with the salvaging of the physical body. Too often this truth is forgotten in the dispute over the viability of civil defence measures against nuclear war. The opponents of civil defence are quite right to highlight the inadequacy of such measures, but what also needs to be emphasised is that the whole discussion is conducted in the light of a very restricted, and even degenerate, concept of 'survival'. Thus, to those who assure me that shelters can provide a measure of physical protection, I am inclined to say: 'So what?' – for the fact that a significant proportion of people might survive a nuclear war physically unscathed seems to me largely irrelevant to the question of human survival.

We should be clear that if we are going to allow ourselves to talk about 'surviving' nuclear war, then we are not talking about survival in any recognisable form. The life that any physical survivors of nuclear war would be condemned to live out, cannot be compared, as some have suggested, to the life of the Middle Ages, nor even to that of the Stone Age. Those who lived in those periods were not reproducing themselves in the knowledge that their entire familiar world had but latterly, and by human agency, been blown apart – the world of their production and consumption *was* their familiar world. Nor were they 'struggling' for existence with a nature contaminated, possibly beyond repair, by the effects of radiation. To survive nuclear war would not be to regress to some earlier stage of civilisation; it would be to live *after* the development of civilisation had come to an end. It would in that sense be to live outside history. Even if a minority of survivors were to scratch together enough to satisfy their physical needs, their life would be one without the distinction between work and leisure, without any sense of community and without any culture. It would be the most physically tortuous life imaginable, and either emotionally barren or wracked by grief, remorse and longing. I do not believe that there would be many who could see their lives in such circumstances as anything but a waiting period before death, as a failure of *human* survival.

We have somehow to summon up within ourselves the will to confront this possible death of human existence. We have also continually to remind ourselves of *how* possible it is: some thousands of missiles are waiting in their silos to make it come true; whole military establishments exist to put them into operation; there are scores of people who are ready and willing to execute whatever orders they receive. I do not think one can dwell on this impending disaster very long without awakening the need to rescue humanity from it. This at any rate is my 'optimism of the will'. Nuclear disarmament can be achieved. The numbers demanding it are already massive. Provided they continue to multiply at the current rate, then the balance of history can be tipped in favour of the forces of sanity. We must stop thinking of a world without nuclear weapons as a kind of impossible Golden Age. Either we make it come true in our epoch, or we are living in the last epoch.

THE WOMEN'S PEACE CRUSADE
The History of a Forgotten Campaign

One morning towards the end of April 1915, a small knot of women stood on the Tilbury dockhead, gazing across the Thames estuary and out towards Holland. Haunted by the thought of events taking place beyond the North Sea, they seemed hardly able to drag themselves away.

Among these two dozen anxious women were some of Britain's leading suffragists. They had devoted the past decade of their lives to fighting for the vote. They were influential members of the large non-militant group, the National Union of Women's Suffrage Societies, which had a long history of peaceful campaigning.* The previous summer it had staged a highly successful national suffrage pilgrimage in which women had walked from all corners of the country to London for a rally in Hyde Park.

One of the group at Tilbury was Margaret Ashton, Manchester's first woman city councillor. Despite her family's wealth and immense respectability within the city, she had not flinched from chalking the pavements and speaking on lorries to demand votes for women. Another was Catherine Marshall from the Lake District, the National Union's Parliamentary Secretary whose natural political flair had considerably sharpened the suffragists'

* The suffragists differed from the suffragettes in that they did not agree with using militant tactics to win the vote. The major group of militant suffragettes was the Women's Social and Political Union, led by Mrs Pankhurst and her daughter Christabel. The major non-militant group was the National Union led by Mrs Fawcett.

effectiveness over the last few years. A third was Maude Royden, the daughter of a Liverpool shipowner; a magnetic public preacher, she too had channelled her energies into winning women the vote.

Together with the others, these three remarkable women stood forlornly on the dockside. They had all made their way to Tilbury with the same shared purpose: to join an International Congress of Women then gathering across the sea at the Hague in Holland. These two dozen women had even managed at the last minute to obtain passports — no easy thing in the ninth month of the war. Then, just as they reached Tilbury ready to step on board, the Admiralty had — by some strange coincidence — closed the North Sea to all shipping.

They waited on the docks, negotiating a reprieve. But hope drained away: all their determined efforts to leave Britain and reach the Hague were in vain. They had to turn round and make their sad way back home, conscious of missing this historic gathering of women.

To understand why reaching the Hague in April 1915 mattered so much to these women, and why the International Congress of Women opened up a new and exciting chapter in women's history, we must go back, beyond the outbreak of war nine months earlier, to the last years of peace.

The suffrage campaign had long linked together voteless women across the world. Despite barriers of distance and of language, they became united in the common fight against male politicians who obstinately refused them access to the ballot box. As early as 1902, an International Woman Suffrage Alliance had been formed to strengthen these links. Two years later in Berlin the Alliance held its first congress. The British delegation was headed by Mrs Fawcett herself, president of the National Union of Women's Suffrage Societies, and included twenty-two-year-old Margery Corbett Ashby. Newly graduated from Cambridge, this young woman was profoundly moved by the meeting of suffrage pioneers from around the world; her Berlin experiences shaped the internationalist direction that the rest of her long life was to take.

In the last few peacetime days of summer, 1914, before Britain slid into war with Germany, support was widespread in the country for Britain to remain neutral. Among the groups pleading with the Liberal government to do everything in its power to avoid the horrors of war was the International Woman Suffrage Alliance. On 31 July, Alliance leaders delivered a manifesto to the Foreign Office and foreign embassies in London. It was signed on behalf of twelve million women in twenty-six countries by Mrs Fawcett and Chrystal Macmillan – a suffragist who had earlier pleaded before the House of Lords the right of Scottish women graduates to the vote. The Alliance's manifesto is moving testimony to the despair felt by women across the globe as their countries sped blindly towards war:

We, the women of the world, view with apprehension and dismay the present situation in Europe, which threatens to involve one continent if not the whole world, in the disasters and horrors of war. In this terrible hour, when the fate of Europe depends on decisions which women have no power to shape, we, realising our responsibilities as the mothers of the race, cannot stand passively by. Powerless though we are politically, we call upon the governments and powers of our several countries to avert the threatened unparalleled disaster ... We women of twenty-six countries ... appeal to you to leave untried no method of conciliation or arbitration for arranging international differences which may help to avert deluging half the civilised world in blood.

Millicent Garrett Fawcett
Chrystal Macmillan

The following day Germany declared war on Russia. Soon news came through of the German invasion of Belgium: Britain responded with a declaration of war on Germany. The desperate plea of voteless women to 'avert deluging half the civilized world in blood' had been thrust aside by the men of war. Much of the energy invested in trying to avoid war was now diverted into trying to win it.

Women, exhausted by fighting the long suffrage campaign against an obstinate Liberal government, responded to the war in a great variety of ways. Many suffragettes led by Mrs Pankhurst and her daughter Christabel made a speedy peace with the government and diverted their energies into helping Britain win the war. Likewise, many of the loyalist Liberals within the National Union of Women's Suffrage Societies – including Mrs Fawcett – felt they must support their government in its war commitment. Along with so many other patriotic women, Margery Corbett Ashby, whose husband immediately joined his regiment when war was declared, began doing war work first in a hospital and later on a farm.

Other women felt a surge of anger at the way their country was now wallowing in war-crazy jingoism, blind to the slaughter that loomed ahead. For instance, Emmeline Pethick-Lawrence, a leading suffragette who had worked closely with the Pankhursts in the Women's Social and Political Union until she was edged out, opposed the war and hoped to be able to bring about peace through a negotiated settlement. It was important for her to enlist the support of people in neutral countries such as America. So Mrs Pethick-Lawrence set sail for New York and helped form a Women's Peace Party there. Others, members of the National Union of Women's Suffrage Societies, felt that they had campaigned for the vote as passionately as they had partly because they wanted the principles of nonviolence to be represented within national politics. But now they were being dragged unwillingly into a war in which they had absolutely no voice. One incensed suffragist, a dressmaker called Harriette Beanland from the Lancashire town of Nelson, which boasted a strong anti-militarist tradition, wrote to her local newspaper three days after war was declared, protesting angrily against:

the erroneous impression that this and other countries are at war with one another. They are not. Their governments, composed of men and responsible only to the men of each country, and backed by the majority of men who have caught the war and glory fever, have declared war on one another. The women of all these countries have not been consulted as to whether they would have war or not . . . If (men) deliberately shut out women, the peace-loving sex, from their rightful share in ruling their countries and Churches, then all the appeals and sentiments and prayers will be of no avail in preventing hostilities . . .

Yours, etc . . .
H. M. Beanland

Since women responded to the crisis in such a variety of ways, some throwing themselves patriotically behind the war effort and others passionately opposing it, it is hardly surprising that there were now strong tensions growing both within the International Woman Suffrage Alliance and within the National Union of Women's Suffrage Societies. The International Alliance had been planning to hold another congress in Berlin in the summer of 1915 – but now the German women withdrew the invitation and the meeting was cancelled.

A few Alliance members, more resistant to nationalistic war fever than others, refused to accept this defeatist decision. The rebels were led by Aletta Jacobs, Holland's first woman doctor and founder of the Dutch suffrage movement. When she received the letter cancelling the Congress, she resolved that 'just because there is this terrible war the woman *must* come together somewhere, some way, just to show that women of all countries can work together even in the face of the greatest war in the world'. So, despite frowns from Alliance officials, in February 1915 Aletta Jacobs called women from across Europe to meet in Amsterdam. Four women came from nearby Belgium, four from Germany and five from Britain – including Chrystal Macmillan, Catherine Marshall, and Kathleen Courtney, the Secretary of the National Union of Women's Suffrage Societies. 'People have no idea what a shock war was to us then. We knew nothing about foreign affairs, we had no ideas of the causes of war,' Kathleen Courtney reminisced years later. 'I felt we must try to learn.'

Together with Dr Aletta Jacobs and other Dutch women, they decided – despite the raging of war all around them – to organise the International Congress of Women at the Hague for the end of April. Chrystal Macmillan stayed behind in Holland, and was soon rejoined by Kathleen Courtney, to help with the organisation. Meanwhile Catherine Marshall and the other two returned home to rouse enthusiasm among British women and to arrange the delegation that would make the difficult crossing to Holland.

A British committee was soon formed and its membership reads like a roll-call of all the well-known women radicals of the day. It included Margaret Ashton, Margaret Bondfield (who later became the first woman Cabinet Minister), Kathleen Courtney who chaired the committee, Margaret Llewelyn Davies of the Women's Co-operative Guild, Charlotte Despard of the Women's Freedom League, Isabella Ford, the Leeds suffragist and Quaker, Helena Swanwick, the writer, Eva Gore-Booth the Irish poet, Catherine Marshall, Lady Ottoline Morrell, the political hostess and confidante of Bertrand Russell, Maude Royden, Sylvia Pankhurst, the East London suffragette, Olive Schreiner, the South African writer – and many, many others. This committee rushed out a manifesto urging those women who could do so to leave their homes and set out on the journey to Holland:

Ever since the outbreak of war, the question has been repeatedly asked, 'What are the women going to do?' The most terrible war in history has come at a time when women's organisations are highly developed and when their voice is heard on all public questions . . . The way has now been shown by women of neutral nations: the American Women's Peace Party has gathered thousands of the best women in the United States together in support of active propaganda for laying the basis of a lasting peace . . . The women of the Netherlands are so strong and united in their movement to bring about better international relations that they are organising a conference of women of all countries to discuss aspects of war and peace, of peculiar and vital importance to women . . .

Women cannot disregard the appeal sometimes expressed, as in letters from . . . soldiers, who from the battlefield call upon them to save civilisation; but more moving and more terrible is the silent appeal from the daily growing cemeteries, from the devastated villages and ruined homes, the orphans, the outraged, and the starving.

It is much more difficult for men to meet in conference; they are in the silent armies. Women as non-combatants have this right, and as guardians of the race they have this duty.

Across the world women readily responded to such appeals. Impressive delegations were mustered. German suffragists were particularly enthusiastic and many of them set out for the Hague; but they were stopped at the Dutch border and only twenty-eight got through. Because of the fighting, no French or Russian women attended. However, Britain mounted a delegation of no fewer than 180 women, all keen to break through the military barriers they so hated. Among them were Sylvia Pankhurst, Olive Schreiner and many other committee members. They all steeled themselves in readiness for the difficult journey, but the suspicious British government decided to demand a dossier on each of them. Then it decided to refuse passports to all but two dozen.

It was, as we know, these two dozen women who managed to arrive at Tilbury in late April 1915. But, even as they reached the dockside, they learnt that they would never reach the Congress.

Luckily three British delegates *did* manage to squeeze their way into the Congress. Chrystal Macmillan and Kathleen Courtney were, of course, already there. And Emmeline Pethwick-Lawrence travelled back across the Atlantic with the big American Women's Peace Party delegation, led by the influential social reformer, Jane Addams from Chicago. Even though Mrs Pethwick-Lawrence had no passport — she had never in her life even see a passport — she somehow smoothed over this problem and arrived with the Americans just as the Congress was due to begin.

These three British women joined over a thousand other delegates from a dozen countries. A day after the Congress opened the five Belgian women managed to arrive despite enormous difficulties. Enthusiastically welcomed by the assembled delegates, they were — at the suggestion of the German women — invited to sit up on the platform. Messages of support poured in from as far away as Brazil and South Africa, India and Russia.

This historic and symbolic Congress, presided over by Jane Addams, adopted resolutions which laid the firm basis for an international women's peace movement. They reflected a commitment both to the women's suffrage campaign from which the idea for the Congress had sprung, and to the search for peaceful means by which international disputes could be settled. The two parts were closely interwoven: there should be machinery for international arbitration, and women's voices should be heard at it.

Despite the nervous strain felt by the delegates at such a time, one particularly ambitious proposal was hurriedly endorsed at the close of the last long session. 'This Congress delegates envoys,' it was agreed, 'to carry the message expressed in the Congress resolutions to the rulers of the belligerent and neutral nations of Europe and to the President of the United States.'

'Surely never since Mary Fisher, the Quakeress, set out on her mission to preach Christianity to the Grand Turk,' marvelled Catherine Marshall after hearing of this last Hague proposal, 'was such an adventure undertaken by women!'

No time was lost. During May and June 1915, the envoys — Aletta Jacobs, Chrystal Macmillan, Catherine Marshall, Kathleen Courtney, leading Hungarian suffragist Rozsika Schwimmer and others — visited European prime ministers and foreign secretaries. In August Jane Addams, whose name carried considerable weight in the United States, managed to interview President Wilson in Washington. The Congress resolutions, the President apparently declared, were 'by far the best formulation which up to the moment has been put out by anybody.'

By October the envoys, now gathered together safely in New York, were able to report that they had been listened to with respect by the American President and European heads of state. They still believed as firmly as ever that the war had burst upon the world partly because women were excluded from the counsels of the nations. It was this logic that fuelled their towering optimism. 'Women will soon have political power,' Aletta Jacobs informed a sympathetic American journalist:

Woman suffrage and permanent peace will go together. When the women of a country are eagerly asking for the vote, and a country is in the state of mind to grant the vote to its women, it is a sign that that country is ripe for permanent peace.

Yes, the women will do it. They don't feel as men do about war. They are the mothers of the race. Men think of the economic results; women think of the grief and pain.

However, in the middle of this most terrifying war, no statesman dared to take up the women's suggestion of calling a conference of neutral nations to offer immediate and continuous mediation as a means to end the barbarous fighting. Peace was not going to be easy to achieve. Even among non-militant suffragists there remained many who looked coldly on the Hague delegates' lack of patriotism. Not only did the cautious International Woman Suffrage Alliance prefer not to risk a meeting in wartime, but many members of the National Union of Women's Suffrage Societies took a similar view. For Mrs Fawcett and Margery Corbett Ashby international peace took second place to the claims of women's suffrage and the duty of a patriot. Mrs Fawcett had even opposed the sending of official delegates to the Hague Congress. But many of the National Union's members, organised into 500 local suffrage societies around the country, fiercely disagreed with her. When the decision not to support the Hague Congress was relayed to the local groups, a furious howl of protest rose up. Resignations flooded in from all quarters. Among influential suffragists who had resigned from the National Union by mid-1915 were Catherine Marshall, the Parliamentary Secretary, Kathleen Courtney, the Secretary, and Executive Committee members Margaret Ashton, Isabella Ford and Helena Swanwick.

Since its formation in 1897, the National Union had been quietly but surely building up its strength and by the outbreak of war it was able to boast about 54,000 members. Now it was split savagely and dramatically down the middle; the split was not, ironically, over the issue of suffrage tactics, but over war versus peace, nationalism versus internationalism. The heart of the women's movement in Britain was now divided. The more conservative portion under Mrs Fawcett's guiding hand continued to run the National Union and to press women's claims to the vote. The more radical portion was now organised around the women's peace movement that sprang from the Hague Congress: the Women's International League for Peace and Freedom.

The British section of the Women's International League was born at a conference held in Westminster in autumn 1915. Despite fierce opposition, it could within a year claim two or three thousand members organised into thirty-four branches around the country. The spirit that moved these women during the testing years of the war is captured in their first annual report; it proclaimed the urgency of

linking together two movements felt to be vitally connected: the Women's Movement and the Pacifist Movement. The first has been recognised as one of the greatest of world movements towards liberation; it is time the second should be recognised as another. Only free women can build up the peace which is to be, themselves understanding the eternal strife engendered by domination, and, by their teaching, liberating the minds of their sons for active, creative, beneficent cooperation.

Brave words – the women's movement and the pacifist movement glorious and indivisible. But the immediate way forward prickled with difficulties. Early in 1916 military conscription was introduced in Britain, and local military tribunals began to hear the cases of conscientious objectors. The Women's International League vehemently opposed the very principle of conscription and in this fight – as in the broader opposition to the war itself – it joined with other more established groups to combat the growing influence of militarism.

Keir Hardie's Independent Labour Party (ILP) had long championed internationalism. Now it provided a vital focus for those men and women within the labour movement who declared themselves to be pacifists. A newer organisation, formed after a few months of war and now thrown into the limelight by the military tribunals, was the No-Conscription Fellowship. Despite all the Fellowship's efforts to safeguard men of military age, there were, before long, few young men available to help run its organisation. Women, of course, were in little danger of being marched off to military prison or the trenches and to them fell an increasing amount of organising responsibility. Most notably, Catherine Marshall now brought all her years' experience of suffrage campaigning to the daunting task of running the No-Conscription Fellowship. During the spring of 1916 she wrote beseeching letters almost daily to Bertrand Russell until at last she won his valuable commitment. The two of them worked side by side in 1916 and 1917, Russell buckling to as Catherine Marshall presented him with lengthy agendas, certain items of which were just marked 'B. R. to do'.

Catherine Marshall and others who opposed conscription had hoped that the conscientious objectors' courageous stand against militarism might hasten the end of the war. Yet by early 1917 the prospects for peace still seemed hopelessly remote. Food shortages led to long queues, while the casualty lists from the Front touched families in every street and every community across the country.

Then into this gloom arrived exciting news of a revolution in distant Russia. Reactions to this – and to the second, Bolshevik revolution later that year – varied enormously. Christabel Pankhurst and her mother stumped the country, warning of the evils of Bolshevism, pacifism and 'shirkers'. The International Woman Suffrage Alliance and what was left of the National Union of Women's Suffrage Societies seemed to fix their gaze steadfastly at some point well above such troublesome events which cast doubts on their time-honoured aims and procedures.

But more radical women welcomed the news of spring 1917 with wild enthusiasm. They were overjoyed to learn that revolutionaries in Russia desired exactly what they in Britain desired: an end to war and an end to tyranny. 'My sisters, I cannot use the ordinary commonplaces,' declared Charlotte Despard in an open letter to Russian women. 'To say that I congratulate you would be out of place. Rather – I am with you – we are one.' The Women's International League was equally enthusiastic, and gladly accepted an invitation to attend the June 1917 Convention in Leeds to honour the first Russian Revolution. At the same time it decided to organise a deputation to go to Russia and see at first hand what was really happening there and to congratulate the Russian women. Charlotte Despard, Margaret Bondfield, Emmeline Pethick-Lawrence and Ethel Snowden, wife of the Labour politician Philip Snowden, were selected to go. But the Foreign Office once again refused them passports while allowing one to pro-war Mrs Pankhurst – to the intense fury of the Women's International League which believed neither in her claim to speak for British women nor in the purpose of her journey.

The women who had launched the women's international campaign were, we can sense, highly educated women who had the money and leisure to leave their homes and travel battle-strewn Europe with their peace proposals. Certainly Helena Swanwick, Kathleen Courtney and Maude Royden were all well-to-do women with an Oxbridge education, as was Margery Corbett Ashby.

Yet this was far from the whole story. The labour movement had split over its response to the war with many trade unionists and Labour Party members sharing in the anti-German mood; some working women within the socialist movement vehemently opposed militarism and the introduction of conscription. Sadly their stories are less well known than they deserve to be.

One of their major campaigns was the Women's Peace Crusade; formed earlier in the war, it took off in 1917-18, bringing together radical anti-war women at a grassroots level. Although it cooperated readily with local branches of the Women's International League, its greatest strength seems to have lain in industrial towns far from London, many of them too small to have a League branch of their own. Certainly this is the impression Charlotte Despard gained as she travelled the country during 1917-18, speaking for the Women's Peace Crusade. Her diary for January 1918, for instance, notes packed meetings at textile towns on either side of the Pennines:

January 6th. Keighley, Yorkshire . . . Afternoon held our Crusade meeting in a large dingy hall — packed! At first there were signs of disturbance, but it passed and I had a very attentive meeting . . .

January 8th. To Blackburn. Almost all women in the [Quaker] meeting house — rapt attention. A young fine factory girl was in the chair — her sweetheart is in prison. I am finding a fine, spirited audience in these women of the north.

Glasgow was one of the major centres of mass support. Here on 'Red Clydeside' in the summer of 1917 the Women's Peace Crusade was launched. Much of the initiative came from two socialists, Agnes Dollan, who later became one of Glasgow's councillors, and Helen Crawford, a suffragette and now Scottish organiser for the Women's International League. Their plans met with an immediate response from local women, embittered by the loss of sons and husbands and angry at having to shiver for hours in endless food queues.

So, on Sunday, 8 July, the Women's Peace Crusade mounted a

historic demonstration in Glasgow. As a result of a campaign of open-air meetings during the previous month, over 12,000 people joined in. 'Sunday was a day of triumph for the Women's Peace Crusaders', noted one Labour paper. 'From two sides of the city great processions came with music and floating banners, and as they neared Glasgow Green they merged into one – a symbol of their unity of purpose and resolve.' Agnes Dollan and Helen Crawford, Ethel Snowden and Helena Swanwick all spoke. 'Though the webs of appeal and argument they wove were varied in workmanship and in design, there was ever present the gold thread of Peace! Peace! Peace!' the ILP newspaper reported. The resolutions were carried unanimously and included the message, 'This mass meeting of Glasgow citizens, summoned by the Women's Peace Crusade, sends to the Russian Revolutionary Government warm sympathy and congratulations.'

Later that summer other towns followed Glasgow's lead. ILP women in Manchester met to plan *their* demonstration. A series of outdoor meetings was organised in Bradford. In Leeds, a local Crusade group formed, with Isabella Ford as secretary. By early autumn the ILP paper could boast that no fewer than thirty-three local Women's Peace Crusade groups had sprung up.

The Crusade won a ready response among working women who wanted an end to the war, but still met with formidable opposition. Patriotic newspapers circulated scare stories of rowdy crowds at meetings. The police seized from the printer the Women's Peace Crusade's first leaflet, 'Casualties'. Individual members were harassed, and in Manchester the police banned a meeting planned for Stevenson Square, the city's traditional meeting site.

In Nelson, a demonstration held in August also had an undertow of violence. A thousand women marched through the crowded streets, bearing their proud banners: 'Peace our Hope' and 'Hail the Russian Revolution'. The mood was hostile and mounted police plus reinforcements on foot were called in to help quell the menacing crowd of 15,000. Margaret Bondfield and local women tried to speak from the platform, but their voices were drowned by rowdy singing of 'Rule Britannia' and 'God Save the King'.

Preaching peace, even by working women who could hardly be accused of being 'conchies' or 'shirkers', was no easy matter. It certainly seemed far harder than demanding the vote. Gwen Coleman had been an organiser for the National Union of Women's Suffrage Societies in the west of England, and after war broke out, became a convinced internationalist. Her memories of 1918 give a vivid picture of the exhaustion women like herself felt at the end of four years of unrelenting warfare:

I think when war was declared over and I was very weary – I'd fought against the war and knew they hadn't fought for the land of freedom and brotherhood they were told they were fighting for . . . We were living in Leeds, Mother and I, and things were pretty bad, we couldn't get any fire-wood or anything. I went for a walk on the moor, gathering firewood. I came to a wall, I stood by this wall and just the other side a lark went up singing. I put my head down on that wall and I sobbed and sobbed. It was just something that this lark had, you know, that we'd done without for so long. Working for peace during the war wasn't easy, it was harder, much harder than working for the suffrage movement, that was child's play compared with what one put up with during the war. I mean you were a traitor to your country, you should have been shot at dawn.

After the war women over thirty were at last able to vote in parliamentary elections. Where, then, did the women who had fought the suffrage battle for so long now invest their energies? Part of the answer is already well known. Some continued to lobby Parliament to rid British law of any hindrances to women's complete equality with men. Some campaigned for birth control information to be made available, or fought for family allowances to give mothers financial independence. Others turned to party politics, working with the men who had previously run the party machines: a few were even elected as councillors or MPs. Some retired completely from the political fray, exhausted by the years of struggle.

What is less well known is how many of the suffragists went on to devote their lives to proclaiming their internationalist faith. Haunted by a grim memory of casualty lists, of soldiers' graves, of harrowed young widows and bereaved sweethearts, some women determined to say 'never again'. They pledged to devote themselves to establishing an international mediating system to prevent future wars, and to urge the powerful nations of the world to lay down their fearful weapons and disarm.

To this end, women worked in various ways during the 1920s. Some chose to work through women-only groups as they had done in the suffrage days, believing that men's experience of – and attitude towards – war was fundamentally different from women's; and that therefore women brought to questions of peace and nonviolence a humane clarity that would be less effective if watered down. Others held that now most women were enfranchised, the logic of separatist organisations grew weaker as each year passed; what was most important, they felt, was that the widest possible 'never again' anti-war campaign should be mounted and that women should add their voices to the other pressure groups. Such women joined their local branch of the League of Nations Union formed in 1918 and tried to ensure that women were represented in League debates at Geneva. Others joined smaller groups like the pacifist No More War Movement formed three years later.

Amidst this general feeling that war must at all cost be avoided, the existing women's organisations continued to meet. The International Woman Suffrage Alliance at last met again – in Geneva in 1920. Margery Corbett Ashby, who acted as recording secretary and interpreter, remembered it as a tricky occasion: the Belgian delegation refused to work with the German and so stayed away, while the French women came only on condition that the German delegation apologise for war atrocities. Only gradually were friendly relations re-established and the Alliance able to celebrate the large number of countries which had given votes to women in recognition of their war service.

The younger Women's International League of Peace and Freedom was more nimble on its feet. It was able to meet again in 1919. This time the twenty-five strong British delegation (including Ethel Snowden, Helena Swanwick, Catherine Marshall and Ellen Wilkinson) managed to arrive in Zurich. However, because of visa difficulties only two French delegates were at the opening of the Congress; then a third delegate, from a devastated region of the Ardennes, arrived dramatically. A German woman on the platform immediately sprang to her feet, clasping the Frenchwoman's hands and pledging her German colleagues to work for reconciliation. An American delegate rose up too and raising her hand solemnly proclaimed, 'I dedicate my life to the cause of peace!' Immediately every woman present stood, hand raised, and joined her in her pledge. 'I have never witnessed or imagined,' Helena Swanwick confessed, 'so remarkable an affirmation.'

Much of the Women's International League's strength lay in its local branches: by the end of the war its British section alone had recruited 4,000 members into fifty branches. Particularly impressive was Manchester, a city where socialism and women's suffrage had long gone hand in hand. Among the local suffragists who joined the 500-strong branch were Hannah Mitchell, author of the autobiography *The Hard Way Up*; two others were Ellen Wilkinson and writer Ada Nield Chew, both of whom had worked as organisers for the National Union of Women's Suffrage Societies before the war. So quickly did the branch grow that by 1918 it was able to employ Arnot Robinson, another National Union worker and socialist, as its organiser.

Although the Women's International League had originally welcomed the first Russian Revolution, by 1919 it had begun to have doubts about the use of violence to achieve political change. By just one vote the Zurich Congress determined that the League would henceforth support only peaceful methods for change, believing that 'it is their special part in this revolutionary age to counsel against violence from any side'. So when the Manchester branch came to hear alarming news from Ireland of the violence of the Irish rebels and vicious reprisals by the British troops, the notorious 'Black and Tans', it suggested the League should send a delegation to investigate.

The idea caught on, and in October 1920 a group of ten women set out to cross the Irish Sea. Among those from the Manchester branch were Helena Swanwick, Ellen Wilkinson and her friend Arnot Robinson; they were joined by Agnes Dollan and another Glasgow woman. In order to counter the stories in the British press of the Irish rebels' alleged crimes, the women tried to publicise the violence done to Irish people in the name of British law and order. Their conclusion was uncompromising: after the success of the Sinn Fein at the recent election, 'the British Government can only pretend to govern by force and fraud, leading to the moral injury of Great Britain and the injury of her reputation throughout the world.' They advocated the release of political prisoners, the withdrawal of the armed forces, and the placing of government in the hands of local elected bodies. But the League's commitment to passive resistance was not to be the way taken by many nationalist leaders.

Equally thankless was the task set by the Women's International League and other anti-war groups to persuade strong nations to commit themselves to a system of international arbitration and a programme of disarmament. At last, in 1925, the League of Nations Disarmament Commission was established, and this gave a useful fillip to the Women's International League's demand for total, universal disarmament.

The British section organised a particularly spectacular campaign. Here, in the summer of 1926, a peacemakers' pilgrimage was staged by the Women's International League and over two dozen other women's and peace organisations. The inspiration for this countrywide pageant came, of course, from the great suffrage pilgrimage organised by the National Union of Women's Suffrage Societies thirteen years before. As in 1913, pilgrims walked from all corners of the country down about eight main routes, all converging on London and Hyde Park. Each route had its own colour and was headed by a great two-poled blue banner with the route names, followed by thousands of flags of different nations and women carrying staffs mounted with a dove of peace on top.

Although it followed hard on the heels of the General Strike, the members of the pilgrimage found that wherever they went passers-by came out to greet them and join in the meetings they held along each route. Local newspapers would report how far the nearest group of pilgrims had got each day. 'Tanned and Tired but Triumphant' ran the *Western Mail* headline about the South Wales women. Even women unable to leave home for more than a few hours could join in. In Halifax, for instance, the local Women's Liberal Association organised charabancs to take women to York to join the pilgrims in a service in York Minster. 'Fare 7s 6d return', ran the advertisement, 'This Is Not A Party Political Campaign'.

Across the Pennines in Nelson, the Labour Party Women's section was alerted early to the pilgrimage, and a demonstration was held in the Weavers' Institute in support of disarmament and international arbitration. Two local women even managed to get away and join the pilgrimage on its last leg; one, a weaver called Emily Murgatroyd, was a veteran of the 1913 suffrage pilgrimage. The rest of the Nelson women pinned their blue and yellow rosettes on to their coats, unfurled their wartime 'Peace our Hope' banner, and clambered into a blue and yellow charabanc destined for Manchester. Here a service was held in the crowded cathedral, followed by a march through the city to Platt Fields where 2,500 people joined in the demonstration. 'Law can be substituted for war,' Kathleen Courtney told the crowd, 'as law has been substituted for duelling.'

The Manchester demonstration was billed to coincide with the first contingent of marchers reaching the outskirts of London. The first to arrive had walked from Brighton, Hastings and the Sussex villages; they carried long staves bearing the names of the three dozen communities which had passed resolutions calling on the government to settle all international disputes by peaceful arbitration. They marched on to an open-air meeting at Crystal Palace; another was held at Fulham Palace for the pilgrims from Land's End and Wales. Thousands of women were now pouring into the city. The following day, 19 June, 10,000 women marched to Hyde Park through the brilliant sunshine of a midsummer heat wave. Many more thousands joined them in front of twenty-two platforms to listen to the speakers: Emmeline Pethwick-Lawrence, Margery Corbett Ashby, Mrs Fawcett, Margaret Bondfield, Ellen Wilkinson and others. At the end of the day a bugle was sounded and from every platform the resolution was put urging the government to support disarmament and international arbitration. With hardly a murmur of dissent, both were carried.

As in 1913, politicians were genuinely impressed by the peaceful women pilgrims. The Foreign Secretary received a deputation from the organisers and listened sympathetically to what they said. He pointed out that preparations for the Disarmament Conference were already under way; but he was wary of the suggestion of international arbitration, for he was conscious that Britain was still a major colonial power and wanted to retain a free hand to settle disputes in her territory.

It was also disheartening that the promised Disarmament Conference took a further six years to materialise. In the meantime, the Women's Peace Crusade was revived to keep up the pressure; and, when the League of Nations eventually agreed that the World Disarmament Conference should meet at Geneva in 1932, millions of women's signatures were collected on an international disarmament petition.

But the great potential for peace of this historic conference was already overshadowed by dark and ominous events. The depression was pushing millions into unemployment. Japan had invaded Manchuria, and this act of aggression began to cast serious doubts on the ability of the League of Nations to impose effective sanctions on aggressor nations. The clear-cut 'never again' certainties of the early post-war years now grew clouded. The chroniclers of the Women's International League in their book, *Pioneers for Peace*, vividly captured the tense atmosphere in Geneva in February 1932:

War raged in the Far East, unemployment blanketed the USA, Europe shivered on the threshold of new chaos – and as the 'peacemakers' assembled, the world held its breath and waited for the words and deeds of hope. What hopes were there for success? The hope of the 'ordinary people' of the world were perhaps of little account. They lay piled in despatch boxes in the library of the conference hall – those millions of petitions, collected during the international disarmament campaigns of the past two years by peace societies and ex-servicemen; by religious and labour organisations; above all by the women, mothers of one slaughtered generation and another now threatened. From the women's organisations alone, eight million signatures were presented at the receiving ceremony . . .

But it became all too clear, as the statesmen at Geneva unfolded their briefs and expounded their compromises, that no spectacular progress would be made.

The Disarmament Conference ended with tragically little achieved: the big powers were reluctant to weaken their own military position relative to their neighbours'. The verb 'to disarm', one French statesman joked cynically, is 'conjugated only in the future tense, and it has only the form of the second person'. Events in Germany cast an even more alarming shadow over Geneva: by the end of 1933 Hitler had become Chancellor, and Germany had walked out not only of the Conference but also from the League of Nations itself. Progress appeared impossible. Even the ever-patient Margery Corbett Ashby, Britain's substitute delegate at the Conference, resigned in complete despair. She sent a bitterly critical letter of resignation to Ramsay MacDonald, the Prime Minister, about the way the British Government had stonewalled at Geneva.

By then the advance of Nazi Germany challenged head-on the anti-war faiths of the earlier group of women who had helped form the Women's International League of Peace and Freedom. Before long that pioneer generation began slowly to pass away: Chrystal Macmillan and Margaret Ashton died in 1937, Helena Swanwick and ninety-five-year-old Charlotte Despard in 1939, Dr Maude Royden in 1956, Catherine Marshall in 1961, Dame Kathleen Courtney aged ninety-six in 1974, and Dame Margery Corbett Ashby, the longest-lived of them all, in April 1981, aged ninety-nine.

Yet the candle of hope they lit at the Hague in 1915 has never been completely extinguished. The Women's International League still exists and was, for instance, among the groups that pressed for the First United Nations Special Session on

Disarmament in 1978. However it has inevitably lost some of its earlier momentum to newer campaigning groups: the membership of its British section has now shrunk right down to under 500 members.

Its history still deserves to be better known. In this country, we have experienced neither a major war nor military conscription for well over a generation now. So, when the women's liberation movement sprang up in the late 1960s, our concerns tended less towards international nonviolence and more towards consciousness-raising and sex discrimination, abortion and eqal pay. These priorities, then, helped shape the way feminists in the 1970s set about uncovering their own history. We now know about women's long struggle for the vote and about women's traditions of work and trade unionism. Yet still too little is known about the story of the magnificent fight by this earlier generation of women against the inhumanity of war and the insanity of stockpiling armaments. The names of Catherine Marshall, Chrystal Macmillan and other women have passed into near-oblivion yet deserve to be remembered. We have to renew their fight to ensure that, half a century later, the powerful nations of the world put away forever their weapons of mass murder.

|Many friends read an earlier draft of this article and I am very grateful for all their comments. I would like to thank in particular Gwen Coleman, Doris Nield Chew, Sheila Rowbotham, Jean McCrindle and members of the Halifax Nuclear Disarmament and Manchester Women's History Groups.

This article has sketched the history of the Women's International League and Women's Peace Crusade, and suggested the links between suffrage and the later anti-war campaign. It has not attempted to assess their effectiveness or raise the more theoretical questions about the relationship between feminism and pacifism; nor has it tried to describe the responses of women in, say, the Labour Party or Women's Co-operative Guild, or those outside any formal organisation; these need further research and will, I hope, be part of a longer study of the subject.|

WOMANPOWER AND NUCLEAR POLITICS
Women and the Peace Movement

This is a book about nuclear disarmament. It is also a book directed particularly towards women. Isn't this paradoxical? To succeed, the movement for nuclear disarmament surely requires the participation of every one, without distinction of class, race or sex. Might not singling out Janet against John work against the cause? If there were no one speaking to John, the answer would be 'yes'. We feel, however, that not only is it *not* counter-productive but it is indeed vitally important for at least one book on this subject to concern itself with and to direct itself towards women. Of course we hope it will be read by men too, and that perhaps it will lead some of them to think again about the relative tasks of men and women working together.

In past times, it has been during wars that the relative powerlessness of women in affairs of state has reached its apogee. Women – wives and mothers – were characterised as 'non-combatants'; their first duty was to their families, whilst that of men was seen to be to their country. The extent of the exclusion of women from wartime activity has varied in differing circumstances. At its most extreme, when the war was fought in another country, the wife stayed at home with the children while the man went away to fight. The man suffered the horrors of the battlefield, the woman experienced the bitter anxiety of ignorance, waiting. We have seen this happening very recently. While young men were losing their lives in the South Atlantic, their wives were kept on tenterhooks, ill-informed and anxious. Some lost people they loved.

More recent divisions of gender roles in wartime took place when women moved to take the place of absent men in the workplace. Women were suddenly seen by statesmen and employers to have skills and capacities they were hitherto supposed not to possess. In Britain, in the Second World War, eighteen million women took on jobs, most of which had been performed up till then by men. Whereas in peacetime they were housewives, or they performed clerical work or 'low-skilled' part-time work, in wartime they took on more 'skilled' full-time work. The civilian population often saw women driving buses and operating machinery. Whereas in peacetime, these tasks are seen to be relatively important (and therefore 'men's' work): in wartime, the 'real action' takes place on the battlefield.

Sometimes, indeed, women have joined the military. But here their tasks often reproduced, in slightly modified form, the role of woman as housewife and mother. Often they service men in the army; or they perform duties that enable men to 'go to the front'. The role of the women in the WRNS and the WAAF was sometimes described as that of 'freeing the men for action'. Although it would be ridiculous to say categorically that their roles disadvantaged women, Ian McEwan's television play *The Imitation Game* graphically illustrates the subordinate position occupied by women in the ATS — their exclusion from access to information, their relegation to positions where they service men, and ultimately, their powerlessness.

In nuclear war, of course, things would be dramatically different. Gone would be the distinction between 'combatants' — legitimate targets for attack, who can also be blamed for acts of aggression — and 'non-combatants'. Effectively, everyone becomes a combatant — in the sense of being a possible target — but also a non-combatant insofar as she or he plays no active role in military action or decision-making. In a nuclear war there would be no conscription, no volunteers for the army, no agonising about whether or not to 'choose' to 'participate'. There would be no possibility of principled pacifists opting out. Whereas in the past governments have required the cooperation of their people to wage war, this time the decision would be taken out of the hands of the populace, of the vast majority of men and women. *Everybody* would become powerless in a much stronger sense than ever before. Gender divisions between men and women's occupational roles would be wiped out. Together they would be placed alongside objects, buildings, machinery, all recipients of undiscriminating missiles.

But in the society we now inhabit, these gender differences are still very much present. Feminist women have, in various ways, been working to eliminate inequalities between the sexes, particularly to eradicate the unequal power relations between men and women. Some of these attempts to remove differences, however, may be seen as a capitulation to the 'male' values of militarism and aggression. For example, earlier this century, some women, fighting inequality and subjection, campaigned for a woman's 'right' to be conscripted into the army. In the shadow of nuclear war, one might expect such ideas to have disappeared. But this is not so. Recently, in the United States, the Civil Liberties Union has been campaigning for the conscription of women (albeit unsuccessfully). Some of the campaigners saw this as an activity critical of an aspect of Reaganism and the New Right. Reagan, whose recent military budget was the largest ever in peacetime, is committed to militarism and nuclear arms; he is also dedicated to nurturing the traditional (nuclear) family. Some feminists, in arguing for women's conscription saw their actions as undermining this dedication to the patriarchal family.

But their campaign was surely misplaced. Militarism runs counter to the interests of nearly everyone in society, women and men. The culmination of militarist thinking is militarist problem-solving — war. Even in peacetime, the diversion of resources to weapon-making must be at the expense of homes and hospitals. Even in a world without nuclear weapons it would surely be a step backwards for women to adopt the vices of men. There is something not only misplaced but *perverse* about women taking on militaristic roles. Those American feminists were doing nothing to undermine the militarism of the New Right. They were indeed encouraging the kind of thinking which must inevitably lead to the possibility of nuclear war, which could mean the destruction of the whole of their society, perhaps of the human race. Rather than aping men's worst actions, women should build on the positive side of their historical experience in their work for peace.

By not being in the armed forces, women have in fact had a measure of freedom. Although the rhetoric may suggest otherwise, those in the military are among the least free members of society. Subject, as they are, to superior authority, they lose their identity, their individuality, their right to information along with their right to question orders. The stereotypical man in the army is said to be assertive, virile, aggressive and powerful. Women outside the army retain certain liberties denied to men – including freedom to think for themselves, to resist authority and to behave as individuals.

It has often been pointed out that women tend to be more passive than men, to have less access to sources of power in society, and that they are often isolated in low-paid work or in the home. They tend, so the conventional wisdom runs, to have less confidence in themselves than do men; they are more imaginative, less logical. Simone de Beauvoir and others have argued that women are not only more passive than men, they are more disposed to be masochistic: they are more prone to self-mutilation and self-denigration. And, as Dale Spender has argued, women tend to occupy relatively subordinate positions in their use of language, in conversation. She points to a 'division of linguistic labour in conversation', where women are likely to talk less, to 'talk on someone else's topic'.

Women must continue, as they have done in the past, to draw on their creativity and their pacifism, qualities they already possess, while becoming more assertive, less self-denigratory, and making peace a positive political aim. Their nurturant, pacific traits must be transformed into active support for the peace movement. This point has been made by women campaigners in the past. Jacquetta Hawkes, in a poem published in the *New Statesman* in 1938, wrote

Women have seldom been the great creators
Rather we have been the containers, the protectors, the lovers of life.

A few men seem possessed by the devil
But many more . . . have remained as boys, just boys
Heedlessly playing. But the spring of the toys they are winding is death
We must take power from these madmen, these prisoners, these
perilous children.

And one of the best-known campaigners for peace in her generation, Dora Russell, lamented the persistence of aggression in what was so markedly a man's world, and the denigration of women as subjective and illogical.

Many women feel that as wives, and even more as mothers, they have an especial concern with peace, But just as it has been suggested that women's roles in wartime organisations tended to reproduce their roles in the home, there is a danger that a similar thing can happen within the peace movement. The peace movement today has many hundreds of thousands of women in it, but for many of them their role remains that of tea-maker and cake-stall holder at fund-raising efforts. Of course there is nothing wrong with women doing these jobs. The movement welcomes everyone, and can make use of every skill on offer. The domestic skills are essential to the smooth running of events, and women, many with a lifetime's experience, are usually better at them than men. Woe betide any movement that undervalues its typists, cake-bakers and tea ladies. But of course, this is the rub. These skills often *are* undervalued. They are seen as far less important than the front jobs of speaking, organising or writing manifestos. And although there are very many women in the modern peace movement who do take these more public and leading roles, many of us feel that we are still expected to work in a domestic role, whether we want to or not.

Women's arguments for peace are not always the same as men's. Both must be heard within the movement. If women tend to be more nervous of public speaking, this must not prevent their voices from being heard. A large number of small meetings may be a much better way of exchanging ideas than a few mass rallies. The two are not mutually exclusive, and everyone in the movement with something to say should be given the opportunity, should indeed be encouraged to work out for herself the best way in which she can get across her own arguments. The most recent phase of the movement, since 1979, has seen many examples of the participation by women in the movement at all levels. National officers include women, and much of the most important work of research into the politics and technology of weaponry has been done by women. But even more interesting has been the number of initiatives which could only have been introduced by women. That is to say, although women can do the same things as men can in a great many fields, there are some peace initiatives which are peculiar to our sex.

The Peace Camp movement is a very good example of this. A march of a small number of women, undertaken as the response to a bigger international women's march, arrived at its focal point, the US air base and proposed Cruise missile site at Greenham Common, and the women asked for a discussion with a member of the government. The days of marching, the discussions among themselves, the arguments and conversations with sympathetic or doubtful members of the public in the various towns and villages through which they had passed, had produced in the marchers a new confidence in their case and in their ability to put it to those in authority. Their request for a debate was turned down, and in protest they picked up a tactic from an earlier women's movement, the suffragette movement, and chained themselves to the railings of the air base. Soon they decided to set up a permanent camp, not only until they got a public discussion, but until the decision to base the Cruise missiles was reversed. The initiative, the style and the tactics of the whole operation were female – argumentative, determined, nonviolent. And the public demonstration of these qualities caught the imagination of people all over the world, so that the peace camps have become part of the vocabulary of action of the world peace movement. In the same way, the march through the USSR of 300 women in pink robes was a gesture which challenged both the suspicion of aggressive intent and the fear of open discussion which has characterised so much of the Soviet response to independent peace initiatives from outside their borders. However threatening our arguments may be to superpower psychology, no one can present a group of women – unarmed and probably incapable of handling firearms – as in any way physically threatening.

The main British peace movement, CND, is a broad, all-inclusive popular movement; it is not a political party. If we believe that the successful elimination of nuclear weaponry requires other, broader changes in society, we can put the case for this within CND. If we believe, by contrast, that every nuclear missile can be destroyed without other alterations in the world, our view will be accommodated. Participation in CND requires one belief and one only, and that is a conviction that we need to rid the world of nuclear weaponry.

A world without nuclear weapons would be a very different one from the world of today. It would be as different, indeed, as is the space age from the eighteenth century. It is unlikely that the thinking of the peoples of the world could alter so fundamentally as to eradicate nuclear weaponry without there being other changes in the world. Other devices for killing, for example, would be challenged too. The participation of women in the disarmament movement *will* contribute to other alterations in society;

their participation in the movement will help break down gender divisions outside CND.

Campaigning to rid the world of nuclear weaponry is a start in the process of changing people – a vital jumping-off point, because without it there can be no starting point. But it is only a start. Accepting the arguments of the campaign could constitute the beginning of a change in human nature. Each person who is convinced of the case and begins to act on her belief in her own small way is beginning the process of changing human beings. Human nature is not static.

Men, women and young people of both sexes have important parts to play in the peace movement. Every individual has her or his own contribution to make, each sex can contribute particular strengths. There are separate organisations for women who want to work exclusively with other women; but most of us take part with other members of our family and with neighbours. Women do a great deal of the organising work, and they also have a particular strength in most kinds of neighbourhood work. Parent-teacher associations are in a position to ask for peace studies in schools (how many of us realise that our government agreed to this by signing the Helsinki agreement?), and to resist the use of the classroom for war propaganda or the justification of atomic weapons. Women trade unionists can put their case in union meetings. Youth clubs, play groups, Women's Institutes and Townswomen's Guilds – all the social and educational groups to which women belong are made up of people to whom this question is urgent and disturbing. We must be able to marshal our arguments and to offer people some hope of a future. The other side may have a disproportionate share of the media, but among concerned people who have taken the trouble to look into the question, teachers, social workers and parents, we have an overwhelming majority. Personal persuasion is, in the end, the most powerful form of persuasion, and the most likely to last because it is arrived at cooperatively by questioning and discussing, and is not imposed.

If women's special qualities are still not represented in the world peace movement in full proportion to the concern felt by women for peace, we must change this situation. As women we must gain more confidence, speak out more and take more organising initiatives. We must persuade all women to stop taking part in events which reinforce or support aggressive or militaristic government actions. We must back our instincts, and do all that we can to take peace – the only sane option for the world – into practical politics, beginning with the absolute renunciation of nuclear weapons. And perhaps the experience of playing a full part in the peace movement will help women to challenge and change obsolete gender divisions outside the peace movement too.

INTERESTING TIMES
A Chronology of the Nuclear Age

'**May you live in interesting times**' – ancient Chinese curse.

The greater part of the preceding information comes from the reports gathered in Keesing's Contemporary Archives; items from other sources are marked*.

1945
6 August: Hiroshima bombed.
9 August: Nagasaki bombed.
9 August: President Truman's statement:

The atomic bomb is too dangerous to be let loose in a lawless world. That is why Great Britain and the US, who have the secret of its production, do not intend to release the secret until means have been found to control the bomb so as to protect ourselves and the rest of the world from the danger of total destruction.

18 October: Oppenheimer to US Senate: 'Temporarily the advantage is ours, but actually the advent of atomic power has weakened the military position of the USA . . . No countermeasure, and very little secret.'

1946
Acheson-Lilienthal Report (USA) calls for UN Atomic Energy Commission to have genuine power with unconditional American support.
June: Truman's advisor, Bernard Baruch, presents plan including

call for full international inspection (control to precede prohibition).

December: Gromyko: 'An urgent decision on the prohibition of atomic weapons would constitute the first practical step.'

1947

January: Baruch advises Truman that US should continue to manufacture atomic bombs until the ratification of the proposed treaty.

January: Agreement on UK-US airforces cooperation: exchange of officers starting with 30-40 and increasing to not more than 100.

1948

July: 'Two Boeing B-29 (Superfortress) medium bomber groups . . . totalling in all 60 aircraft', coming to UK for 'short period of temporary duty, part of the normal long-range flight training programme instituted over a year ago' by the US Strategic Air Command. About 1500 men involved.

August: Numbers increased (in view of Berlin airlift). In Europe 466 aircraft, 18,000 men, including 6,000 to be based in Britain. USA, UK and Canada agree on common policy on atomic research.

August: UN commission on conventional armaments breaks down after sixteen months of disagreement. Soviet Union and Ukraine vote against breaking it up, and want to extend its considerations to include atomic weapons and destruction of stockpiles.

1949

USSR explodes atomic bomb. Statement in TASS, 25 September (referring to Molotov, November 1947): 'This secret has long ceased to exist'; reiterates: 'The Soviet Government . . . adopts, and intends adopting in the future, its former position in favour of the absolute prohibition of the use of the atomic weapon.'

September: NATO set up.

November: Soviet proposal of five-power pact (USSR, USA, UK, France and China) — rejected.

1950

January: Truman authorises development of hydrogen bomb.

February: (US) Senator McMahon calls for a stop to the atomic armaments race, and Senator Tydings calls on President to initiate an international disarmament conference.

Twelve leading scientists: 'We believe that no nation has the right

to use such a bomb, no matter how righteous its cause.'
June: Invasion of South Korea by North Korean Communist forces. UK supports USA; USSR boycotts Security Council.

1951

US tests: Nevada (5 tests); Eniwetok (Marshall Islands, Pacific) – thermonuclear (hydrogen), March, April and May.

Second Soviet nuclear expolsion.

November: UK, USA and France present disarmament plan to UN General Assembly; proposals rejected by USSR, whose delegate calls them 'spurious, nugatory and trifling'.

October – November: Further US tests in Nevada.

Western disarmament proposals accepted at UN. USSR agrees with three Western powers on establishment of new UN Commission on Disarmament.

October: Gordon Dean (Chairman, US Atomic Energy Commission) says development of tactical atomic weapons has altered previous concepts of atomic warfare, and suggests that 'atomic weapons could be used henceforth, as occasion demanded, in the same manner as other weapons'.

1952

Continued deadlock on cease-fire negotiations in Korea.

October: First British atomic weapon exploded at Monte Bello, NW Australia; acclaimed on account of British independence and scientific prestige.

November: USA tests hydrogen bomb at Eniwetok.

December: Churchill, statement to Parliament on changes in defence programme:

These difficulties are being partially alleviated by the orders we are receiving for defence equipment from our NATO allies, the Commonwealth and other friendly countries. These will not only contribute to the security of the free world but will also help to maintain the war potential of British industry and help the balance of exports.

1953

US tests in Nevada, March and April.

5 March: Malenkov speaks on peaceful coexistence.

20 August: Pravda reports explosion of first Soviet hydrogen bomb.

October: British tests at Woomera range, Australia.

1954

April – May: Parliamentary debates on production of hydrogen bomb; Labour amendment to bring debate and decision-making into the open, and the whole matter under the direct scrutiny of Parliament – defeated (Labour party divided on this issue).

26 April: Malenkov, in speech to Supreme Soviet: speaks on peaceful coexistence between capitalist and communist systems, while warning that strength will be met with strength; fears resurgence of militarism in Germany and Japan, and war in SE Asia; stresses need for European security, based on wartime pacts between USSR, Britain and France; states that 'we have no intention of isolating the United States from Europe', and that USSR is willing to join NATO 'under proper conditions'.

Conclusion of US tests at Bikini Atoll.

14 May: Petition to UN from Marshall Islanders: 'that all experiments with lethal weapons within this area be immediately ceased.' They describe medical effects, removal of populations, loss of lands and livelihood.

Reply, same day, from Mr Cabot Lodge (US representative at UN): 'The US Government were very sorry indeed that some of the inhabitants of the Marshall Islands had apparently suffered ill effects from the recent thermo-nuclear tests.'

15 July: Trusteeship Council adopts resolution asking USA to take adequate precautions to safeguard the security and welfare of the inhabitants ... expresses regret for the damage, notes that compensation has been paid for the damage, and also notes 'with satisfaction' that all those affected have now recovered.

1955

USSR continues to propound theory of peaceful coexistence, offers to disclose data on peaceful uses of atomic energy, offers aid in atomic research to Eastern European countries and to China.

Warsaw Treaty: In March it is announced that proposed agreement on defence between Eastern European states would be put into effect if NATO (Paris) agreements were ratified; in June the Warsaw conference sets up a 20-year mutual defence treaty.

7 May: USSR abrogates treaties with UK (1942) and France (1944) in view of Paris agreements on militarisation of West Germany and setting up of NATO.

August: International conference on peaceful uses of atomic energy.

November: USSR tests hydrogen bomb: 'Cannot discontinue the production and testing of nuclear weapons so long as the US and Britain continue to manufacture such weapons and to test them.' Dulles comments that the US government had for many months been studying the possibility of an agreed suspension of tests, but so far no formula had been found to meet two essential criteria: whether any agreement on the suspension of tests would be dependable; and whether it would be in the best interests of the US and the world.

1956

Exchange of letters between Bulganin and Eisenhower: USSR proposes friendship treaty, wants reduction of armaments to precede 'open skies' policy.

At the United Nations, Rapacki (Polish Foreign Secretary) proposes plan for nuclear-free zone covering Poland, Czechoslovakia, East and West Germany, inspected by joint NATO, Warsaw Pact, and non-aligned powers. Rejected by the Western powers on grounds that it did nothing to reunify Germany or to cover conventional arms.

More Soviet tests in March and April.

July: US B47 bomber crashes at Lakenheath, Suffolk, into building in which three nuclear bombs were stored. Report (not public until 1979, and denied by the US military authorities) states that while a nuclear explosion was unlikely, plutonium could have been released sufficient to have made much of eastern England a desert. The fire was contained.

May, June and July: Series of US tests in Pacific.

August – September: Further series of Soviet tests.

3 – 10 November: Suez crisis.

10 – 24 November: Hungarian insurrection and Soviet invasion.

US provides West Germany with tactical nuclear weapons.

1957

January and March: Soviet tests.

Canada, Japan and Norway propose registration of nuclear tests.

March – June: Series of British tests in Pacific.

1 March: Mass rally in Tokyo demanding suspension of tests by Britain, USSR and US. Japanese letter to Macmillan: 'The wish of the Japanese people for the prohibition of nuclear tests is one of humanity, which transcends all such considerations (of coping with aggression).'

Gromyko places responsibility for tests on Western powers, and Britain describes this as the latest move in the Soviet propaganda campaign.

March—September: London disarmament talks deadlocked.

3 October: Revised Rapacki plan presented at UN General Assembly.

11 October: Report of accident at Windscale, Cumbria (production of plutonium for military use). Enquiry set up: '. . . as Windscale is a defence plant, the committee will not meet in public. For the same reason the report will not be published.'

ICBMs accepted in Western Europe and Turkey.

Russian Sputnik launched.

1958

February—March: Soviet tests.

March: Anti-nuclear demonstrations in German cities.

31 March: USSR unilaterally suspends tests. Eisenhower calls this a gimmick. Report from Denmark that tests have been broken off because of a catastrophic accident whose nature was not defined.

February: CND launched in Britain. First Aldermaston march in April.

*11 March: A-bomb accident in South Carolina.

August—September: British series of tests.

October: US reports successful conclusion of its series of tests; USSR resumes tests.

Quemoy crisis and US build-up of forces in West Pacific.

Revised Rapacki plan proposes phased approach to arms reduction in Central Europe. Rejected by Western powers.

*Serious nuclear disaster at Kyshtym near Sverdlovsk in the Urals — thousands of square miles of wasteland. Reported in US in 1977.

Ministry of Defence statement:

In order to provide insurance against future defence needs, certain of the civil nuclear power reactors now in early construction or design stage are being modified so that the plutonium produced as a by-product is suitable for use, if the need arises, for military purposes. These modifications will not delay the construction of the reactors and will not effect their normal operations as civil power stations. This decision does not affect power stations at Bradwell, Berkeley and Hunterston where construction and installation are already well advanced. Hunterston is so designed as to be suitable for this purpose anyway.

This decision represents a reversal of previous policy, the UK having been the only country in the world with a substantial programme of nuclear power stations operated solely for civil use. Hunterston, Hinckley Point, Dungeness, Sizewell, and Calder Hall and Chapelcross would thus be dual purpose, producing electricity and plutonium.

1–4 Sept: Second UN conference on peaceful uses of atomic energy.

1959
17 January: First European congress for nuclear disarmament, London.

March: Second Aldermaston march.

1 May: U-2 incident – unarmed US reconnaissance plane shot down near Sverdlovsk (having flown from base in Turkey, via Peshawar, and aiming to reach N. Norway). Khrushchev demands apology from Eisenhower and doesn't get one; Paris conference of Heads of State collapses (May 16–17).

Eisenhower:

These activities had no aggressive intent but rather were to assure the safety of the US and the free world against surprise attack . . . These flights were suspended after the recent incident and are not to be resumed.

June: Khrushchev condemns establishment of US bases in Italy and warns against proposed US bases in Greece. Proposes nuclear-free zones in Balkans and Baltic area.

24 June: British Labour Party rejects unilateral disarmament and emphasises need to stay within NATO.

September: Khrushchev visits US, and offers, at UN General Assembly, new proposals for general and complete disarmament. Satellite launchings by USA and USSR.

1959–60
Record-breaking voyages by US nuclear-powered, missile-launching submarines.

Further proposals for establishment of nuclear-free zones offered by China and Ireland.

1960
June: Bucharest conference of Communist leaders. Soviet rift with China who sticks to hard line on inevitability of war so long as

American imperialism exists, and condemns Yugoslav 'revision-
ism'; Khrushchev reaffirms theory of peaceful coexistence.
France plans nuclear striking force.

September: UN General Assembly: Denmark proposes complete
reorganisation of disarmament negotiations, steps on verification
to precede or to go alongside steps on disarmament; appeal from
five neutral nations to USA and USSR.

October: Labour Party controversies on Clause Four (nationalisa-
tion) and unilateral disarmament; victory for unilateralists at
Scarborough conference, (reversed in the following year).

November: Polaris submarines to be based on the Clyde.

1961

April: First manned space flight by Soviet cosmonaut, Yuri
Gagarin.

April: Abortive invasion attempt on Cuba by anti-Castro exiles
(Bay of Pigs).

June: Antarctic Treaty comes into force: the region to be kept free
from any military installation.

Berlin crisis: USSR increases military budget and suspends demobil-
isation; Kennedy increases US arms budget by three thousand
million dollars, and announces expansion of Skybolt, Minuteman
and Polaris programmes. East Germany closes Berlin border and
builds wall. USSR announces decision to resume nuclear tests, thus
breaking moratorium which had obtained since 1958. Geneva disarmament conference adjourns after three years of deadlock.

September: Fifteen Soviet atmospheric tests. US resumes underground tests. In October, Soviet rocket tests in Pacific.

British trade fair in Moscow, followed by Soviet exhibition in
London and visit to London by Gagarin; trade negotiations and
cultural agreement.

October – November: More Soviet tests in Arctic, including (30
October) the biggest ever man-made explosion, fallout affects
USSR, Canada, Alaska, northern US, Iceland, Japan, Britain and
Scandinavia. Denunciations and appeals to stop testing from India,
Ghana, Ethiopia, Yugoslavia, Japan and the Socialist Inter-
national.

Resolution on denuclearisation of African continent adopted at UN.

1962

Manned space flight by US astronaut John Glenn.

USSR claims to have solved problem of intercepting missiles.

March: Proposals for US-USSR cooperation in outer-space research; joint launching of earth satellites in December.

April—July: Series of US tests in Pacific; underground tests in Nevada continue from Sept '61 to July '62.

July: USSR announces more tests.

Cuban missile crisis:

3 September: USSR announces military aid to Cuba.

14 September: US Congress passes bill for mobilisation.

24 October: USA blockades Cuba; Kennedy threatens 'full retaliatory response' upon USSR.

28 October: USSR agrees to dismantle missile bases; US inspection of the process is achieved without difficulty. Blockade is lifted.

New version of Rapacki plan proposed at UN and rejected by Western powers.

1963

June: At Geneva disarmament conference (which latest version had been sitting for sixteen months) agreement between US and USSR for establishing a 'hot line' between Washington and Moscow.

July: Discussions in Moscow on Partial Test Ban Treaty, successfully concluded. USSR, UK, and US agree to ban all tests, except those underground. Treaty contains 'escape clause' giving each party the right to withdraw if it decided that 'extraordinary events . . . had jeopardised the supreme interest of its country,' e.g. if nuclear tests other than underground had been held by any other power, such as France or China.

Treaty ratified in October.

1964

October: China explodes its first atomic bomb.

State of emergency in South Vietnam, increased fighting in months following; US military aid to South Vietnam, USSR protests against US bombing of North Vietnam.

USSR introduces SS 5 ICBM, range 2,300 miles, single warhead.

US continues to develop increasingly sophisticated missiles (Minuteman, range from 5,000 to 6,300 miles; Polaris, range 2,500 miles; Poseidon, the submarine-launched ballistic missile; plans for fleet of 41 Polaris submarines, each to carry 16 missiles, complete by July 1966).

1966

*Stockholm Peace Research Institute founded by Swedish parliament to celebrate 150 years of peace.

March: West Germany puts forward comprehensive proposals for peace and disarmament – welcomed by West, refused by Soviet bloc.

December: Outer Space treaty agreed, after US-Soviet negotiations, started in May '66 and conducted in private; unanimous approval at UN.

1967

January: Secretary of State Macnamara, on defence:

The most demanding test of American 'assured destruction capability' was the ability of the strategic offensive forces to survive a well-coordinated surprise Soviet first strike directed against them. Even if the Soviet Union in the 1972 period were to assign their entire available missile force to attacks on US strategic forces (reserving only refire missiles and bomber-delivered weapons for urban targets), more than one half of the total US forces planned in 1966 for 1972 would still survive and remain effective. After absorbing such an attack, therefore, America could still 'destroy the Soviet Union as a viable twentieth-century society'. The detonation of even one-fifth of the total surviving weapons over Soviet cities would kill about 30 per cent of the Soviet Union's total population – or 73,000,000 people – and destroy about one half of her industrial capacity; doubling the number of warheads delivered would increase fatalities and destruction by considerably less than one-third; and further increments of warheads would not appreciably change the result, as smaller and smaller cities would have to be brought under attack, each requiring one delivered warhead.

Increasing split between China and USSR. Attacks on foreign diplomats in Peking, Soviet Embassy besieged, troops on frontier (estimated 40 Soviet divisions and two million Chinese troops), 'incidents' on Amur river.

Eighteen-nation disarmament committee in Geneva deadlocked on extension of test-ban treaty to cover underground tests, the problem being on-site inspection. Various proposals:

USSR: 'nuclear umbrella' – agreement on retaining visible land-based weapons, to be inspected on launching pads; the reduction of military budgets.

US: freeze on delivery vehicles and destruction of bomber aircraft.

UK: establishment of observation posts.

1968

May: Opening of Paris Conference on Vietnam.

August: Soviet invasion of Czechoslovakia, follows intensive activity in Soviet bloc concerning Premier Dubcek's liberalisation. Condemned by Yugoslavia, Rumania, China, and Italian communist party, as well as by Western powers, and at UN.

At UN Rumania reiterates plan to denuclearise Balkans — rejected by Western powers.

24 August and 8 September: French explode two thermonuclear bombs in Pacific.

September: Canada agrees to sell plutonium to France.

27 December: Chinese test 3-megaton bomb.

Treaty of Tlateloco prohibiting nuclear weapons in Latin America — not signed by Brazil or Argentina.

15th session of Disarmament Conference:

  Soviet proposals: comprehensive eight points and draft treaty on prohibition and use of sea bed for military purposes;

US presents draft treaty on same matter;

  UK proposes convention prohibiting microbiological warfare, and on procedures aimed at overcoming Soviet suspicion of espionage in the matter of on-site verification; Sweden presents draft treaty banning underground tests.

US-Soviet agreements on minor topics (consulates, teleprinter 'hotline', cultural agreements on environmental studies, space cooperation) between 1968 and 1970.

1969

June: International conference of communist parties in Moscow emphasises support for peaceful coexistence, states that the primary contribution of communist parties in the struggle against capitalism lies in economic development, while stressing that this does not involve abandonment of support for revolutionary movements.

20 July: Apollo moon landing by USA.

Strategic Arms Limitation Talks (SALT): President Johnson had in 1967 indicated US desire for talks to start, but then a year's delay because of Soviet invasion of Czechoslovakia. USSR made fresh approach at time of Nixon's inauguration, Jan 1969. Preliminary talks Nov-Dec '69; second round of talks in Vienna, April-Aug 1970.

US Defence Secretary Laird states that ABM strength must be maintained in face of Soviet threat.

5 March: Non-proliferation treaty in force, with 47 signatories; 50 more had signed but by this date had not ratified. It was not signed by France or by China, and others who had not signed included Algeria, Argentina, Brazil, Chile, Cuba, India, Israel, Pakistan, South Africa, Spain and Uruguay.

USSR and West Germany sign treaty on renunciation of use of force.

June: Soviet orbital space flight of 17 days sets new record.

May – August: Eight French tests in Pacific, including one thermonuclear. Vietnam peace talks continue in Paris from November '69 to July '70.

26 – 27 October: 'Preliminary exchange' talks between USA and USSR on space cooperation, both being in this period engaged in successful space probes, lunar landings, plans for sky labs, manned satellites. Craters on the far side of the moon are named to commemorate Soviet and American cosmonauts, distinguished British scientists, and famous scientific figures of the past from many nations.

1971

May – September: Secret peace talks in Paris (resumed April '72).

9 November: USA carries out underground nuclear test at Amchitka, Aleutian Islands. At five megatons this is the biggest ever, with the probable exception of a Soviet test in September '71, reported in the US to be of six megatons. Strong protests against US test, before and after, by Japan and Canada. No earthquakes or tidal waves reported, but the shock registered on seismographs all over the world; 7.1 on Richter scale recorded in Berkeley, California.

Atmospheric tests on various occasions by France and China.

1972

February: President Nixon visits Peking; USA supports entry of Communist China to the United Nations.

March: USA announces defence programme for next five years, stressing modernisation and expansion.

May 8: USA intensifies bombing of North Vietnam and mines the ports; controversy over alleged US bombing of North Vietnamese dykes. Nixon:

Abandoning our commitment in Vietnam here and now would mean turning seventeen million South Vietnamese over to Communist tyranny and terror . . . An American defeat in Vietnam would encourage this kind of aggression all over the world.

22–30 May: Nixon visits Moscow, signs interim treaty on limitation of ABMs (SALT I), and a number of other agreements on cooperation in space research, science and technology, and commerce.

Treaties in force prohibiting use of the sea bed for siting of nuclear weapons, and prohibiting use of biological weapons.

1973

February: Britain's Defence White Paper notes that the political alignments of the post-war world have become less rigid; that the first major agreements between the US and USSR have been reached (SALT I), and that the second phase of the talks are under way and expected to lead to further constraints; that Chancellor Brandt's *Ostpolitik* has enabled ratification of treaties between West Germany and Poland and the USSR, and of the Basic Treaty between East and West Germany; and that exploratory talks have been arranged on Mutual and Balanced Force Reductions. It also states that the USSR shows no sign of anticipating the outcome of negotiations by a slackening of its defence effort. 'Only negotiation from strength was likely to produce equitable agreements with the Soviet Union, and there must therefore be no unilateral reduction of defence capabilities in the West.'

Campaign against dissidents, launched by Soviet authorities in 1972, reaches a climax in August–September '73. Violent press campaign against Andrei Sakharov (founder of Committee for Human Rights) and Alexander Solzhenitsin – suggestions that they might be brought to trial.

June: Brezhnev visits USA. Agreement on basic principles of negotiations on the further limitation of strategic offensive arms. A White House statement on 21 June emphasises that this was a solemn commitment at the highest political level to limit strategic arms permanently, and to complete agreement for this purpose before the end of 1974.

11 September: In Chile, overthrow of President Allende by military coup. Condemnation in many countries. Edward Kennedy:

The US government had given no aid to the freely elected government of President Allende, and had even prevented any initiatives in this direction; it should not hasten to give economic aid to a regime which had seized power in a brutal military coup.

6 October: Yom Kippur war (the fourth between Israel and Arab states since 1948). Nuclear alert, reinforcements from USSR to Egypt and from USA to Israel, both superpowers increase their Mediterranean fleets.

*Brawdy Surveillance Station in southwest Wales is completed (the site of the largest US underwater surveillance centre out of 21 others world-wide).

*1974 Campaign against the Arms Trade (CAAT) founded in Britain – directed mainly towards conventional armaments.

1975

Helsinki: Conference on Security and Cooperation in Europe (Declaration of Human Rights).

March: Convention on prohibition of bacteriological weapons ratified and in force.

May: Nuclear non-proliferation conference – 1968 Treaty ratified by 94 countries.

Starting in April, secret talks in London between USA, Britain, Canada, France, West Germany and the Soviet Union, with an observer from Japan, to discuss safeguards which would prevent a nation from using its nuclear energy industry to produce explosives, or from using technology transferred from civil purposes to build secret plants for the production of weapons. It is thought that the US government, with Canadian consent, was induced to convene this conference as a result of the Indian nuclear explosion, which had been carried out in 1974 on the basis of plutonium 239 obtained from its reactor, using Canadian technology.

1976

Soviet SS20 comes into production.

Secretary of Defense Schlesinger to the US Congress:

We continue to deploy our own theatre nuclear forces in both Europe and Asia. In the case of Europe, we have three basic reasons for our deployments. First, the maintenance of theatre nuclear capabilities in NATO is essential to deterrence as long as the Warsaw Pact deploys theatre nuclear forces of its own. They help to deter the use of nuclear weapons by the Pact and, along with our strategic nuclear and conventional forces, provide a general deterrent across the entire spectrum of possible aggression. Second, should deterrence fail, our theatre nuclear capabilities provide a source of limited and controlled options other than the early use of US and allied strategic forces. Third, in keeping with NATO's flexible response strategy, we do not rule out the use of nuclear weapons by the United States and its allies if that should prove necessary to contain and repel a major conventional attack by the Warsaw Pact.

May: Ninth round of East-West talks on Mutual and Balanced Force Reduction opens in Vienna − these talks began in 1973 and have as yet reached no settlement.

1977

US development of MARV begins.

USSR development of mobile ICBMs (SS-x-16).

April: At the Nuclear Suppliers' Group (15 leading countries who export nuclear technology − includes USA and USSR), US announces intention to limit severely and seek to prevent the spread of nuclear weapons − mentions Israel, South Africa, South Korea, Taiwan, Yugoslavia, Brazil, India, Iran, Spain, Argentine, Egypt, Pakistan and North Korea.

SALT I interim agreement due to expire in October. President Carter says (24 March), 'All previous SALT agreements have been in effect limitations that were so high that they were just ground rules for intensified competition and a continued massive arms growth in nuclear weapons.'

Gromyko (31 March), 'We shall not depart from the principle of equality.'

May: SALT II negotiations resumed in Geneva.

June: US announces cancellation of the B−1 bomber, but intends to proceed with cruise missile and to allocate funds to develop neutron bomb.

November: Review of ABM Treaty − both sides agree that it needs no amendment at this time.

1978

February: Terms of proposed SALT II agreement announced.

April: President Carter announces decision to defer development of neutron bomb.

The ultimate decision on the incorporation of enhanced radiation features into our modernised battlefield would be 'influenced by the degree to which the Soviet Union shows restraint in its conventional and nuclear arms programmes and force deployments affecting the security of the US and Europe.'

May 23−July 1: UN Special Session on Disarmament. Final

document defines goal of nuclear non-proliferation as: 'to prevent the emergence of any additional nuclear weapon states besides the existing five,'
and 'progressively to reduce and eventually eliminate nuclear weapons altogether.'
Britain, France, USA and USSR agree to the creation of a new Committee on Disarmament.

July: Paul Warnke (US negotiator in SALT II process) explains how arms reduction negotiations should be quite separate from any 'linkage' with human rights.

It is essential . . . we remember one main principle: effective and verifiable control over strategic arms is not a reward for Soviet good behaviour. I think you can prove the inherent fallacy of an attempted link . . . if you turn the linkage argument upside down: if all the Soviet personnel were to leave Africa tomorrow, and bring every Cuban with them, if the Soviet leadership were to free all political prisoners and extol the American Bill of Rights, should we then accept Soviet arguments at Geneva for further limits in our forces? No. It is clear that strategic arms control has to stand on its own feet.

December: USA recognises Communist China, opens way for supplying arms to China while reducing US commitment to Taiwan. USSR takes sceptical attitude to President Carter's assurances that American move is not directed against Soviet Union.

1979
May: Lord Mountbatten's Strasbourg speech.

. . . In the event of a nuclear war there will be no chances, there will be no survivors — all will be obliterated . . . I have heard the arguments against this view, but I have never found them convincing. So I repeat in all sincerity as a military man that I can see no use for any nuclear weapons which would not end in escalation, with consequences that no one can conceive . . . As a military man who has given half a century of active service, I say in all sincerity that the nuclear arms race has no military purpose. Wars cannot be fought with nuclear weapons. Their existence only adds to our perils because of the illusions which they have generated.

February—November: Iranian hostage crisis.
October: Brezhnev proposes Soviet troop and tank withdrawal from East Germany (up to 20,000 troops and 1,000 tanks).
June: US go ahead with development of MX mobile missile system.
December: NATO decision to instal new long-range theatre nuclear weapons in Europe.
Soviet invasion of Afghanistan. (Instability in the region largely caused by events in Iran.) 85,000 troops there by January 1980.

USA defers ratification of SALT II Treaty, imposes sanctions and grain embargo, and attempts to organise boycott of Moscow Olympics (due in June 1980).

1980

18 January: General Bastian dismissed from West German army after publicly declaring his opposition to deployment of new nuclear weapons in Western Europe.
Serious industrial unrest in Poland.
In USSR arrests and trials of human rights activists; Sakharov condemned to internal exile.
April: European Nuclear Disarmament appeal launched.
17 June: Greenham Common, Berkshire, and Molesworth, Cambridgeshire named as sites in Britain for cruise missiles.
MFBR (Mutual and Balanced Force Reduction) talks continue in Vienna.
November: CSCE (Conference on Security and Cooperation in Europe) − meeting to review progress since Helsinki (1975) opens in Madrid. War breaks out between Iran and Iraq.
US reinforces its naval presence in Indian Ocean.
In Belgium, political deadlock over defence spending and the siting of Cruise missiles.

1981

Bitter controversy in West Germany over commitment to instal 108 American Pershing II missiles and 464 ground-based Cruise missiles. USA critical of low level of West German defence spending.
Britain decides to buy US Trident missile system to replace Polaris.
30 June: Brezhnev says USSR would be prepared to suspend the deployment of new medium-range missiles in the European part of its territory on the day when arms limitation talks opened, provided the US notified the Soviet Union of a reciprocal intention. (He had till now insisted on an actual US/Soviet agreement to stop new deployments during negotiations.)
October: New government in Greece led by socialist Papandreou aims at setting out a 'firm timetable' early in 1982 for the withdrawal of US forces from Greece, and at creating nuclear-free 'zone of peace' in Balkans − it would be the first state to implement withdrawal of nuclear weapons from its territory (previous

Greek governments had refused to confirm that nuclear weapons were stationed there).

November: Coalition government in the Netherlands issue statement postponing final decision on siting of nuclear armaments (including 43 Cruise missiles), because no substantial arms limitation talks had so far taken place.

Second phase of Madrid Conference on Security and Cooperation in Europe devoted to discussion of new proposals for more effective confidence-building measures, and for a European Disarmament Conference.

*10,000 nuclear warheads estimated to be present for use in Europe (SIPRI Yearbook 1981).

Notes

In the decades preceding the Second World War, research in pure physics concerned with the structure of the atom had made dramatic progress, notably in Germany, France and Britain. The neutron was discovered in 1932. The end of the 1930s saw migration of some key scientists from Europe, among them Teller and Fermi to the United States, and Frisch and Peierls to Britain.

In 1939 Einstein wrote to Roosevelt, urging that the United States devote attention to the production of the atom bomb.

After that date, work proceeded with each side in ignorance of what the other was doing. Germany had the capability to produce the bomb, with sufficient uranium from Czechoslovakia, and scientists of proven expertise, but not (as emerged eventually) the correct calculations: in England, Frisch and Peierls found that a very significantly smaller amount of uranium was required than had been anticipated. This was what made all the difference.

The 'Manhattan Project', to produce an atom bomb, was initiated in the United States in 1942. US policy from the start was that the involvement of foreigners should be kept to the minimum: US suspicion of Britain and of Churchill persisted throughout, and indeed after the end of the war, British and American atomic research continued for several years quite independently (cf. Margaret Gowing). It is no surprise that there was little, if any, notion given to ideas of cooperation on research matters with the Russians.

After the defeat of Germany in May 1945, the Manhattan Project scientists were ready to test an atom bomb, and did so in Alamogordo, New Mexico on 16 July. Some of them at that point wanted the Japanese to be invited to see the test, in the hope that that would lead them to sue for peace. But this notion was overruled.

The Allies agreed to divide the remaining task, with the Russians clearing the Asian mainland, and the United States the Pacific and Japan itself. This was expected (bearing in mind the past record) to involve heavy American losses, and this is the official explanation of the decision to drop the atom bomb. Churchill was unequivocally in favour of this military decision. Argument continues to this day as to the reasoning behind the bombing of Hiroshima and Nagasaki. The Russians had entrained eighty divisions to the East; for President Truman it was a priority that they should not gain a foothold on the Japanese mainland.

*   *   *

In a memorandum written during the early period of their collaboration, Frisch and Peierls described the potentiality for making a super-bomb. They also made clear the moral issues, and stressed the unsuitability of such a weapon on account of the great numbers of civilians who would die from the effects of radiation. Shelter would be impossible, they said.

Oppenheimer, who led the Manhattan Project until 1945, and who after that date remained a central figure in American atomic research, moved right away from his hawkish wartime stance, and refused to support American development of a hydrogen bomb; the story of his hounding during the febrile years of the McCarthy era, and his subsequent trial and downfall, is well known.

There is a dark side to the neutron, leading to the bomb and nuclear weapons. There is a neutral side, that associated with neutron beams and pure science aspects; and there is a positive side, in application of the neutron to power generation, isotope production, and medical treatment.
Royal Society's programme describing scientific exhibits,
London, June 1982

The threat of the nuclear weapon has been used a number of times since 1945, with the intention of ending a crisis and of bringing an enemy to the conference table. American presidents have made such threats publicly on three occasions: Truman in 1950 (Korea); Kennedy in 1961 (Berlin crisis), and in 1962 (Cuban missile crisis).

According to Daniel Ellsberg, in an interview in 1980 (*Conservation Press*, Berkeley, California; see for detailed references), secret threats have been made by Truman in 1946; by Eisenhower in 1953 (Korea), in 1954 (when he offered nuclear weapons to the French in Indochina), and twice in 1958 (when he ordered secret preparations in response to crises in Iraq/Kuwait, and in Quemoy/Taiwan Straits); when Kennedy's chiefs of staff recommended use of nuclear weapons in Laos in 1961; repeatedly, during the Vietnam war, by Johnson in 1968, and by Nixon, 1969–72.

However, in his memoirs, President Nixon explains why he decided against using tactical nuclear weapons in Vietnam:

The domestic and international uproar that would have accompanied the use of either of these knock-out blows (the other was the bombing of the North Vietnamese dykes) would have got my administration off to the worst possible start.

(cf. *Defended to Death*, Chapter 10, Penguin, 1983)

Ellsberg further suggests that the Russians must have used the nuclear threat against Third World countries and against countries in Eastern Europe; the closed and secretive nature of the Eastern bloc makes it unlikely that information on this will become available.

*   *   *

On nuclear or near-nuclear accidents, information comes only sporadically. In 1980, the Pentagon admitted to twenty-seven accidents besides those listed as follows:

(Reported American accidents in the military context)

1956 (July) Lakenheath, Suffolk (see above);

1958 (March) B-57 drops atomic bomb over South Carolina – conventional, non-nuclear explosion (not all the triggers worked);

1960 fire at McGuire airforce base – radioactive leakage;

1961 Palomares, Spain – us bomber with four nuclear bombs crashes;

1968 (January) B–52 with four nuclear bombs crashes in Thule, Greenland;

1980 fire aboard B–52 carrying 30 nuclear weapons, at Grand Forks, North Dakota.

*   *   *

Since 1945 statesmen of both superpowers have relentlessly proclaimed their devotion to peace, and have equally relentlessly devoted more and more of their countries' resources to the production of bigger and better weapons.

Throughout this period, there has been an almost continual series of disarmament conferences, whose practical effect has been minimal while engendering at the same time a comfortable feeling that something serious and genuine was being done. Modest, limited peace initiatives (such as those put forward by Poland, to denuclearise one area at a time) have not been taken up; treaties such as the one on Non-Proliferation have been neutralised by non-signatory nations and their acquistion of ostensibly peaceful nuclear capability; as soon as a SALT treaty is signed, the search is on for 'Salt Free' weaponry.

The widespread understanding is that nuclear weapons are safely stored in deep and distant places, with, at the very most, one man's finger on the trigger − instead there is an ever-proliferating industry, with continual up-grading, development, replacement, and movement from place to place − and very many fingers.

At the time of the United Nations General Assembly's first session on disarmament in 1978, there was a general consensus on the goals of arms control; even this has by now disappeared. The second special session, in June 1982, has been a failure. Summing up, its president, Mr Ismat Kittani, of Iraq, said, 'We cannot be proud of our achievements here. They were too few, and too insubstantial. The hopes of countless millions of people have remained unfulfilled because of the sad state of the world in which we live.'

[I am indebted to two intrepid consciousness-raisers, Professor Christopher Cornford and Dr Gwyn Prins.]

GLOSSARY

ABM – anti-ballistic missile: a defensive interceptor missile for use against ICBMs (see below). The AMB treaty was one of the documents produced by the SALT discussions (see below) by which defensive AMBs were limited by agreement between the superpowers. The USSR is said to have 64 of their own ABMs (known as Galosh) stationed around Moscow.

airburst: a nuclear bomb exploded in the air as opposed to on the ground or underground.

atom bomb: popular name for a fission bomb: a nuclear weapon that produces an explosion by the uncontrolled fission of uranium or plutonium.

ballistic missiles: *see* ICBM. The initials BM often refer to ballistic missiles, as in ICBM (below), ABM – anti-ballistic missile, BMD – ballistic missile defences, etc. The most common use is in ICBM.

battlefield nuclear weapons: weapons with a range of less than 150 km.

beta particle: a type of radiation: the particle emitted in beta decay – either an electron ($\beta-$) or a positron ($\beta+$) can cause skin burns and, when ingested, cancer.

bilateral talks: talks or negotiations between two powers only. Usually nowadays means between the two superpowers, the USA and the USSR (as opposed to multilateral − involving many nations or interests).

biological warfare: the use of living organisms and chemicals which act on or spread disease amongst populations or growing plants.

Britain's independent deterrent: an expression used to describe Britain's nuclear weapons.

cesium 137: a biologically hazardous beta-emitting fission product. It has a half-life of 30 years and concentrates in muscle tissue.

chemical and biological warfare: non-nuclear methods of war of which a great number have been considered which involve the use of highly poisonous chemicals as weapons of destruction. Biological warfare can include anti-foliants which destroy growing plants, microbes or other disease-bearing organisms, used to spread disease amongst the populations under attack.

conventional weapons: in general, non-nuclear weapons, but usually excludes chemical and biological weapons as well. Perhaps should be taken to mean the type of weapons which have already been used in the two world wars.

counterforce: a nuclear strategy whereby attack missiles are targeted against the opponent's military emplacements. Embodied in PD 59 (see below).

Cruise missile: sometimes shortened to CM − as in ALCM − air-launched Cruise missile, GLCM − ground-launched or SLCM − submarine-launched missile whose flight is controlled from launch to impact. Cruise missiles have wings and fins and are best envisaged as small pilotless aircraft.
The Tomahawk (the US Navy's sea-launched CM) can travel 1,500 miles and has a 200 kiloton warhead. Guidance is provided by radar in the missile. Its ability to hug the ground makes it difficult to detect.

detente: French world meaning relaxation. Often used to describe the policies of those US statesmen who favoured some negotiations with USSR and the easing of tensions between the superpowers.

deterrence: the threat of immediate retaliation in the case of aggression or other hostile act. It is the concept which has replaced that of military defence in the vocabulary of most politicians when discussing nuclear strategy.

EMP – electromagnetic pulse: an effect produced by the explosion of nuclear weapons in the atmosphere. This is a calculated effect, since it has never been possible to test it, but many scientists believe that the effect of such explosions over cities would be to interfere with or destroy a whole range of electric and electronic communication systems – radio, telephone etc.

enrichment plant: a factory or plant in which enriched uranium is produced.

first strike: this literally means what it says – simply the first attack by either side. As a tactic, however, it is based on the latest developments of super-accurate nuclear missiles. The doctrine of MAD (see below) was based on a concept of massive retaliation: if either power sent off a single missile the other would retaliate with large-scale bombardment of cities. The doctrine of the first strike, however, is based on the possibility of one side sending across such accurate and massive missiles that they could destroy the enemy's ability to retaliate by destroying his weapons in their silos, making a retaliatory strike impossible. This doctrine can be assumed to make the possibility of a nuclear war greater for several reasons. Firstly, the original MAD situation included a strong disincentive to any first strike. Some people saw the main danger of the MAD situation as an exchange resulting from an accident or computer fault, since the certainty of massive retaliation would deter any rational command from beginning an exchange. The first-strike doctrine, however, would give victory to the side which launched enough weapons to knock out all or most of the enemy's weapons before they were launched. In a situation of crisis, the temptation to gain this advantage could be considerable. Secondly, it makes more credible the idea of a 'limited' nuclear war – since accurate missiles, even if they did not succeed in destroying all the enemy's retaliatory potential, could be expected to reduce it so significantly that the side which struck first could hope to limit the weapons used in number and in range. It also of course removes the main incentive for delay and negotiation, since speed of attack becomes crucial.

gamma ray: a high-energy, short wavelength electromagnetic radiation emitted by a nucleus during gamma decay.

Greenham Common Peace Camp: the first women's peace camp established in Britain in 1981 to protest against the proposed siting of Cruise missiles at Greenham Common in 1983.

ground zero: the point directly below the centre of a nuclear explosion.

Hard Rock: code name for a nationwide Civil Defence exercise planned by the Home Office for summer 1982, but cancelled because of lack of cooperation by local authorities.

hydrogen bomb: the popular name for a thermonuclear bomb. It produces its destructive power largely from atomic fusion.

IAEA – International Atomic Energy Authority: a UN-sponsored body, based in Vienna, set up in 1957 in order to promote the peaceful uses of atomic energy, to control safety and proliferation of nuclear materials throughout the world.

ICBM – intercontinental range ballistic missile: a land-based missile capable of reaching the USA from the USSR or vice versa (range 2,500 miles upwards).
'Ballistic' means that once its fuel is exhausted the missile's trajectory is determined by the speed and direction at the moment the rocket motor cuts out.

intermediate nuclear weapons: includes weapons with ranges below 5,500 km down to 150 km.

ionisation: the process of adding or removing electrons so as to form ions. Ionization can be caused by high temperatures, electrical discharges, or nuclear radiation.

ionising radiation: radiation which removes circumnuclear electrons from atoms, e.g., alpha, beta and gamma radiation and x-rays.

irradiation: exposure to radiation, e.g. to neutrons in the core of the nucleus.

isotope: atoms of the same element having different atomic weights owing to differences in the number of neutrons in their nuclei. A radioactive variant of a common element with a different atomic weight but similar characteristics. Isotopes are created by the fission process. Also known as (radio)nuclides.

kiloton: a measure of destructive capacity equivalent to 1,000 tons of TNT. The Hiroshima atom bomb was a 12 kiloton weapon equal to 12,000 tons of TNT.

Lance system: surface to surface artillery missile which can deliver a conventional or nuclear warhead up to 75 miles at 1,900 mph. It can be filled with a neutron warhead.

Laser: a highly concentrated beam of light. Acronym of *light amplification by stimulated emission of radiation*. Work is in process in both the USA and the USSR to harness the properties of laser beams for the destruction of aircraft and of ballistic missiles in flight.

LOW — launch on warning: *see* Pershing II.

Lucas Aerospace: leading British arms firm whose shop stewards took the lead in investigating programmes for conversion to peaceful uses of technology.

MAD — mutually assured destruction: an aspect of the policy of 'deterrence'.

MARV — manoeuvreable alternatively targetable re-entry vehicle: like MIRV but each warhead can alter course and change targets in order to evade anti-ballistic missiles.

megaton: the energy of a nuclear explosion that is equal to one million tons of TNT (or 1,000 kilotons).

MIRV — multiple independently targetable re-entry vehicle: like MRV but each warhead can be separated from the re-entry vehicle independently so that it can be aimed at a different target. Thus one missile can destroy several targets.

MRV — multiple re-entry vehicle: the final stage of a missile carrying more than one warhead, the cluster of warheads 'spraying out' over the target.

multilateralist: a supporter of disarmament by negotiation between all armed powers. Often used to mean some one who mistrusts unilateral action. Thus all unilateralists are also multilateralist but not all multilateralists are also unilateralist.

MX — missile experimental: a type of ICBM which it was planned would be deployed by 1985–6 in the US. 200 of the MX missiles were to be deployed, one possible system involving a mobile transporter and 23 launch sites for each missile. A Soviet first strike would necessitate destroying all 23 shelters to be sure of hitting the missile. The system is under scrutiny and may not go ahead.

NASA – (US) **National Aeronautics and Space Administration**: the body directing US space research.

NATO – **North Atlantic Treaty Organisation**: the main military alliance of the West formed in 1949.

neutron bomb: a type of nuclear weapon that produces a comparatively low explosive yield but emits a very high number of potentially lethal neutrons. Although usually referred to as a bomb, this kind of explosive may also be used in shells and other battlefield weapons.

non-aligned: not bound by permanent treaty obligations to either of the two main superpowers. Countries like Yugoslavia and India prefer to remain non-aligned, and to take up positions on international questions as they arise.

NPT – **non-proliferation treaty**: an international treaty, endorsed by the UN in 1968, designed to prevent the spread of nuclear weapons and technology. Signed in March 1970 by 42 nations.

nuclear proliferation: the increasing acquisition of nuclear weapons and energy sources by states throughout the world, whether by their own development, by purchase, gift, or by illicit means.

nuclear reactor: a plant in which a neutron-induced fission chain reaction can be maintained under close control.

Pershing II: one of the new US weapons which it is intended to station in West Germany in the near future. The particular feature of this intermediate-range weapon is its speed and accuracy. It is said to be able to reach Moscow from West Germany in 6 minutes. The greatest danger of such weapons is that they bring nearer the situation known as launch on warning (LOW) which involves computer-activated launch systems. No one today needs to be warned of the dangers of computer faults, and it should perhaps be pointed out that the Soviet Union is behind the US in the development of computers, a fact which massively increases the dangers of LOW.

PD 59: **Presidential Directive 59** – issued by President Carter in 1979 – first leaked to the press in August 1980. The first official recognition of a change in US nuclear weapons policy from the strategy of MAD — the targeting of massive ICBMs on Soviet cities — to the strategy of 'Counterforce', i.e. the targeting of nuclear weapons on Soviet missile silos and other military targets.

plutonium 239: a heavy, highly toxic, radioactive metallic element, man-made, used as breeder reactor fuel and for atomic weapons. Highly carcinogenic.

Polaris: the United States' first nuclear-powered ballistic missile submarine, also the first US submarine-launched ballistic missile which has a maximum speed of 6,600 mph, with a range of 2,875 miles. It has a shorter range than an ICBM and is intended for launch close to the enemy coast. A Polaris submarine carries 16 missiles, and in 1980 the US had 10 Polaris submarines in service.

Poseidon: is slightly larger than Polaris, with a similar range but more accurate. The Poseidon can carry between 14 re-entry vehicles, the normal system carrying 10. Like the Polaris, the name is used for the submarine itself and for the missiles. The Poseidon was developed from the Polaris, and was seen as its successor.

precision-guided munitions (PGM): electronics-based weapons which find their targets by a variety of built-in means, as opposed to old-fashioned targetting. They have the advantage that they can be operated at great distances and by comparatively unskilled personel. Although they have been to some extent deployed in recent conflicts in the Middle East and the South Altantic, they are still largely an unknown factor, with regard to actual performance.

pre-emptive first strikes: a nuclear first strike launched on the presumption that the other side is about to attack. The target of this strike is supposed to be the enemies' silos and weapons rather than cities or military bases. It is a strategy which depends on nuclear missiles which can be targetted with great accuracy.

Rad: a measure of exposure to radiation; the absorbed dose.

radiation: the emission of neutrons, alpha particles, beta or gamma rays from a radioactive source.

radioactivity: the spontaneous decay of an unstable atomic nucleus accompanied by the emission of ionizing radiation.

R & D — research and development: the preliminary

investigation and testing, including the building of prototypes, before manufacture can be started.

Rapacki plan: a proposal for the establishment of demilitarised zone in Central Europe put forward in 1956, 1957 and 1968 by the Polish government.

ss 20 – the Soviet medium-range nuclear weapon that is targetted on Europe: nearly all Soviet nuclear weapons are known in the West by code names beginning with SS, since information about them comes from Western intelligence sources rather than from official Soviet publications. Weapons which are submarine-launched are given the cole SS–N followed by a number. For a quick run-down on the significance of other SS designations see Robert C. Aldridge, *The Counterforce Syndrome* (Institute of Policy Studies, 1978–81).

SALT – Strategic Arms Limitation Talks – (Treaty.): talks between the USA and the USSR on potential limitation of major weapons and defence systems. SALT 1 signed 1972, SALT II never ratified by US. These agreements did not lessen the number of weapons, but proposed a limit on the number of new ones to be installed. (President Reagan proposed acronym S*T*A*R*T for his talks with USSR, suggesting they represent Arms Reduction rather than simply limitation. Nothing has yet emerged to suggest that they will.)

Schlesinger Doctrine: doctrine proposed by US Secretary Schlesinger in the 1970s of the possibility of fighting and winning a 'limited' nuclear war.

second strike: a response to a first (nuclear) strike. May be aimed at either nuclear installations or at more generalised targets in retaliation for a nuclear first strike.

Sputnik: Russian word for spacecraft. Sputnik 1 was the first satellite to be put in orbit.

Square Leg: code name for a Civil Defence exercise held in autumn 1980.

strategic nuclear weapon: weapon with a range of 5,500 km or more (the shortest distance between the USA and USSR). *Strategic* indicates to do with strategy, the planning and directing of large-scale military operations, as opposed to tactical, which means operating on a lower and more localised level of decision-making. Thus nuclear operations within Europe, for example, are seen by the US as 'tactical' or concerned with one theatre of operations only, hence 'theatre' weapons.

strontium 90: a biologically hazardous beta-emitter, which can cause bone cancer.

tactical nuclear weapon: a relatively small nuclear weapon ranging from less than a kiloton to over 50 kilotons and of range below that of strategic weapons, intended for battlefield, anti-ship and similar uses.

take out: military jargon for 'destroy'.

theatre nuclear weapons: medium-range nuclear weapons which, in theory, might be utilised in a continental rather than global conflict.

TNT – trinitrotoluene, (or toluol): powerful non-nuclear explosive, which forms the basis of most conventional forms of bombardment.

Trident submarine: Britain's modernised independent weapons system, proposed for introduction in the 1990s. By then the Chevaline programme which is the modernisation of Poseidon, will have been in operation for some eight years. The Trident is a totally new system, using missiles manufactured and serviced in the US, mounted on submarines at present proposed to be built under contract in British shipyards. The system represents a massive expansion of the existing system both in the number of warheads, manoeuverability and reach of targets. Also, it goes without saying, in cost of installation and maintenance. The Labour Party is on record as guaranteeing to cancel the programme when it is returned to power.

unilateral disarmament: a voluntary decision to reduce arms taken by one nation. It may be related to negotiations with other powers, or be an independent gesture of renunciation of a particular weapon – particularly a nuclear weapon.

ultra-violet ray: a ray lying beyond the end of the visible colour spectrum. An important part of the sun's light, this ray can be harmful, but is at present filtered through the ozone layer of the upper atmosphere.

UN Special Sessions: meetings of the whole of the UN especially convened to discuss world disarmament. First, in 1978, proposed restriction of atomic weapons to existing 'nuclear' states, and a programme for the progressive reduction and eventual abolition of all nuclear weapons. Second, in 1981, ended with very few specific proposals.

uranium 235: the main current source of nuclear reactor fuel.

Warsaw Pact – Warsaw Treaty Organisation (WTO): the main military alliance of Eastern and Central Europe under Soviet leadership.

x-ray: a penetrating form of electromagnetic radiation emitted when a metal target is bombarded with high-speed electrons. X-rays can cause cancer and are an over-used and abused medical practice.

Yalta Agreement: Agreement signed by Churchill, Roosevelt and Stalin in 1945 by which Europe was divided into 'Eastern' and 'Western' spheres of influence. The terms of the agreement were open to more than one interpretation (for example, it was agreed that there should be free elections in Eastern Europe at the earliest possible time), but over the years it has been taken to have established the division of Europe into exclusive spheres of influence for the two superpowers.

NOTES ON SOURCES AND CHAPTER NOTES

BOOKS, NOTES AND SOURCES

We have not used footnotes in this book, partly because they slow up reading for a lot of people, and partly because we are not discussing scarce or even debatable material. All the information in the various chapters has been obtained from easily accessible sources. Where possible we have indicated these in the text, and in some cases additional notes to chapters will be found below.

Our main source of information, like that of any citizen, is the communication media – daily, weekly and monthly press and the radio and television news. There are also specialist journals for the study of peace and disarmament, some of which are listed below. Most big libraries subscribe to these journals, and to *Hansard* – the regular report of all debates in the Houses of Parliament. The handy *Weekly Hansard* is the best place to find out what government spokesmen and women, as well as your local MP are saying. As far as daily newspapers and weeklies go, news on these crucial questions tends to get left out of most of the popular ones, and it is to *The Times* and the *Guardian* among the dailies, and the *New Statesman* and *Tribune* among the non-specialist weeklies, that you have to go for more regular information. The *Guardian*, in particular, gives regular coverage to issues of nuclear war and disarmament on its woman's page as well as its news and feature pages.

There are now several first-rate journals containing news of the peace movement and information about activities. The Campaign for Nuclear Disarmament (CND) (11, Goodwin Street, London N4) publishes *Sanity* and also handles, through its bookshop, a great variety of publications, journals, books and pamphlets. European Nuclear Disarmament (END) (227, Seven Sisters Road, London N4) publishes a *Journal* containing news, discussion and information mainly from Europe and concerned with the campaign for a nuclear-free Europe. *Peace News*, published fortnightly, presents the pacifist case, but also a great deal more in the way of information and discussion about all aspects of peace and disarmament. There are in addition a number of excellent local newsletters and journals being produced in all parts of the country. Official publications as well as *Hansard* may be obtained from HM Stationery Office, through your local stationer, and are usually to be seen in your local library. The Circulars on Civil Defence mentioned in Suzanne Wood's article can be obtained by writing to the Home Office for copies (ES Memoranda, 1973 – 81).

Information about weaponry and tactics and about plans and decisions by governments is continually being updated. There are several specialist institutions whose work is to keep in touch with these questions and to report on them. These include the semi-official Institute for Strategic Studies (23, Tavistock Street, London WC2) which publishes a bi-monthly journal, *Survival*, as well as annual reports, including one called *Military Balance* which presents the most up-to-date assessment of the strength of various countries. Although the Institute is NATO-oriented, its publications are scholarly and extremely useful. The Stockholm International Peace Research Institute (SIPRI, Bersrama S-17173, Solna, Sweden) produces an annual yearbook which is the most useful source of information about weaponry and strategic policies. The current yearbook (1982) is especially valuable. All libraries should be persuaded to subscribe to it. In addition, the Armaments and Disarmament Information Unit (Mantell Building, University of Sussex, Falmer, Brighton) provides information through its bi-monthly *Report*. This is particularly valuable as a running bibliography of books, papers and articles published in this wide and expanding field.

In spite of the low level of 'mass media' coverage of the disarmament movement, there is a growing library of first-rate material available in books and articles. By the time this list is published, no doubt it will already be out of date, so what follows is a very short list of especially recommended books currently in print. Most of them have lists of further reading in them.

Several chapters in this book have been influenced by the remarkable study of the objective possibilities of nuclear damage in the event of a war by Jonathan Schell, first published in the *New Yorker*, and published in 1982 as a book, *The Fate of the Earth* (Picador, 1982).

For a good, readable outline of the whole case against nuclear weapons, and an account of attempts to control them, Paul Rogers, Malcom Dando and Peter van den Dungen's *As Lambs to the Slaughter* (Arrow Books, 1981) is excellent, and Richard Wilson's savage and brilliant drawings should be especially mentioned. Robert Neild *How to Make up your Mind about the Bomb* (Andre Deutsch, 1981) is a clearly argued presentation of the case for and against nuclear weapons by a notable Cambridge academic which will leave little doubt in anyone's mind. And Dan Smith and E. P. Thompson's collection, *Protest and Survive* (Penguin Special, 1981) which includes the seminal pamphlet of the same name as well as a number of other articles, is by no means out of date. Another Penguin, *Defended to Death*, produced by the Cambridge Disarmament Seminar, edited by Gwyn Prins, will be published early in 1983. Important books on the subject by women writers include Alva Myrdal's *Game of Disarmament* (Manchester University Press, 1977) the basic text for an understanding of the problems of disarmament negotiations, and Mary Kaldor's *The Baroque Arsenal* (André Deutsch, 1981) which looks at the effect of the massive diversion of resources and the irrationality of the nuclear arms programmes.

ADDITIONAL NOTES TO CHAPTERS

Chapter 2: How I Learnt to Start Worrying and Hate the Bomb

Helen Caldicott, *Nuclear Madness* (Bantam, 1978)

Radical Statistics Nuclear Disarmament Group, *The Nuclear Numbers Game* (1982) 9, Poland St WIV 3 DG

Anthony Tucker and John Gleisner, *Crucible of Despair: the Effects of Nuclear War* (Menard Press, 1981)

Robert Jungk, *Brighter than a Thousand Suns* (Penguin, 1982)

The Medical Consequences of Nuclear Weapons — issued in 1982 by the Medical Campaign against Nuclear Weapons (MCANW), 7 Tenison Road, Cambridge CBI 2DG

Chapter 3: The Balance of Terror

E. P. Thompson, *Beyond the Cold War* (Merlin Press, 1982)

Ken Coates, *European Nuclear Disarmament* (Spokesman Press, 1981)

(eds) Frank Barnaby and Geoffrey Thomas, *The Nuclear Arms Race – Control or Catastrophe?* (contributions by Barnaby, David Owen, E. P. Thompson, John Erickson, Nicholas Sims) (Frances Pinter, 1982)

Solly Zuckerman, *Nuclear Illusion and Reality* (Collins, 1982)

Weekly Hansard, 3 March 1981; 16 March 1982 debates.

Chapter 4: The Illusion of Protection

'Civil Defence or Internal Defence', in *State Research Bulletin*, vol. 2, no. 8 (October-November 1978)

Phil Bolsover, *Civil Defence, the Cruellest Confidence Trick* (CND, 1981)

Martin Spence, *Civil Defence and Nuclear War in the North East* (Days of Hope Bookshop, 1982)

Michael Pentz, *A Provisional Brief on Civil Defence* (Scientists Against Nuclear Arms, 1982)

Chapter 5: Defend Us Against Our Defenders

Rights (Journal of the National Council for Civil Liberties), *passim*

Robert Jungk, *The Nuclear State* (John Calder, 1979)

(ed) Gari Donn, *Missiles, Reactors and Civil Liberties* (Glasgow Council for Civil Liberties, 1981)

E. P. Thompson, *Writing by Candlelight* (Merlin Press, 1982)

Chapter 7: Fuel for the Nuclear Arms Race

Robin Cook, *No Nukes* (Fabian Tract 475, July 1981)

S. Croall and K. Sempler, *Nuclear Power for Beginners* (Writers and Readers, 1978)

Robert Jungk, *The Nuclear State* (John Calder, 1979)

W. Patterson, *Nuclear Power*, (Penguin, 1980)

S. Lovins, *Soft Energy Paths* (Penguin, 1977)

Nigel Calder, *Nuclear Nightmares* (BBC Publications, 1979)

p 67, line 33 Estimates of the cost of dismantling a reactor vary from the £20 million put aside by the Central Electricity Generating Board to cover the decommission costs, to the £½ million put aside by the Scottish Electricity Board.

p 69, line 3 The first reactor to be built for domestic use was in fact at Obninsk in the USSR in 1954. The Cold War resulted in the Western powers' consensus focussing on Calder Hall as the 'first nuclear power station'. This claim is only defensible if size is the criterion, since Calder Hall was much larger than the Soviet plant.

A. Kramish and E. Zuckart, *Atomic Energy for Your Business: Today's Key to Tomorrow's Profits*, (David McKay, New York, 1956)

Warren H. Donnelly, *Commercial Nuclear Power in Europe: the Interaction of American Diplomacy with a New Technology.* Science Policy Research Division, Congressional Research Service, 1972.

K. Kehoe, 'Report to Environmental Policy Center. The US Nuclear Industry' (quoted in Anne Gorgynyetal, *No Nukes*, Southend Press, 1979)

Maria Korchmar, 'Carter, Congress cave in on Indian Exports', *Critical Mass Journal*, July 1978.

Chapter 8: Letter to My Neighbour

'Square Leg' map on p. 90 is from Bob Fromer's teaching pack 'Nuclear Weapons' (Mary Glasgow Publications, 1982)

The maps on pp. 98 and 99 and much of the detailed information in the chapter is from *Ambio* (Magazine of the Royal Swedish Academy of Sciences) vol. XI, no. 2–3, (1982), articles by G. M. Woodwell, Paul Crutzen and John Birks, Yves Laulan, Frank Barnaby and Joseph Rotblat, Lindop and Coggle, Hugh Middleton.

Anthony Tucker and John Gleisner, *Crucible of Despair* (Menard Press, 1981)

Jonathan Schell, *The Fate of the Earth* (Picador, 1982)

Undercurrents, no. 54

Norman Landsell *The Atom and the Energy Revolution* (Philosophical Library, New York)

Jim Garrison, *From Hiroshima to Harrisburg, SCM Press Ltd, 1980.*

Chapter 9: Take the Toys from the Boys

Margaret Gowing, *Independence and Deterrence: Britain and Atomic Energy 1945–1952* (Macmillan, 1974)

Peter Pringle and James Spigelman, *The Nuclear Barons* (Michael Joseph, 1980)

The Times, 4 May, 1960

Daniel Ellsberg, 'Putting out the Light', *Peace News*, 28 Nov, 1980

Laurence H. Shoup and William Minter, 'Shaping a New World Order' in *Trilateralism: The Trilateral Commission and Elite Planning for World Management*, edited by Holly Sklar (South End Press, 1980)

David A. Rosenberg, 'American Atomic Strategy and the Hydrogen Bomb Decision', *Journal of American History*, June 1979

(ed) Holly Sklar, *The Trilateral Commission* (Southend Press, 1980)

A. Cockburn, J. Ridgeway and A. Cockburn, *END Bulletin*, Spring 1982 Interview with Robert McNamara by Robert Scheer, *Guardian*, 9 August, 1982

A. Cockburn and A. Cockburn, 'The Myth of Missile Accuracy', *New York Review of Books*, 20 November, 1980

Robert F. Coultram, 'Inter-service Weapons Rivalry', *Bulletin of the Atomic Scientists*, June 1977

(ed) Rita Arditti, Pat Brennan and Steve Cavrak, *Science and Liberation*, (Southend Press 1980)

McGeorge Bundy, 'The Missed Chance to Stop the H-Bomb', *New York Review of Books*, 13 May, 1982

Charles Schwartz, 'The Corporate Connection', *Bulletin of the Atomic Scientists*, October 1975, p. 16.

Harold Jackson, 'New Doubts About Faulty Cruise', *Guardian*, May 11, 1982

Chapter 10: Alternative Defence

Each title gives further documentation.

Gene Sharp, *The Politics of Nonviolent Action*, (Porter Sargent, Boston, 1973)

Peace Pledge Union: *Studies on Nonviolence* (series, obtainable from Housmans Bookshop, 5 Caledonian Road, London N1)

International Seminars on Training for Nonviolent Action (ISTNA), *Alternatives to the use of arms*, 1982

Michael Randle – *Training for Direct Action: Bibliography on Training for Nonviolent Action* (ISTNA, Box 515, Waltham, MA 02254, USA)

Chapter 16: Contemplating a Nuclear Future

Jonathan Schell, *The Fate of the Earth* (Picador, 1982)

R. Lifton and K. Erikson, 'Nuclear War's Effect on the Mind', *New York Times*, 15 March, 1982 *p 142, line 27* The catalyst for this 'conversion' was reading E. P. Thompson's pamphlet, *Protest and Survive*, a document that has had historic import in the resurgence of the peace movement in Britain.

p 146, line 17 It is true that some individuals (e.g. complete hermits) deny themselves such resources. Others may 'perversely' want to 'take everyone else with them' when they go. But the point is that these cases are exceptional and arguably therefore to be understood as pathological.

p 146, line 33 Perhaps it will be said that there will be consolation in religion. Not being a religious person, I would not want to pronounce on this. I have sometimes wondered, however, to what extent religious people are able to reconcile the hell that would be nuclear war with the inheritance of the Kingdom of Heaven which they presumably believe would be its sequel.

Chapter 17: The Women's Peace Crusade

Helen Ward, *A Venture In Goodwill, Being the Story of the Women's International League 1915–1929*, Women's International League, London 1929. This little known booklet tells the early story of the British section.

Gertrude Bussey and Margaret Tims, *Pioneers For Peace, Women's International League for Peace and Freedom 1915–1965*, reissued Women's International League, London 1980. This book tells the international story; it was first published by Allen & Unwin in 1965 but sadly by 1968 had gone out of print.

Arnold Whittick, *Woman Into Citizen*, Athenaeum with Frederick Muller, London 1979. An account of the International Woman Suffrage Alliance and Margery Corbett Ashby's role in it.

Andro Linklater, *An Unhusbanded Life: Charlotte Despard, Suffragette, Socialist and Sinn Feiner* (Hutchinson, London 1980)

Jo Vellacott Newberry, 'Anti-War Suffragists', *History*, 1977, vol 62. Amanda Sebestyen, '67 Years A Feminist: an interview with Gwen Coleman' (*Spare Rib*, no 23)

Manchester Guardian, Nelson Leader, Labour Leader.

Women's International League for Peace and Freedom, British section, annual reports.

Additional League material, Catherine Marshall papers, Cumbria Record Office, Carlisle.

NOTES ON CONTRIBUTORS

Women talking about Disarmament
Meeting at 43 Abbey Gardens

Edith Simon 1982

Note: this list includes women who contributed to all aspects of this book as well as the authors of the articles.

Alison Assiter teaches philosophy at Thames Polytechnic. She has been involved with CND for about a year.

Jeanette Buirski was born and educated in Liverpool. She read Chemistry and Physiology at Manchester University and taught these subjects in secondary schools and technical college for a period of ten years. She took a degree in Philosophy at London University in 1972, and would have completed her Bar exams by now had it not been for the birth of her two children. She is married, lives in London and has worked for the peace movement for three years.

Angela Carter was born in 1940. She is a novelist, living in London. She has no children.

Gay Clifford is an editor of the magazine *Writing Women*. She is Lecturer in English Literature at University College, London, has published poems in various journals, and is the author of *The Transformations of Allegory* (Routledge 1974).

Jill Craigie has been, along with her entire family, an ardent supporter of CND since its inception. An authority on the women's struggle for political emancipation, she has written several articles on this subject for various newspapers.

Janet Dubé: 'was born in London in 1941. My father was a prisoner of war at the time. He lost an eye and had other injuries. Both my grandfathers were foot-soldiers in the First World War. When my first two children were born in 1964 and 1966, I was conscious that they were the first children to be born in 'peace time' for three generations (in our family at least). This was one of the things that set me thinking . . . '

Jenny Edwards is a full-time worker for the Campaign for Nuclear Disarmament. Her main areas of activity are work with trade unions, with the campaign for nuclear-free zones and on the questions raised by civil defence. She is a member of Westminster CND and a supporter of the Women's Peace Alliance.

Lisa Foley was born in the United States. She now works as a research assistant for the Alternative Defence Commission, and as a librarian for the Commonwealth Collection linked with the School of Peace Studies, Bradford University. She lives in Bradford, where she is active in the local Labour Party and women's groups.

Inge Goodwin was born in Germany and came to England as a child in the 1930s. She read Natural Sciences at Cambridge and worked for a time in laboratories. Has published a novel, several short stories and a number of translations. She is married with two children and has been an active Labour Party worker for many years.

Philomena Hingston is a former SRN turned handloom weaver and designer. Married to a busy GP in Bradford, she is the founder and now the treasurer of her local peace group and has been an active member of the peace movement in Yorkshire for several years.

Sue Hirst is an archaeologist, specialising in the medieval period. A keen supporter of the peace movement, she commutes between London and Herefordshire and spends her time writing reports, digging and looking after her young son.

Lynne Jones is a doctor who has recently given up her job to work full time in the peace movement. A pacifist and a feminist, she is involved in the Medical Campaign against Nuclear Weapons, European Nuclear Disarmament, and the Women's Peace Movement. Spends most time and energy on the last of these, particularly in connection with the Peace Camp at Greenham Common, since she sees it as offering the most positive approach to the problem of nuclear weapons and other connected problems.

Evelyn King is a pianist who has performed and given radio broadcasts in New Zealand, the country in which she was born. She has been living in London for the last three years, and has given concerts there, and travelled with her chamber music trio. She has been working with the peace movement for the last two years.

Jill Liddington lives in West Yorkshire and is a member of the Halifax Nuclear Disarmament Group. She teaches local history for the Workers' Educational Association and is co-author of *One Hand Tied Behind Us: the Rise of the Women's Suffrage Movement* (Virago Press 1978).

Maggie Lowry is twenty, and comes from an Irish family. She has interrupted her studies as a student of Applied Social Sciences at Coventry Polytechnic to work full-time in the peace movement. Was connected with the Upper Heyford Peace Camp since it started, and is now there all the time, helping to run the camp, organise demonstrations and resist the threat by the council to evict the campers.

Connie Mansueto is twenty-seven and is a lesbian radical feminist. She belongs to the feminist disarmament network, Women Oppose the Nuclear Threat (WONT), is involved in anti-racist struggles, and is raising two children and two cats in North London.

Bel Mooney is a journalist who contributes regularly to newspapers such as the *Times* and the *Sunday Times*, as well as appearing frequently on television and radio. She has written a book about children, books for children, a novel, and is presently working on a biography of George Eliot. She is married to television reporter Jonathan Dimbleby, and they have a son and a daughter.

Marjorie Mowlam has received her doctorate and now teaches Political Science at the University of Newcastle upon Tyne. She has worked in the Anti-Nuclear Movement, primarily in opposition to nuclear power, for the last ten years.

Ann Pettitt has a science degree, has been a school teacher and an inner London squatter. She now runs a tiny smallholding in Wales, with her husband and two young children. She was the initiator of the Women for Life on Earth march which led to the setting up of the Peace Camp at Greenham Common in the summer of 1981.

Cathy Porter has published books on women in Russia and is at present at work translating the diaries of Countess Tolstoy. She has worked in the Soviet Union, and has travelled in a number of other European countries.

Beryl Ruehl was born in Birmingham in 1930 and has lived there ever since. She is married to an ex-German prisoner of war, and they have two daughters and a son. She has worked in the CND, the Committee of a Hundred and in the Labour Party, and has been a coopted member of the Education and Library committees of Birmingham City Council. She worked for two years as general secretary of the Socialist Medical Association, and when over forty, took a degree in History at the University of Birmingham. Since then she has worked as a research assistant and Open University tutor.

Diana Shelley, Lesley Merryfinch and *Sheryl Crown* are all members of the Feminism and Nonviolence Study Group which has just written a pamphlet on feminism and nonviolence published by *Peace News*.
Diana is a freelance journalist and historian. She has been active in a number of campaigns over the last twenty-five years including the Committee of a Hundred, British Withdrawal from Northern Ireland Campaign, the squatting and women's movements. She is currently active in CND.
Lesley works at the Campaign Against Arms Trade and is a member of her Local Women Oppose the Nuclear Threat group. She has contributed to a handbook 'Law and Sexuality', 'Shrew; Feminism and Nonviolence' and 'Loaded Questions; Women in the Military'.
Sheryl works in Theatre in Education and in community theatre. As an active socialist feminist she works within CND, WONT and the Labour Party. She is involved in nonviolent direct action training in both the anti-nuclear power and peace movements.

Edith Simon began as an art student, but then turned to writing and is the author of seventeen works of fiction and non-fiction. She returned to the visual arts some years ago, and has held seventeen one-woman shows in Britain and abroad, including exhibiting in Edinburgh as part of the Festival. Married with three children. Her work is in private and public collections in Britain, the Americas, Germany and France.

Myrtle Solomon trained for drama, but was interrupted by the 1939 war. She worked in an armaments factory from 1941 – 1945. Gained her political training in the Women for Westminster movement. She became a pacifist in 1946, and has worked for the Peace Pledge Union from 1952 – 1972; she is now the chairwoman of War Resisters International. She is 61.

Kate Soper is a philosophy teacher, writer and translator. She has three children. Until recently she was co-secretary of Brighton CND and is now active with the Lewes group. She is the author of *On Human Needs* (Harvester Press, 1981), and is currently writing a book on the concept of 'humanism'.

Fran Stevens works in the London Borough of Islington as an organiser of children's pre-school activities. She is married with two children and has been a supporter of the peace movement as long as she can remember.

Marian Sugden graduated in English at the University of London. She has worked as a school teacher and in mental welfare and for a long period has been an artist working in mosaic. She has been a magistrate since 1970. She has recently been working as a research assistant for the book *Defended to Death*, a study of the arms race. She is married to a scientist and has one son, also a scientist.

Dorothy Thompson was born in London. Her work for a History degree at Cambridge was interrupted by two years as an industrial draughtswoman during the war. Worked part time and freelance in adult education, social surveys and writing while she and her husband were bringing up their three children. Since 1968 she has held a full-time appointment in Modern History at the University of Birmingham. Is the author of several books and articles on British working-class history.

Hilary Wainwright has written about trade unionists in the arms industry. She is co-author of *The Workers Report on Vickers* and *The Lucas Plan; a New Trade Unionism in the Making*? A socialist feminist and a co-author of *Beyond the Fragments*, she is at present a member of the Greater London Council's new Economic Policy Group, working with trade unionists and community groups on plans for jobs.

Maxine Wombwell is a designer and craftswoman in jewellery. She studied at Colchester School of Art and Kingston College of Art. She has worked as an art therapist with physically disabled and mentally ill people, and is at present lecturer in jewellery design at North Essex Art School. Married with two children, she is thirty-five.

Suzanne Wood is in her early thirties. She has worked at various different jobs, including six years in an architects firm. Recently she has returned from fifteen months travelling Latin America.

If you would like to know more about Virago books, write to us at Ely House, 37 Dover Street, London W1X 4HS for a full catalogue.

Please send a stamped addressed envelope

VIRAGO
Advisory Group

Andrea Adam
Carol Adams
Sally Alexander
Rosalyn Baxandall (USA)
Anita Bennett
Liz Calder
Beatrix Campbell
Angela Carter
Mary Chamberlain
Anna Coote
Jane Cousins
Jill Craigie
Anna Davin
Rosalind Delmar
Christine Downer (Australia)

Zoë Fairbairns
Carolyn Faulder
Germaine Greer
Jane Gregory
Suzanne Lowry
Jean McCrindle
Cathy Porter
Alison Rimmer
Elaine Showalter (USA)
Spare Rib Collective
Mary Stott
Rosalie Swedlin
Margaret Walters
Elizabeth Wilson
Barbara Wynn

Book Tokens

Give them the pleasure of choosing
Book Tokens can be bought and exchanged at most bookshops